Sunbonnets and Shoofly Pies

The Pennsylvania Dutch sunbonnet, which I believe can serve as an index of our culture, was no static thing. It developed from the bonnet worn by Mrs. L. Friedrich Hermann, wife of the pastor at the Reformed Church in Easton, to the bonnet worn by a twentieth-century child. Moreover, bonnets varied from summer to winter, sect to sect, and even within sects to distinguish various choirs or age groups. Some wore prayer caps in the house and sunbonnets outside. For others they were simple utilitarian protection against the hot sun. In any event, they are Pennsylvania Dutch.

Sunbonnets and Shoofly Pies

A Pennsylvania Dutch Cultural History

John Joseph Stoudt

South Brunswick and New York: A. S. Barnes and Company
London: Thomas Yoseloff Ltd

© 1973 by A. S. Barnes and Co., Inc

A. S. Barnes and Co., Inc.
Cranbury, New Jersey 08512

Thomas Yoseloff Ltd
108 New Bond Street
London W1Y OQX, England

Library of Congress Cataloging in Publication Data

Stoudt, John Joseph, 1911–
  Sunbonnets and shoofly pies.

  1. Pennsylvania Germans. I. Title.
F160.G3S76   917.48′06′31   75–39348
ISBN 0–498–01124–0

By the same author:

*Consider the Lilies, How They Grow—An Interpretation of the
Symbolism of Pennsylvania German Art*
Jacob Boehme's The Way to Christ *in Modern Translation*
Pennsylvania Folk Art—An Interpretation
(Reprinted as *Pennsylvania German Folk Art*)
Pennsylvania German Poetry, 1685–1830—An Anthology
Private Devotions for Home and Church
Sunrise to Eternity—A Study in Jacob Boehme's Life and Thought
(Reprinted as *Jacob Boehme—His Life and Thought*)
Devotions and Prayers of Johann Arndt
Caspar von Schwenkfeld's Passional and Prayerbook in Modern Translation
(With James Ernst) *Ephrata, A History*
Ordeal at Valley Forge
Early Pennsylvania Arts and Crafts

Printed in the United States of America

For Melinda

Contents

Preface

*T*wo amused city slickers had come to the Pennsylvania Dutch folk festival to see how their country cousins behaved. They were standing in front of the information booth. When their turn came one asked, "When do they start to *hex?*"

The frame of reference from which this question was posed suggests that a factual book about the Pennsylvania Dutch—or, if you are a purist, the Pennsylvania German—is needed. Misinformation clouds the picture. Untruth is being spread about hex signs, distelfinks, powwowing, Amish blue gates for marriageable daughters, "papa is all," "plain and fancy," "chust fer nice," and "that what chumps over the fence last." Clever journalists rediscover the Pennsylvania Dutch and then we read another book about this peaceful land of plenty that is inhabited by plain Dutchmen with bobbed hair. The dramatic conflict between those who accept modern technology and those who oppose it—*progress* is the word—seems perennial.

Nor do specialists in Pennsylvania Dutch studies—and there are some good ones—always maintain sober objectivity. Some grind axes. Some seem to imply that being born a Pennsylvania Dutchman makes them expert on all themes. One archivist said of such a specialist that his one contribution to the field was the distelfink, and that was a mistake!

Under the title *Sunbonnets and Shoofly Pies* I here offer a work that means to tell things as they are, based on facts that stand the tests of the laws of historical evidence, giving a sound account, as honest as I can make it,

without wallowing in sickly filio-pietism or sitting in the scorner's seat.

Sunbonnets were worn by all women, sectarian nonconformists as well as more orthodox church people, in differing styles, of course. So Gilbert Stuart, while living in Germantown, painted the portrait of Susanna, wife of Colonel David Deshler, wearing her sunbonnet. Moravian women, Mennonites, and Ephrata sisters wore bonnets of differing styles, just as the dressier women of the denominations wore bonnets of brighter colors. By the same token, with either wet or dry bottoms, shoofly pies were ubiquitous among us.

Pennsylvania Germans have been orphans in American studies. Although in 1790 they were one-twelfth of the American population, we may read a work like the *Harvard Guide to American Studies* with little illumination on the subject. Histories of American literature are scarcely any better.

The main barrier to better understanding has been language. Pennsylvania Dutch culture has been viewed as "strange" and "foreign" by authorities in American studies. The field has no academic home, for it belongs neither to German nor to history departments. Some rubricate it with folklore. Now, since two of our sons have occupied the White House, we Pennsylvania Germans may perhaps be allowed to assert our Americanism!

We do not mean to boast. We do not need to. For the image of the Pennsylvania Dutch has changed from the "dumb Dutch"—or, as Benjamin Franklin called them, "boors"—to a "vigorous strain in American culture." I

9

plan to give facts, plain and unadorned, as befits the theme.

I shall not romanticize. I shall not build a *Heimathimmel* of pious imagination. The fertility of the land was God given. Our culture was well known, the product of many minds. And opposition to technology by some dissenting sectarians is not necessarily prophetic. Some of us have been over-pious, many overbearing. We have been good farmers, good craftsmen, good cooks—and better eaters! Yet, during the earlier period at least, our public services were meager. I shall not point out how so-and-so was successful, or made the first thingumajig, or reached this high position. I shall not make a list of famous Pennsylvania Dutchmen, an arrogant business. While some of us did indeed succeed to the White House, others have been more docile citizens. The Amish have had running battles with the Pennsylvania Department of Public Instruction and sporadic bouts with the Social Security Administration.

As the story unfolds, a new focus may perhaps come. We may come to see that the main thrust of Pennsylvania Dutch culture was not so much in the heartland as beyond it. In the Americanization process, we gave more than we took.

Significantly, there has never been a Pennsylvania Dutch nationalist movement like the one in French Quebec. The nearest we came to this was the whiskey rebellion of the 1790s. We may have had cause!

Now for a question that has clouded the area for more than a century: shall we say *Pennsylvania German* or *Pennsylvania Dutch?* The argument is that the Pennsylvanians are not Hollanders; they come from what is now called Germany. But the fact is that Hollanders are not Dutch either, but Nederlaenderer! The answer to the question, which is as far as some people get in Pennsylvania German studies, lies in whether you are a Saxon or a Latinist. When migration to Pennsylvania took place, there was no Germany. Germany as a nation was the product of Bismarck in the nineteenth century. At first we were "foreign Protestants," usually with the adjective "poor" added. And during the eighteenth century we were called both "German" and "Dutch" by our

neighbors in Pennsylvania. Since Hollanders are "low Dutch" and those from up the Rhine "high Dutch," Pennsylvania Dutch was logical. Both phrases mean the same. The first one of us, Francis Daniel Pastorius, used "high Dutch." Is there any earlier authority than that?

The language problem is more formidable. Anglo-Americans have been as skittish about English as the Dutch have been stubborn about German, both dialect and literary. We went to school, church, catechetical instruction, were baptized, married, and buried in High German. Only the forced introduction of English in the schools let German die out. The opposition to Pennsylvania Dutch culture mounted by the Pennsylvania Department of Public Instruction has had tragic consequences. Americanization has meant the death of the old ways. Was there no other way?

All that now remains is dialect. Go to an Old Order Mennonite meeting and listen! The language you hear is no longer vital. Scorned, laughed at, ridiculed by some, praised, cherished, and loved by others, this dialect just will not die. It has been opposed by Benjamin Franklin, by Dr. William Smith, by presidents of colleges; it has been spoken by the first speaker of the House of Representatives and understood by at least two Presidents. It still moves strong men to tears and makes others snicker. But it remains.

Here, then, is a book that tells in text and honest picture the story of Pennsylvania Dutch culture, moving out beyond the colorful arts and crafts to other areas. Recognizing that history can be visually documented, I have added pictures of the Pennsylvania scene that reveal, perhaps better than the text itself, the spirit of one of America's sturdiest peoples. I have not tried to glamorize the Pennsylvania Dutch; rather, I have sought older photographs that tell a realistic story. Fortunately, several collections were available.

So, under a somewhat catchy title, I mean to tell the cultural history of the Pennsylvania Dutch with as much truth as one mind can intend.

John Joseph Stoudt

Stauderhof
Fleetwood, Pennsylvania.

Acknowledgments

I am obligated to the following institutions for their help: The American Museum in Britain, Claverton Manor, Bath, England; the Library of the American Philosophical Society, Philadelphia; the *Call-Chronicle* newspapers, Allentown; The British Museum, London; the Bodleian Library, Oxford; the Boone Homestead, Exeter Township, Berks County, Pennsylvania; the Library of Congress, Washington; the Henry Francis duPont Winterthur Museum, Winterthur; the Haverford College Library, Haverford; The Archives of the Brüder Unitat, Herrnhut, Germany; the Historical Society of Berks County, Reading; the Historical Society of Pennsylvania, Philadelphia; the Historical Society of York County, York; the Metropolitan Museum of Art, New York; the Moravian Archives, Bethlehem; the Pennsylvania German Society; the Pennsylvania Farm Museum, Landis Valley; the Pennsylvania Historical and Museum Commission, Harrisburg; the Pennsylvania State Archives, Harrisburg; the Philadelphia Museum of Art, Philadelphia; the Rare Book Room of the Free Library of Philadelphia; the Ridgway Branch of the Library Company of Philadelphia; the *Eagle,* Reading; the Schwenkfelder Library, Pennsburg; the Shelborne Museum, Vermont; the Valley Forge Park Commission.

I am also indebted to the following individuals: Mr. and Mrs. John Adam, Mr. Richard Adam, Mr. Andrew Berky, Mr. Lester P. Breininger, Dr. Edwin Bronner, Mrs. Hattie Brunner, Mr. Oliver Lewis Christman, Mr. Philip Cowan, Mr. William B. Daub, Mr. David Ellinger, Mrs. Wilmer Greulich, Dr. David Hoffman, Dr. and Mrs. David Hottenstein, Mr. Charles Hummel, Dr. Henry J. Kaufman, Dr. Donald Kent, Mr. Joe Kindig III, Mr. Stephen Kindig, Mr. John Y. Kohl, Mr. and Mrs. Walter C. Moser, Miss Lottie Moyer, Mr. Vernon Nelson, Mr. Arthur J. Sussel, Mrs. Blanche Riegel, Mrs. Leroy Saunders, Mr. Edward W. Schlechter, Mr. Tom Schmoyer, Mr. William Shade, Mrs. Martha Silvernail, Mr. John Y. Stoudt, Dr. Lawrence Thurmond, Mr. Robert Walch, Mr. Donald Wendling, Mr. Wes White, Mr. Paul Wieand, Mr. Edwin Wolfe III, Mr. Arthur Rauch, Mr. Wallace P. Wetzel.

My wife, Nancy Yost Stoudt, is owed my deep appreciation for putting up with pounding typewriters and endless paper-shuffling.

My publisher, Mr. Thomas Yoseloff, has allowed me the freedom to do this book with integrity.

J. J. S.

List of Color Plates

Pennsylvania Dutch rooms, American Museum in Britain
Pennsylvania toleware
Reverse portraits on glass
Lehigh County barn
Mr. and Mrs. Beard of York
Sheriff Getwicks of York
Peter Coffman: pastel portrait of a lady
Hattie Brunner's Winter Scene
Hattie Brunner's Farm Scene
David Ellinger: watercolor of an egg tree

Sunbonnets and Shoofly Pies

Introduction

EUROPE AT THE TIME OF MIGRATION

*A*bout fifty thousand "poor Palatines," as they were called, ancestors of the Pennsylvania Dutch, were moved to leave Europe and to seek new life in Penn's America. Two worlds were then in conflict: feudal Europe was dying, while democratic America offered hope of a new world order.

The mortifying Old World with its worn shibboleths was passing. Inquisitions, religious wars, dragonnades, exile, galleys, intolerance, and moral corrosion were its hallmarks. Overseas a New World beckoned with enlightenment, reason, tolerance, morality—perhaps even with life, liberty, and pursuit of happiness.

The crises that had marked the European conscience during the 1680s were mirrored in, if not the dire result of, the religious question. This issue had divided Europe ever since the time of Martin Luther. Southern and western Europe were Roman; northern and eastern Europe were Lutheran. Between, from Edinburgh to Geneva, was the Calvinist buffer, a mixture of Gallic reason and Saxon fervor.

Three religions were allowed, and the prince decided which; the people had no say. The Peace of Westphalia (1648) reaffirmed the old feudal principle that the ruler might choose among the Roman, the Lutheran, and the Calvinist forms. Others were not allowed in the Holy Roman Empire. Migration was therefore escape.

The buffer separating Lutheran from Roman became the arena of special conflict: Alsace, Lorraine, Baden, and the hapless Palatinate. The cockpit of conflict was the lower Rhine valley, where most "poor Palatines" were to come from.

In 1591 the prince elector of the Rhenish Palatinate was Friedrich III, known as "the pious," an eager champion and advocate of the Calvinist catechism named for his seat at Heidelberg. Friedrich's family, Pfalz-Simmern, had become an ornament of Protestantism; his son, Ludwig VI (1538–1593), who began rule in 1571, was Lutheran. His grandson, Friedrich IV, whose rule began as a regency under Johann Casimir between 1583 and 1593, was followed by Friedrich V, the "winter king," whose election as emperor of the Holy Roman Empire began the bloodiest of wars, 1618–1648. He married Elizabeth, daughter of James I of England, and he championed the Protestant cause. When war came, his lands were overrun, his castle sacked, the population decimated. When he died in 1623, his lands again were Catholic.

After the war the butchery stopped. Karl Ludwig (1650–1680) ruled with tolerant fair-mindedness, a memorable prince during whose reign the ruined lands again were peopled, and Swiss and Alsatian immigrants prospered in those once-ravaged lands.

Prosperity did not last. In 1685, just as Pennsylvania was coming into European consciousness, Karl Ludwig's line died out. It was succeeded by the Pfalz-Neuberg house in the person of Johann Wilhelm, who had been educated in France by Jesuits and who introduced frightful measures. At that time his subjects were in this proportion: one Catholic for every two Lutherans and three Reformed. Sectarians who had been tolerated under

Map of Germany around the time of the emigrations
to Pennsylvania.

Karl Ludwig—a Quaker Meeting had even been established—now had to go underground. Persecution was bitter. Protestants had to bow before the Roman host.

Sectarians fared no better in other lands, for persecution was almost universal. Holland was the exception, for there it was not illegal to believe otherwise than the prince or to go beyond his choice. In 1692 the Amsterdam fathers protested the persecutions that were being made in Zürich by the Town Council. By 1671 the situation was intolerable in Switzerland. Many Swiss sectarians fled to Alsace, for Strassbourg was a free imperial city with some measure of liberty. Soon the Huguenots, now again made illegal by revocation of the Edict of Nantes (1685), fled France. In 1686 Strassbourg fell to the French. One war was "settled" by the Peace of Ryswick in 1697 which, outwardly, gave some semblance of tolerance.

The War of the Spanish Succession followed (1700–1713), during which the armies trooped back and forth over the already-ravaged Rhineland. The fate of Swiss Mennonites was especially blood-marked because they refused to bear arms. Between 1699 and 1743 there was an effort to extinguish them; many were drowned, sent to galleys, or given opportunity to go to America. Listen to Benedict Brechtbühl's account as quoted in Müller's *Bernische Täufer* (p. 273):

It was in the year 1709, January 12th, early in the morning, that the magistrate of Bern sent seven provosts with a court servant to my house, which gave me such a fright that, with my wife, I wanted to hide myself. I hid myself beneath a stack of hay. They searched through all places in my house. Finally they came back to the hay, probed it with their daggers, felt that they had hit upon me, that someone was in it. I came out and they seized me and asked me my name and whether I was a preacher, which I said and confessed to them. Then they brought me into my room, gave me a box on the ears, bound my hands at the back, and led me out of my house. Then my children cried and wailed so miserably that, as they say, a stony heart would be moved thereby. But the provosts took great pleasure in having found me. They led me from there to the city of Bern with two other Brethren and brought me into captivity, and that in a long cold winter. If we wanted to keep warm we had to pay dearly for wood. After six or seven days they brought me to another prison. There they locked me up in iron chains. In addition the magistrates who had jailed me gave me one hundred Thalers which I and mine had to repay. After two days they again brought me into the tower, put me in a special cell, and locked me therein with iron chains. There I lay for eighteen weeks. Thereupon they brought me, with all other prisoners, to the infirmary where we had to work on woolens from four o'clock in the morning to eight at night, and they fed us with bread and water, allowing us no complaints. This lasted for thirty-five weeks. For the remaining ten weeks the work was lighter. So the entire period of my imprisonment in Bern was one year, seven months, and seven days. This took place in the 44th and 45th years of my life.

Benedict Brechtbühl
Born in Emmenthal.

Imprisoned for not bearing arms, their lands ravaged by the enemies of their princes, the people were also oppressed by heavy taxation. Tithes were universal, the French calling this the *décime ecclésiastique,* meaning one tenth of everything—money, vegetables, grain, wine, fruit, animals, butter, milk! Ordinarily one tenth sufficed, being split—two-thirds for the lord, one third for priest or minister. In hard times the priest came off badly, with sometimes another tenth for the lord. When wars ravaged, a third tenth might even be imposed. Also, there was the *mortuarium,* a death tax where the best animals, fowls, and produce were taken. Some peasants are known to have been murdered for this tax. Then there was the notorious *laudenium,* another death tax. Together these taxes made it very costly for a land-owning farmer to die. Nor could he change his residence, even though he had been freed from serfdom for more than a century.

Lords also had special privileges. They had the right of the first night with a new bride, and they could hunt where they pleased. After 1687 a craze for the hunt developed in the Palatinate; nobles chased quarry wherever it went.

Tolls were universal: roads, bridges, even footpaths. The poor peasant also owed several days labor per week, for which he was not paid.

To all this man-made misery must be added that the winter of 1709–1710 was so cold that animals and fruit froze; hardly any crops were harvested that year. The first great migration was then under way.

It might seem that the Four Horsemen of the Apocalypse were riding across the beleaguered land! Wars there were a-plenty, seemingly going on forever. French dragoons came almost every harvest with sword and faggot. Pestilence and the plague were intermittent. London burned, and soldiers of the French king set their torches everywhere. Famine followed. Bitter winters, hard times, unfriendly governments, and always the spectre of war!

Could there be a land of peace?

The hope of a new world order found projection in a new religious movement—known in Roman lands as "quietism" and in Protestant lands as "pietism": a new state of mind that cannot be called new doctrine. Some people reacted against the loss of social and personal morality by an effort to make faith a living thing. Believing that a righteous life was not the consequence of correct doctrine but of love, pietists tried to establish ways by which love might be engendered.

The old argumentative nature of doctrinal religion had brought forth the wars of religion, when men slaughtered in the name of love! The source of human misery, some thought, was rational theology. As John Locke restored the empirical element in human knowledge, so pietists revived an older mystical empiricism, seeking to give life to dead faith. Instead of outer conformity they sought inward love. It was not enough to be merely baptized, they believed; they must be converted, their religious faith revived.

Philip Jakob Spener (1635–1705), in whose Frankfurt circle the migration of Germans to Pennsylvania was to take shape, felt the dry rot of formalized religion, the sickness of faith, and especially the lack of morality. Alsatian by birth, he proposed reform based on intensive study of the Bible, on a spiritual priesthood, on stressing the preached word instead of the doctrinal nature of religion, on avoiding controversy, on doctrinal reform, and on basic preaching. This mood was shared by many others and these "witnesses to truth," as Friedrich Breckling was to call them, were set on fire by the philadelphian ideal, the dream of universal love.

Gottfried Arnold (1666–1714) had written in his challenging "Non-Sectarian History of the Church and Heretics" that heresy was right more often than orthodoxy. Previously heretics had been deemed sons of Satan; Arnold argued for tolerance toward them.

Still the old mocking names continued: "Quaker," "Weigelian," "Boehmist," "Schwenkfelder" (sometimes called Stinkfelder), *"Schwärmer,"* "Enthusiast," and of course "Papist." But to no avail. Calling names was not an act of love! Perhaps there was a place where all who bore these spiteful names might dwell in love?

Was not Christianity itself on trial? Were not morals corroded? The dominant mood emanated from the court at Versailles—a mood that was challenging European modes and manners to imitate its brilliant, liberated paganism, and it was setting the pace for courtly life everywhere.

So I must suggest that migration came about from a religious cause. Still, we dare not thus isolate the drive that pushed so many persons to Pennsylvania. In addition, tight labor conditions made it hard for a young man to find a place in the economic life. Guilds tightly controlled jobs and patterns of work. To keep employed one had to follow the long-winded speeches at guild meetings and get a *Wandersbuch* to secure work.

The need for migration was there. Europe was experiencing the change from feudal to bourgeois values. The Old World was dying and it would not be renewed in Europe without major upheavals. So when Quaker William Penn was given a princely grant of land in the New World, and when his dream of a land of tolerance caught on, new vision arose. Penn had been interested in German dissenting religions, however, before he became owner of Pennsylvania. Between 1671 and 1677 he came to know some sects in Holland and Germany; and even before Penn, Quaker missionary William Ames, as early as 1657, had gathered a Meeting at Kriegsheim near Worms; Stephen Crisp had organized one in Crefeld. Both places were to send settlers to Pennsylvania.

Penn wrote an interesting *Journal* of his 1677 trip. He visited Princess Elizabeth, daughter of Friedrich V of the Palatinate and granddaughter of James I of England, who was the abbess of a Protestant cloister at Hereford, a prototype of Ephrata. Penn had also visited Frankfurt-am-Main, where he was received in the *collegia pietatis* of Spener. Here the Frankfurt Land Company for settling Germans in Pennsylvania was formed. In August 1677, Penn was in Kriegsheim with German Quakers, preaching in a barn; later he was in Duisburg. He also visited the Labadists in Holland.

Penn and other Quaker missionaries at first sought to spread their sectarian faith. However, their work bore strange fruit. The very centers that Penn visited became the places where German migration to Pennsylvania began.

Once William Penn had become the owner of pleasant lands west of the Delaware, his aims and actions became the chief focus of the migration. Both his personal struggle in England and his dream of tolerant freedom in Pennsylvania epitomized the new goals.

After March 4, 1681, Penn was owner of a great province. In this same year there appeared in English, Dutch, and German *Some Account of the Province of Pennsylvania,* which pictured a fertile land of tolerance where a "holy experiment" might take place. The next year, in German and Dutch, there came out *Information and Direction to such Persons as are Inclined to America more Especially those related to the Province of Penn-*

sylvania. This gave precise help to prospective settlers—grand-scale real estate promotion.

Penn had help from several remarkable persons, among whom was Benjamin Furly, Quaker merchant in Holland and Penn's continental agent, who got in touch with those on the Continent who were seeking tolerance. Furly gathered several accounts by early Pennsylvania settlers, and these may have been even more influential than Penn's, for they were written by people who had been there.

Hardly was the German version of Penn's 1681 pamphlet out when three members of the Quaker meeting in Crefeld—Jacob Telner, Dirck Sipman, and Jan Strepers—bought five thousand acres of Pennsylvania land at a cost of forty shillings per hundred acres and one shilling quit rent per hundred. Three months later three more Crefelders—Govert Remke, Lenart Arets, and Isaac van Bebber—bought eighteen thousand acres. These seem to have been independent purchases.

The next year, 1682, pietists associated with Spener in the Frankfurt circle organized a land company and bought twenty-five thousand acres. Originally this group had eight members, among whom were Johann Wilhelm Ueberfeldt, later editor of the 1730 edition of Jacob Boehme's works, and the philadelphians Johann Petersen and Elanor von Merlau. In 1682 or 1683 the agent and general secretary of the Frankfurt Land Company was designated—Francis Daniel Pastorius, son of a Lutheran lawyer from Sommerhausen.

Thus migration began, at first a small trickle. Yet, once people arrived in Pennsylvania, they sent back letters and accounts that described the new land. These became the main cause of new migration.

There were also many accounts of America and Pennsylvania in the public press. These have not yet been studied, but their effectiveness may be gauged from the action of the magistrates in Bern, who forbade publication of newspaper accounts that depicted Pennsylvania in a favorable light.

Among the more influential travel accounts was Pastorius's *Umständige Geographische Beschreibung der zu allerletzt erfundene Provinz Pennsylvanien.* This appeared in 1700 in Frankfurt and Leipzig, and was a composite of letters that the young man had sent home to his parents.

In 1702 the work of Daniel Falckner, also an early settler, called *Curieuse Nachricht von Pennsylvanien in Nord America,* came out in the same places.

In 1704 Pastorius's *Beschreibung* and Falckner's *Nachricht* were combined in a new printing with a new title. These works proved popular and were reprinted even as late as 1782, long after their materials were stale. Falckner's work added from the pietist August Hermann Francke questions that showed interest in broader social, economic, and religious matters.

An interesting publication that encouraged migration to Pennsylvania was the "Golden Book of Queen Anne," so called because it bore a golden image of the good queen of England on its cover, thus implying her interest in migration. This work was written in English and was distributed by British officials in Germany. It is clear that British authorities, especially Ambassador Davenant in Frankfurt, were agents for the migration.

Soon migration proved profitable for ship companies and a special breed of exploiter appeared, the *Neuländer* (Newlander). The significance of these swindling agents

When they came through England on the way to Pennsylvania, the Yoder family of Oley acquired, either by purchase or as a gift, this pair of Queen Anne candlesticks. They have been treasured ever since.

for mass migration to Pennsylvania should not be minimized. They not only drove their business in the harbors but wandered over southern Germany, where distress was greatest, going from house to house, especially where members of the family were already in America. They received seven dollars for each passenger. They carried faked documents and letters that gave glowing pictures of a fertile and prosperous land, thus selling the glories of the New World. Governments tried to stop this business, but the secretive nature of the *Neuländers'* work added to the attractiveness of migration. Christopher Saur I, Pennsylvania printer, vigorously opposed it.

Historian Julius Göbel has collected a group of letters, written by early German settlers in Pennsylvania and sent back to the homeland, under the title *Aus Deutsch-pennsylvanien*. These were reprinted in the journal *Nassovia* 4 in 1903 and they reveal fascinating efforts to approach several princes with the hope of migration, and their responses. At first the princes were agreeable to emigration; soon, when the economic consciences of the rulers had been aroused and depopulation threatened, they opposed it. Therefore, after 1709 edicts forbidding migration were enacted in most principalities, especially Zürich and Bern. These edicts did not succeed in halting migration; they just made it illegal.

For it was a new world that was being hoped for, and these new places in America gave hope that new social patterns might emerge, a note that was clearly expressed in Daniel Falckner's *Curieuse Nachricht*. He saw that Pennsylvania

is a country that supports its labors abundantly; there is plenty of food. What pleases me most is that one can be peasant, scholar, priest, and nobleman all at the same time without interference, which of all modes of living has been found the best and most satisfactory since patriarchial times. To be a peasant and nothing else, is a sort of animal life; to be a scholar and nothing else, such as in Europe, is a morbid and self-indulgent existence; to be a priest, and nothing else, ties life to blunders and responsibilities; to be a nobleman and nothing else makes godless and riotous. . . .

Ye European Churchmen, consider, unless you put off your soiled garments of religion you cannot enter into the Philadelphia which the Lord awakens anew.

Thus was a new age awaited.

However, German magistrates continued to be rough on dissenters, especially those who would not accept military service or who opposed dry and formalized worship. These "awakened" gathered in centers of refuge. Several enlightened princes were minded to fill their half-empty lands with good religious people. One such center was the duchy of Wittgenstein in Westphalia, which was a jumping-off place for Pennsylvania. In 1708 the Dunkards arose under Alexander Mack I and gathered

in Wittgenstein. The small land of Büdingen in Upper Hesse also became a refuge center. In eastern Germany, when bitter Jesuit persecution came, a center arose in Herrnhut in Saxony.

Two of Pennsylvania's sects were to come from eastern Germany. The Schwenkfelders, followers of the Silesian nobleman, Caspar von Schwenkfeld von Ossig, a contemporary of Luther, had been vigorously persecuted by the Romans in Harpersdorf. Some conversions followed and in 1725, when the Emperor withdrew his protection, the Schwenkfelders had to flee. In 1733 they were banished, and they found temporary refuge in Saxony on the estates of Count Nicholas Ludwig von Zinzendorf, who was already gathering his own religious movement from all areas in Germany, the renewed Moravians, as they were called.

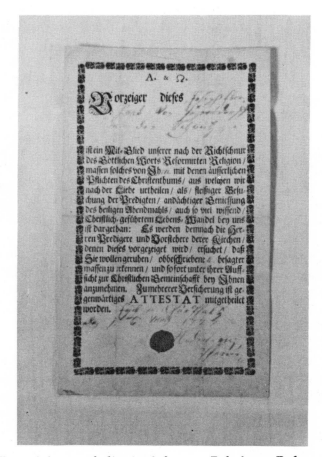

Formal letter of dismissal from a Palatinate Reformed Church for Joseph Ehrhard, born in the Swiss canton of Bern. The name of the pastor who signed it cannot be deciphered. It is dated 1727.

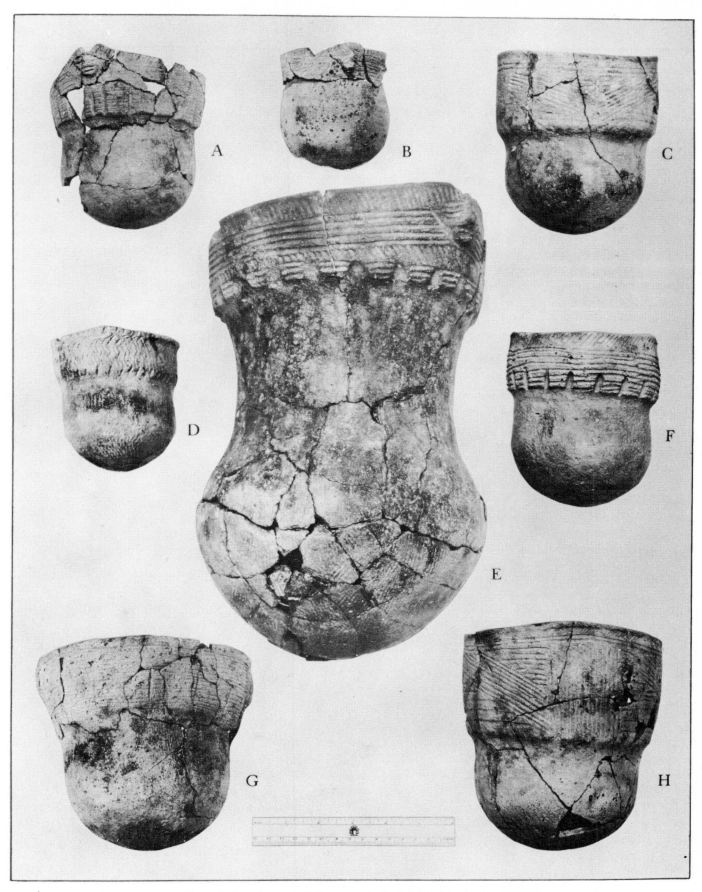

One of the more useful words in Pennsylvania history is *Conestoga,* an Indian word that served to mean many objects. It referred to a river and its valley, to a wagon that became the "ship of inland commerce," to a cigar shape—the celebrated "stogie," and to the long Pennsylvania rifle. Most of these things originated in the Lancaster region where the Conestoga river flows into the majestic Susquehanna. Above are further objects that arose in the Conestoga region—pottery made by the Conestoga Indians, the people who were living in the Pennsylvania Dutch heartland before it was settled by Germans. *Courtesy the Pennsylvania Historical and Museum Commission*

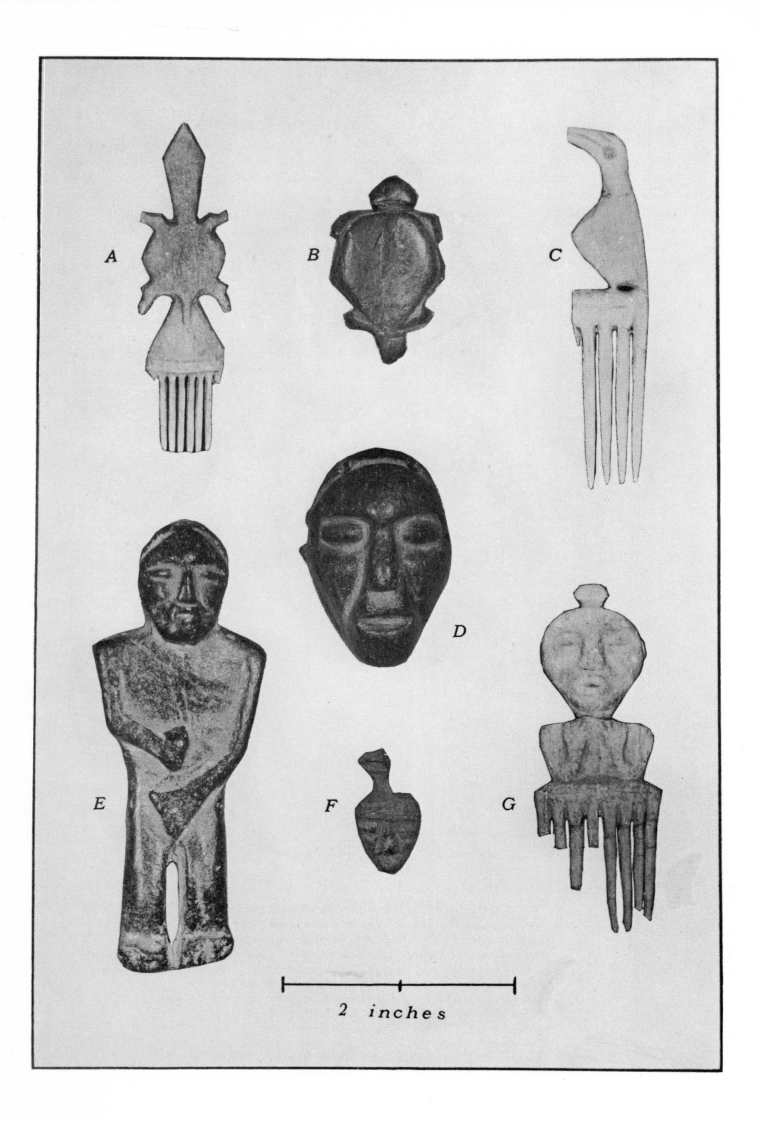

A   B   C

D

E   F   G

2 inches

Thus the Pennsylvania dream caught on. All western Europe was astir. New hopes appeared.

Before the long journey to America could be started, the migrant had to fortify himself with two documents. As head of a family he had to get a civil passport for himself and for his dependents, wherein it was stated that he was a godly, moral man, of good character; he also had to declare that he owed no one anything, asserting that he had paid the migration tax. Then, too, he had to possess a certificate of dismissal from the state church, even though he may have been a suspected sectarian, wherein he said that he had last taken the sacrament on a specified date and place and wherein he made open profession of the "pure Reformed religion," or maybe the "orthodox Lutheran faith," and that he had conducted himself uprightly "without giving cause for scandal." Authorities were allowing only good subjects to emigrate.

Thus Pennsylvania beckoned for the dissenters who were not *en rapport* with established religions and who were not being handled too kindly by magistrate and priest. And they were allowed to migrate, given the benefit of departing their homelands—*beneficium emigrationis*—an act of benign condescension by a magistrate who might have consigned his charges to the Italian galleys.

But Pennsylvania was no empty land; it was the home of generally docile Susquehannocks and Lenni Lenape, who were called "women," both of them conquered peoples. On the north were the Iroquois, warlike and strident, who entered the pages of Pennsylvania history with brash disregard of the tender consciences of its inhabitants. None of these aborigines had emerged from primitive ways of life, and how to deal with them was a factor in Pennsylvania cultural life.

The turtle clan of the Conestogas lived near Washington Borough, Lancaster, even during the period of colonization. They welcomed the new settlers, especially Madame Feree and her group of Huguenots. Here are several carved turtles and a thunderbird, done in bone and dating from about 1450, just about the time when contact with the white man was made. *Courtesy the Pennsylvania Historical and Museum Commission*

1

Migration

The first Pennsylvania Dutchman was already here before William Penn. He was the Mennonite William Frey, who was from Altheim in Alsace and was to settle in Germantown.

However, generally speaking, German migration to Pennsylvania is said to have begun with Francis Daniel Pastorius, a well-educated young lawyer who had been part of Spener's Frankfurt circle of pietists and who was secretary of the Frankfurt Land Company. He arrived August 20, 1683, with several German-speaking families: Jacob Schuhmacher, Georg Wertmüller, Isaac Dillbeck, Thomas Gasper, and Conrad Becker. Several weeks later Pastorius was able to greet the "Concord" with thirteen families from Crefeld, mainly Hollanders, including several merchants who had been Mennonites but who now were Quakers.

On October 12, 1683, Pastorius was granted title to about six thousand acres situated about two hours from the village of Philadelphia, east of the river named the Schuylkill by the Dutch, and near to Mill Creek. When it was surveyed, the tract measured just over fifty-seven hundred acres.

On October 29, 1683, the new town, named Germanopolis by the settlers themselves, was founded. It consisted of a long street, about twenty yards wide, crisscrossed by side streets. Each lot was three acres in size, thus making reproduction of the German agricultural village impossible. Most settlers were linen weavers, knowing little about agriculture.

In 1684 a few more settlers came, chiefly from Mühlheim in the Ruhr, and in 1685 some German Quakers from Kriegsheim in the Rhenish Palatinate came, probably responding to William Penn's visit there. By 1689 Germantown had fifty families, necessitating subdivision into regions: the part nearest the village of Philadelphia was called Germantown, having about 2,750 acres; next was Kriegsheim, with about 880 acres; then Somerhausen (Pastorius's birthplace), with about 900 acres; and finally Crefeld, with more than a thousand acres.

Soon this new Germanopolis became an independent community modeled on Old World patterns but with a somewhat utopian flavoring. It was a German-speaking community, with its own legal statutes and with its charter confirmed by King William in 1691. Its burgomaster and council were elected in democratic fashion.

Pastorius himself was burgomaster in 1691, 1692, 1696, and 1697, holding other municipal offices in other years. His *Grund- und Lager-buch* survives in the Historical Society of Pennsylvania and in it he put his legal education to good use, expressing an ideal of democratic brotherhood fully as significant as any town meeting democracy from New England. The Latin preface was

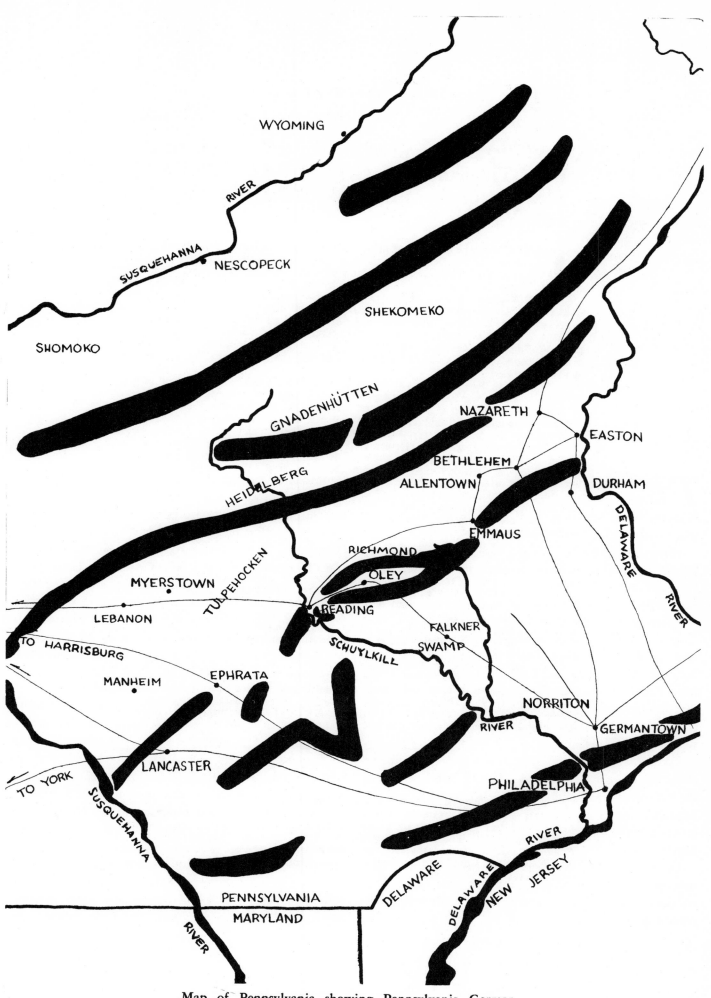

Map of Pennsylvania showing Pennsylvania German
Colonial population centers.

A Brief Reprefentation of the Diftreffed Cafe of above Four Thoufand Poor *German* PROTESTANTS Fled out of the Fruitful *Palatinat* by the *Rhine*, and *Neckar*.

THIS Country has fuffered more than any other during this long and dreadful War, by the frequent Invafions and repeated Conquefts of the *French*; more than Two Thoufand of their greateft Citys, Market Towns, and Villages have been burnt down to the Ground by the *French* Incendiarys, as *Hydleburgh*, *Manbein*, *Worms*, *Spire*, *Frankendale*, *Baccarac*; all their Fortifications, ftately Caftles, and Magnifi ent Churchcs at vaft Expencewere blown up into the Air, the very Graves of Princes laid Open, their Skuls and Bones Kick'd up and Down the Churches and Streets. Their *Vines* deftroyed, and in many p'aces Rooted up, with a defign to make fo fatal a Wafte that this Country might never be Peopl'd and inhabited again : Vaft Numbers of thofe People perifhed in Woods, and Caves, amongft the Wild Beafts, by Hunger, Cold, and Nakednefs.

(Is not Divine Vengeance this Day Judging the Authors and Inftruments of fuch Barbarities?) Thefe Poor Refugees are the Survivers of them, who during a fhort intervall of Peace, had Built up a few Cottages, and began to Cultivate their Country, in hopes of fome means of Subfiftance, but by reafon of the late irruptions of the *French*, who have again ruin'd their Country, carried away their Cattle, and yet do continue to this day to exact Vaft Contributions from them, befides the many Heavy Taxes from their own Government, who have Stript them of all the Enemy leaves; feeing themfelves in a manner Starving, Deftitute of all Conveniencies for Humane Life, have thrown themfelves into the Arms of *Britains* Charity (A Great Honour to the *Englifh* Nation to be own'd the Refuge of the Diftreffed).

Thefe People are efteem'd, by the Wifeft of Her Majefties Counfellors, and by Merchants, and other Perfons of more than Ordinary underftanding, capable of being made a B'effing and great Advantage to this Nation, as being a very Induftrious People, us'd to Hard-Labonr, do confift of Plowmen, Herdfmen, and variety of Mechanicks as *Carpenters*, *Mafons*, *Smiths*, *Weavers*, *Spinners*, *Knitters*, &c. are willing to be at the Difpofition of our Gracious Sovereign, who has incouraged them by her Bountiful Affiftance, and is much concern'd how to difpofe of them after the beft manner. At prefent their Numbers being fo great and more Dayly expected ; it is to be hoped that all pious and Compaffionate Chriftians will take their Deplorab'e ftate into Serious Confideration and imitate fome Noble and Generous Souls, who have already Freely and Liberally Contributed to thefe Diftreffed Refugees, either by Vifiting them Perfonally, who are known to be about *Camberwell*, and *Debiford*; or elfe to fend their Charity to the Perfons named in this Paper or in any other of the Prints.

To the Reverend Doctor *Bray* near *Aldgate* Church, the Reverend Mr. *Tribbeko* at the Golden *Angel* near *Summerfet-boufe* : the Reverend Mr. *Ruperti* Minifter of the *Savoy*. To Mr *Jonathan James* in three King Court *Lumbard*-ftreet, Doctor *Slear* in *Bartlet-Buildings Holburn*, Mr. *Gardner* Diftiller at *Holburn* Bride. Mr. *Trollop* Linnen Draper near *Aldermanbury* Conduit, Mr. *Skate* Brafier *Hounds-Ditch*. Mr. *Cook* Merchant, Mr. *Green* both in *Camberwell*.

P O S T S C R I P T.

THat there are fome Families of *Roman-Catholicks*, who have alfo left this Delicious Country, where their own Religion is favour'd, to come into a Proteftant Nation, is an Argument of their great mifery and Diftrefs, many of thefe being New Converts, are difpos'd to turn Proteftants. The King of *Pruffia* for years paft, received Thoufands of thefe Ruin'd Proteftants, and gave them many Immunities and Priviledges, who are now a Rich and Thriveing Colony and do Contribute thoufands of *Dollars* Annually for the fupport of the Government and carrying on the War againft *France*.

London Broadside from around 1709 describing the plight of the so-called ''Kocherthal Colonists'' when they were encamped in that city awaiting transportation to the New World. *Courtesy the Bodleian Library, Oxford*

addressed to his followers in these words:

> Be greeted, posterity! Descendants of Germanopolis!
> And gather first from the contents of the following pages that your elders and forebears forsook Germany, which bore and nourished them, in full decision, in order to bring forth in this forest-rich Pennsylvania, in a wasted wilderness, the remainder of their lives in the German fashion, as brothers!

Can it be that Pastorius here is suggesting a German source for the ideal of democratic brotherhood?

Economically Germantown portrayed the motto chosen by its founder: *vinum, linum, et textrum*: attempts were made to make American wine but insects here prevented it; flax was grown and the burghers were busy spinning and weaving even as they cultivated generous gardens, gaining some reputation as gardeners. Stocking weaving was performed by women and their products were sold in Philadelphia shops, while the city market featured Germantown vegetables. The first paper mill in America was erected in Germantown by Wilhelm Rittenhausen in 1690. It was forty years before a similar mill was built in New England. Following 1695, yearly market was held which, after 1701, became bi-annual.

Germantown was no utopian experiment, although it did reflect advanced political views; this was doubtless due to Pastorius's sound legal training. Official jobs were enough to go around; one burgomaster, four burgesses, six jurors, one recording secretary, and one each of clerk, master of rents, sheriff, and coroner. No one wanted to serve: the burgomastership was a burden and no one wanted it for more than a year. Fear of fire was lessened by spreading the dwellings and by strict control of chimneys by Leonart Aret and Op den Graeff. Even cows' horns were dulled for safety, and guns could not be fired on First Day.

Thus Germantown partly reflected an Old-World German village without starry-eyed idealism: woods were made into sown fields; dwellings lined its streets; gardens had flowers, and Pastorius made poetical catalogue of them. In 1694 old Peter Cornelius Plockhoy, ill and battered by years of misery, came to Germantown, after having failed to build Utopia in lower Delaware. Indeed, Richard Frame's description of Germantown in his poem of 1692 was accurate when he said there were *High German* and *low Dutch* in the village.

On Saint John's day, 1694, the ship *Maria* landed a group of young immigrants, forty in number, who called themselves "The Woman in the Wilderness," a

biblical name taken from Revelation 12. Convinced that Europe was degenerating, moved by pietist moods, these university graduates came in the hope that they could see a new dawn in Pennsylvania. They had been gathered by a remarkable figure, J. J. Zimmermann of Bietigheim,

At LeVan's mill, Berks County, Count Zinzendorf preached in the year 1742. That makes this mill one of the oldest. *Photograph by W. W. Dietrich*

a prolific writer who had got into trouble because of heretical writings and who died in Rotterdam harbor on board ship. This group was given 175 acres by Thomas Fairman, surveyor, along the Wissahickon, and they built log houses and established a settlement that lasted ten years.

Land speculation soon began. The Frankfurt Land Company now was no longer sole agent for land-purchase by Germans. Daniel Falckner, who had been one of the Zimmermann forty, acquired a tract of 22,025 acres in what is now Montgomery County, still known somewhat sneeringly as "Falckner's Swamp." This was October 25, 1701. Others also were caught by speculative land-fever; Johann Heinrich Sprögel, son of a German theologian and brother-in-law of historian Gottfried Arnold, sought to drive settlers from their Germantown homes, but intervention by Pastorius foiled the effort. Indeed, Pastorius aggressively attacked these land agents with broadsides and other weapons, and when Germantown was granted royal charter in 1717 these schemes collapsed.

By 1702, it is estimated, there were about two hundred families of so-called Pennsylvania Dutch. They clustered around Germantown, Falckner Swamp, and Trappe, even mingling with the Holland Dutch around Whitemarsh. Settlement had been made at Falckner Swamp as early

Front and rear of John Steele's log cabin with hand
pump, paling fences, and blooming fruit trees.

as 1700, for Daniel Falckner held Lutheran worship services there as early as 1703 and 1708. In 1704 the first log church was built there, surviving until 1721. There was also an important Lutheran congregation in New Providence (Trappe) but its beginnings are somewhat obscure. Both Falckner Swamp and Trappe became important Lutheran centers.

While Germantown and Falckner Swamp—and to lesser extent Trappe and Whitemarsh—were growing at the rate of a dozen families a year, a dramatic turn of events took place. Spurred by misery, oppressed by insensitive rulers, and victimized by the cruel winter of 1708–1709—the hardest known in the history of modern Europe—a mass of "poor Palatines" journeyed to Rotterdam where, upon intercession by the Duke of Marlborough then on campaign there, they were transported to the British isles by the British navy, subsistence being provided by charitable friends in Holland. At least thirteen thousand emigrants ultimately reached Great Britain, of whom 2,207 were Roman Catholics who were either returned to Rotterdam or sent to Limerick County, Ireland. London was overwhelmed by the crowding Palatines; inns, taverns, and houses were filled. Queen Anne, whose consort, Prince George of Denmark, had been German, was being urged by the Reverend John Tribecko and others to show favor to these "poor Protestants." The British government assisted the refugees.

The previous year a small migration of forty families had already gone forth to New York State, led by the Reverend Joshua Kochethal, thus giving hope direction.

Rear view of early structures at LeVan's mill, Eaglepoint, Maxatawney, Berks, showing the living quarters and other buildings in use before 1742. *From an old photograph by the* Reading Eagle

Roof tiles made by the Weidner pottery on the spring house of the Hoch farm in Oley. *Photograph by Mr. William B. Daub*

Beginning May 3, 1709, and ending July 27, 1709, six sailings brought a total of eight thousand Palatines to New York in Royal Navy ships, settling them in the Schoharie region along the Hudson, where they were paid subsistence to boil tar for the Royal Navy. Pennsylvania Governor George Keith invited these refugees to Pennsylvania and, having been warned against New York, most accepted this offer. Thus the interior valleys of piedmont Pennsylvania—Oley, Maxatawney, Pequea, Tulpehocken—were filled by settlers from the Schoharie region, who did not enter America through the port of Philadelphia. Some Schoharie settlers, however, remained in New York, among them Johann Peter Zenger who had arrived as a lad of thirteen and who later fought for the freedom of the press.

At almost the same time that these refugees were en-

Roof tiles, one of which was decorated with cross hatch, made in the Oley Valley during the middle of the eighteenth century. *Courtesy Mr. Stephen Kindig*

tering Pennsylvania by way of New York, a second wave came. In 1710, while it still was part of Chester County, settlement of Lancaster by Swiss and German Mennonites began. The Pequea and Conestoga areas had been scouted by a citizen of Bern named Ludwig Michel, who sent back favorable reports about the fertility of the region. This interested two men, Georg Ritter and Rudolph Ochs. Between 1705 and 1707 they were petitioning the Town Council of Bern, as well as the British representatives in Switzerland, to permit them to lead a group to Pennsylvania. In 1710 the Council agreed to pay twenty-five

Roof tile with the initials of the potter and the date, 1756. One of these was generally included in each set of roof tiles. *Courtesy Mr. Stephan Kindig*

dollars per head for deportation of imprisoned Mennonites. First the migrants went to Holland, where their freedom was bought by Dutch co-religionists, and some returned to the Palatinate. But a colony did go to the New World, ending up, not in Pennsylvania, but at New Bern in North Carolina.

In Holland a company was created for aiding distressed Mennonites, with the title: *Commissarissen voor het fonds van buittenlandsche noeden.* This served the needs of the Bern sectarians, who were allowed to leave Switzerland on condition that they would not return. Many put down in Alsace, in the Palatinate, and in the Netherlands before they came to Pennsylvania.

Another area where settlement began during the first decade of the century was Oley in Berks County. Quakers had been there earlier—the Boones, Lincolns, and Lees —but in 1708 Johannes Keim arrived and in 1709, the

same year in which he had come to America, Jean leDee arrived, settling down without land-warrant or survey. About 1711 Isaac deTurk and his wife, the former Maria Weimer, came down from Newburgh, purchasing land from leDee and George Boone. By 1734 Oley had thirty-four land-owners, most of them from the Schoharie and ostensibly members of the Reformed Church, although they were riddled by pietism and even separatism. Many of them had been Huguenot.

On October 23, 1710, a group of Swiss Mennonites who had entered, probably by the port of Philadelphia, the year before, acquired a tract of land of ten thousand acres at the sources of the Pequea Creek in regions eastward from the Conestoga. Its leaders were Hans Herr and Martin Kindig. In 1717 five thousand acres were acquired and smaller parcels were being added until 1730, when Jacob Brubacher got 124 acres. Blooming settlements appeared in the wilderness, which soon became a garden. Groffsdale was acquired by Hans Graff in 1718. Between 1728 and 1729 Earltown was founded. In 1719 Hans Herr built his cabin, the oldest German dwelling of the Colonial period. In 1723–1724 three brothers named Weber (Weaver) founded Weaverstown and about the same time Eberhard Riehm established Reamstown. By 1735, it is estimated, four thousand "Dutch" families lived in Lancaster.

In 1719 a new sect appeared, eventually putting down in Lancaster. Led by the weaver Peter Becker, after a year's sojourn in Crefeld this former congregation of German Baptists came to Germantown. They numbered about twenty families and finally settled in Lancaster. In 1729 a Schwartzenau congregation followed, under the leadership of Alexander Mack. "Awakenings" began, finally centering in the Conestoga, where the leaders came to be fashioned into new fellowships.

Already in 1712 the Ferree family, with others, had arrived in the Pequea region of Lancaster, met by friendly Susquehannocks. A group of individual separatists began to come into the Conestoga wilderness. About 1729 a village near Lancaster appeared that was to become the largest inland town in Colonial America and where the Continental Congress was to meet, having at this later time about four thousand inhabitants. By 1730 poets and solitary were gathering near Ephrata; an organized community appeared around 1734, and by 1723 the village of Strassburg had come into existence.

Meanwhile other areas were beginning to be settled. Around 1720 thirty families came down to Maxatawney from the Schoharie, including many of Huguenot back-

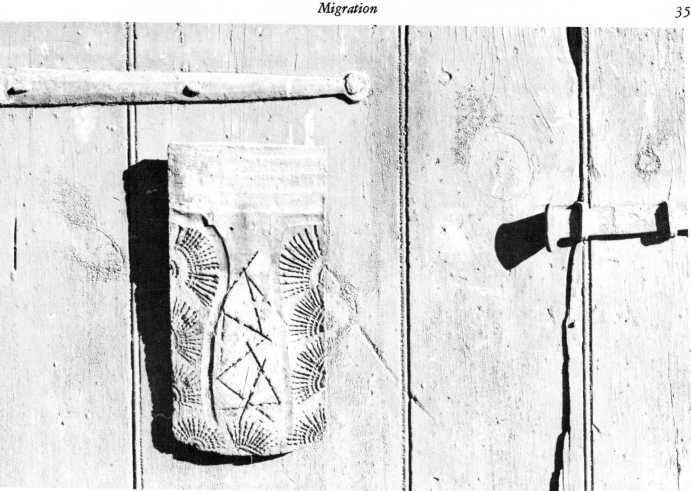

Decorated Oley roof tile on a barn door. *Courtesy Mr. Stephan Kindig*

ground. In 1723 thirty-three families left Schoharie under the leadership of Johann Conrad Weiser, former *Schultheiss* in Württemberg and by following the Susquehanna, and by way of its tributaries, they came to the fertile Tulpehocken, where there arose a settlement called Heidelberg. In 1729 Weiser's son followed with more Palatine families; he became the celebrated Conrad Weiser who was representative of the Provincial Pennsylvania government to the Indians for many years. Indeed, in 1732, in an unusual move, although one with good Pennsylvania tradition, these German families of the Tulpehocken formally purchased their lands from the Indians.

While these somewhat stable communities were emerging, Lancaster was filling up with ruggedly individualistic radicals who called themselves the quiet in the land (*die Stille im Lande*)—of whom I shall be speaking in the following chapter—who were fleeing Euro-

pean corruption for fresh life in the Pennsylvania forests. Fully half a century before Rousseau was to popularize the notion of the noble savage, a group of German pietists, perhaps also quietists, had fled Europe's foulness for the virginity of the Lancaster woods. Among these were Christopher Saur I, who with wife and son first came to Lancaster and later became the celebrated Germantown printer; also the four sons of Michael Eckerlin, former councillor of Strassbourg, an early Alsatian pietist. Some of these individualists also settled in Germantown, like Stephen Koch, friend of the mystical poet Gerhard Tersteegen. As it had been earlier for migrating groups, so now did Pennsylvania become a haven for many of the awakened who came simply as "the quiet in the land."

By now the Pennsylvania authorities had grown increasingly apprehensive about this burgeoning German migration. As early as 1717, a year before Penn's death,

After 1742 foreign Protestants were required, after having spent seven years as good subjects of George II, to swear allegiance to him. They went to the Supreme Court in Philadelphia, before the judge, and took the oath or, if they were Quakers—i.e., sectarians—affirmed allegiance. These lists exist in duplicate in the Public Record Office, London, and in the State Museum, Harrisburg. Some were also printed by Benjamin Franklin.

Governor George Keith had expressed fears in a message to the Provincial Council wherein he suggested that Germans might gain the upper hand, and he proposed listing them as they disembarked. Fears grew. Were not some of these "foreigners" persons with French names, probably papists sneaking into the sacred land of Pennsylvania? Were they not stubborn in manners and morals?

On September 14, 1727, matters came to a head. The Provincial Council decided that all persons entering the port of Philadelphia had to be listed and must pledge allegiance to their new government. Registered migration was to be allowed for those who proclaimed loyalty to the British crown and to the Proprietors of Pennsylvania.

These lists, which began in 1727 and which go down to the American Revolution, survive in the State Archives and have been published by the Pennsylvania German Society, *Pennsylvania German Pioneers* (Norristown, 1934). They tell who entered the port of Philadelphia after 1727; they do not say who came through other ports or came before that date. Most Moravians came through New York or southern ports; many others came through Boston and Baltimore. Nor do these lists tell where the immigrants came from. Just short of forty thousand names are given here, all classed as "Palatines" although they may have come from other places: Alsace, Nassau, Westphalia, Hesse, Zweibrücken, Erbach, Darmstadt, Basel, Mannheim, Hamburg, Hanover. Some refused to take oaths, affirming loyalty instead.

The first ship thus registered brought the Reverend Georg Michael Weiss as head of a colony of one hundred and nine "Palatines" who, with their families, totaled about four hundred. They arrived on the *William and Sarah* and settled as a group in what is now the Perkiomen region of Montgomery County. Friedrich Hillegas, the actual leader, had been in Pennsylvania before, returning to Germany to bring his followers here. This group formed the nucleus of New Goshenhoppen Reformed Church.

If the red tape wrapped around the immigration was intended to curtail it, it failed. The flood increased. Therefore, on May 10, 1729, a second law was enacted, aimed at indentured servants. This law put a tax on the following categories: twenty shillings for Irish immigrants; forty shillings for "foreigners"; five pounds for Negroes. Several efforts were made to reduce the tax, but fears that a hard-working element might be lost led the colony to repeal it.

By the time registration began, settlement was still confined to areas east of the Susquehanna and south of the Blue Mountains. Soon, however, the best lands in this region had been snapped up. By 1731 Germans were in Conewago, and a typically German town, Hanover, appeared in York county. In 1733 the Lutheran congregation at Kreutz Creek on the Codorus was founded, served by Johann Caspar Stoever, one of the itinerant preachers who traveled from log church to log church, serving settlers over a wide area. In 1741 the town of York was established, mostly by Germans; later travelers called it a German-style town. Tensions between Germans and Scotch-Irish in southern York and Lancaster arose.

Soon the areas between Philadelphia and up-country began to fill. In 1727 Whitpain Township, Montgomery County, was already the center of Reformed activity; here lived schoolmaster Johann Philip Boehm, who was ordained a minister after having served as schoolmaster. By 1730 a Lutheran log church had been erected at Indianfield near Sumneytown, surrounded by Germans. By 1734 half of the taxables of Montgomery county were Germans.

On September 24, 1734, a day still recalled as Schwenkfelder memorial day, a group of forty families led by Georg Weiss arrived in Philadelphia, planning to settle down together. However, they were forced to put down in two areas, first in the Goshenhoppen region of Perkiomen and then in the Skippack region.

The Schwenkfelders were a remarkable group, home educated by necessity, having taught themselves ancient and biblical languages, human studies, and sectarian hymnology, not to mention poetry. They were avid copyists of religious verse. Living quietly, even strictly, they were pacifists and moralist, sharing many opinions with the Quakers.

In 1740 an important law was passed in England, "An Act for naturalizing of such foreign Protestants . . . as are settled in any of his Majesty's Colonies in America," including the islands. After seven years' residence these foreigners could receive the rights of natural-born Englishmen by taking an oath or by affirming loyalty to the British crown before a properly appointed judge. Both Quakers and Jews were exempted from the obligation of taking the sacrament.

This list survives in two places: the Public Record Office in London, and the Pennsylvania State Archives. Although printed from both sources, besides some individual printings by B. Franklin (the so-called *laws*), these lists are largely unstudied and are not integrated into historical studies. They tell us much: whether the new citizens were sectarian or churchmen, what township they lived in, and when they took the oath or affirmation.

The first Moravians came to Pennsylvania from Georgia, where they had settled as early as 1735 under Bishop Spangenberg. In 1737, refusing military service against the Spanish, their presence there became unwelcome and they began to appear in Germantown the next year. In 1740, under Peter Böhler, friend of John Wesley, they showed up in the forks of the Delaware, where they took over a school for Negroes that the British evangelist George Whitefield had started in Nazareth. This was on a tract of about five thousand acres. However, they did not stay too long there but acquired five hundred acres along the Lehigh where the Monocacy flows into it, and in the spring of 1741 Bishop Nitschmann directed the erection of a log house for pastors and for missionaries, the first of the Bethlehem buildings patterned on German structures. On Christmas Day, 1742, in dramatic fashion, Count Zinzendorf named the new settlement "Bethlehem." Meanwhile the Nazareth lands became Moravian.

Moravians were organized into "sea congregations" for the journey to America, and most entered through New York from their church-owned ship. The first of these sea congregations put to land at New Haven, where the Yale students welcomed them. In 1742 the second sea congregation arrived, composed of members from Herrnhag, Marienborn, Herrnhut, and various places in England. A third such congregation came in 1739. By 1762 eight hundred Moravians lived in the region around Bethlehem and Nazareth, few of them registered in the lists.

Only Moravians could dwell in early Bethlehem and Nazareth, for these were closed communal villages established and run by the congregation. Their social patterns had been created in Europe. Moravian settlements grew swiftly as more and more brethren came to Pennsylvania. In 1744 a house for single brothers was erected in Bethlehem; in 1748 a new building was built for them and the old one given to the single sisters. In 1768 a structure for widows was built. For that age these were massive structures, several stories tall, large and unusual for early Pennsylvania, where most buildings in rural areas were of logs. These buildings gave early Bethlehem an aura of its own.

Schools appeared early, in line with the Moravian stress on education. In 1743 a school for girls was estab-

lished, the first in the colonies, and in 1748 the first institute for teachers was formed.

The sexes were separated. Marriage was by lot, the way that all important decisions were made.

Moravians dressed alike, plain. Men wore simple dark brown coats with knee breeches and round shoes; women wore capes, with ribbons designating their *Chor* covering simple frocks.

Moreover, Bethlehem was the chief part of a larger settlement, which in fact could have become as significant as other utopian groups. Nazareth was an agricultural and educational center. By 1755 it had a day school, which in 1785 was opened for all Protestant boys; it was a clean town with good, quiet living. Other associated villages were Gnadenthal (1742); Christiansbrunn (1748), which was established chiefly for raising cattle; Schöneck (1757); and Emmaus, which was started in 1742 mainly as a refuge from Indian raids. Lititz in Lancaster later became a center.

These Moravian settlements were bound together by a social vision that had a theological basis, for Moravian views were predicated on the idea that revival of religion and life would some through "little churches within the Church," through an awakened remnant within the comprehensive territorial church. Zinzendorf had gotten his idea from pietist Spener, and he expanded the notion of the "first fruits." He was looking for an association of what he called *tropes,* the awakened among all nations—Arab, Eskimo, Indian, German, English, and West Indian—in an early tolerance.

From the beginning of the settlement of Pennsylvania, even among Quakers and in Germantown, there had been a considerable, submerged, Huguenot element. In areas that were basically Germanic, these French families followed the usual custom of Huguenots in the *diaspora,* hiding their French identity. Many were second and third generations of the dispersion, having fled France around the time of the revocation of the Edict of Nantes (1685), settling in the Palatinate and elsewhere. Others were Alsatian Lutherans and Lorrainers, and some even members of the tightly organized French Reformed groups in France.

Huguenot migration was steady. Small parties were on nearly every ship. Here are the names of several ships, with dates of arrival and the number of heads of families with French names: *Princess Augusta,* 1736, 11; *Loyal Judith,* 1741, 6; *Neptune,* 1746, 9; *Brotherhood,* 1750, 7; *Patience,* 1751, 7; *Phoenix,* 1751, 9; *Patience,* 1752,

17; and the *Nancy* in 1754, with 34 from Lorraine. The migration of Huguenots was more than a trickle.

Most Pennsylvania Huguenots were already German-speaking, coming from Alsace and Lorraine. Those who had settled in the Palatinate, as in Franckenthal, which had a vigorous French-language Reformed church (to which Abraham deTurk belonged), sought to hide their Gallic spirits. Stapleton's *Memorials of the Huguenots* lists about six hundred and fifty heads of families of Huguenot origin in Pennsylvania. They settled in all areas and among all religious groups, with Quakers and Moravians, in Oley, Tulpehocken, Maxatawney, Lancaster, Bucks, and Northampton. A goodly number remained in Philadelphia. Quite a few celebrated Pennsylvania families have Huguenot background: deBenneville, Benezet, Boudinot, deHaas, DuSimitere, Griesemer, Hillegas, Pershing, Reno, Ritner.

Soon the back country next to the Blue Mountains had German-speaking churches. While Moravians were building Bethlehem, Lutheran and Reformed churches arose at Allemängel (1742), Saucon and Upper Milford (1743), Whitehall (1744), Jordan, and Salisbury. Towns like Hecktown, Hellertown, and Weisenberg show their Germanic origins. Easton was founded at the concourse of the Lehigh and Delaware rivers in 1750.

In 1748 Reading was founded, seat of Berks County, although its Lutheran church had been built a year before. In its neighborhood were Alsace, Schwartzwald, Heidelberg, and Bern. Within a few decades other towns were established: Kutztown, Boyertown, Bechtelsville, Hamburg, and so on.

Lebanon also started to take shape by 1750, and in 1755 the colorful Schaefferstown was founded.

By 1750 the German migration to Pennsylvania had become a flood. The year 1749 saw 7,020 immigrants and the figures for the next years were similar. (In estimating the length of the voyage to America after September, 1752, we must realize that calendar change had taken place and that Philadelphia now was on new-style reckoning; previously the voyage had taken eleven more days.) Soon, however, war between England and France made migration difficult. Apparently by 1750 Germans made up one-half of the population of Pennsylvania, being just under eighty thousand persons. The newer settlers, finding most land before the Blue Mountains already occupied, had to spread out, illegally, to regions beyond, which were in part already settled by Scotch-Irish.

Some unusual groups appeared. From Gimbsheim there came a colony of "awakened" who went to Ephrata. In 1750 another group of both sexes arrived in Philadelphia, led by a scholar named Ludovici. These were followers of the German philosopher Christian Wolff, and they disappeared into the general settlements.

One of the uglier practices of the migration, one on which its increase in large measure depended, was the custom of traveling now and paying later. The system of indenture did not originate in Pennsylvania; as it had been used a century earlier in Virginia to fill that labor-hungry land with dependable workers. There seem to have been two ways of proceeding: a person might sell himself to whomsoever would pay his passage, or else he might solicit funds from friends and relatives already in the New World. William Penn had been advised to adopt this means if he wanted his lands to be a haven for the oppressed; this offered a practical way to get settlers. So he published a broadside in which he offered to the first purchaser of an indenture a tract of fifty acres. Several laws were enacted in early Pennsylvania to regulate this business.

During the first fifty years the indenture system was not much used; this was the period of the migration of sectarians. Most could pay their passage. After 1730, however, change occurred and almost every third immigrant was a redemptioner.

The Newlanders took all sorts of people to the ships. They swindled them, locked them on board, fed them slop, robbed their baggage, and did everything to impoverish them so that they might sell their services when they got them to the New World. When they arrived in Philadelphia notices were put in the newspapers that so many "Palatines" were to be sold for freight. Quaker merchants were active in this business, and in the popular mind there was little difference between indentured servants and slaves.

What was the deal? If an immigrant could not raise his passage money he was obligated to work for a period, first of seven years, later of four years. Children under five could not be made to work, but from ages five to twenty-one service was obligatory. Unity of families meant nothing; many were separated permanently, as notices in Colonial newspapers suggest. In his turn the master was obligated for food, clothing, and housing. At the conclusion of the contract, "freedom" was granted, along with suits of clothes, one of which was to be for dress, as well as some hand tools like broadaxes and hoes. Children were to be given some education. Stern legal

An ACCOUNT of the Births

and Burials in CHRIST-CHURCH PARISH, in *Philadelphia*, from *December* 24, 1750, to *December* 24, 1751. By CALEB CASH, Clerk, and SAMUEL KIRKE, Sexton.

Viz. Christened	Males	58	Buried	Males	70
	Females	60		Females	76
In all		118	In all		146

Under One Year	24	From Forty to Fifty	13
From One to Three Years	34	From Fifty to Sixty	14
From Three to Five	14	From Sixty to Seventy	5
From Five to Ten	7	From Seventy to Eighty	1
From Ten to Twenty	5	From Eighty to Ninety	4
From Twenty to Thirty	13	From Ninety to a Hundred	1
From Thirty to Forty	11		

The DISEASES and CASUALTIES this Year.

Apoplexy	1	Gravel	1
Aged	5	Hives	2
Cholick	1	Hooping Cough	6
Casualty	4	Imposthume	2
Consumption	26	Mortification	2
Convulsion	1	Pleurisy	9
Child-Bed	7	Quinsy	4
Dropsy	2	Small Pox	47
Fever	7	Surfeit	1
Flux	4	Teeth	5
Fits	9		

Still Born 14. *Note*, These are exclusive of the above Numbers.

Christenings Increased	2	Burials Increased	17

Burials Increased or Decreased, *viz.*

Swedes	27	Increased	14
Presbyterians	48	Increased	22
Baptists	28	Increased	19
The People called Quakers	107	Increased	3
Dutch Lutheran Church	56	Increased	28
Dutch Calvinist	40	This Account from *May* only, Inc.	1
The New Building	30	Increased	11
Roman Catholicks; Males 10 Females 11	21	Increased	6

Burials in the Strangers Ground, *viz.*

Strangers, *viz.* Dutch, and other white People	319	Increased	69

Lutherans Christened	150	Increased	82
Swedes Christened	42	Increased	32

Burials in the Negroes Ground, *viz.*

Negroes		84

This interesting document lists the number of burials in Christ-Church parish, Philadelphia, 1750–1751. Note especially the second last item: "Burials in the Strangers Ground" of strangers, "Dutch, and other white people"! Where were these interred? Could it be that here were recorded the names of those who died at sea? *Courtesy the Historical Society of Pennsylvania*

measures prevented servants from running away, and, if caught, the runaway had to serve out his whole period. Differences between Irish and German "indentured" servants soon arose, the latter being used more for farming and the former for household duties.

The indenture system was not all bad. The immigrant came to an established farm and he did not need to go into the bush and grub for himself. Work was hard, abuses many, but not universally. Thus the congregation from Hamburg in Berks county acquired its schoolmaster

Delaware had a hospital for treating sick immigrants. In 1750 a law was passed requiring each passenger to have enough room on board ship. On December 26, 1764, the German Society of Pennsylvania was founded with the main purpose of helping these poor redemptioners. Captains were required to maintain physicians; half the passage money had to be paid in advance; and if the ship were delayed thirty days, free board was to be allowed.

The indenture system brought such hardships that

A group of farm buildings near Blandon in Berks County, photographed before 1900. The building on the left is combination house and barn, of logs. In the center is the stone house etrected before advent of the Georgian. Note also the paling fences for gardens and rail fences for fields.

by paying passage for Johann Friedrich Schrock and binding him to teach school for three years and four months. Many an indentured servant married well and some were even able to buy out their masters.

Nonetheless, opposition increased. In Saur's newspapers, in letters to the Governor, and in petitions, the attack was mounted. In 1742 one of the islands of the

Germans helped themselves. Pastor Heinrich Mühlelberg and Christopher Saur I, otherwise opponents, were energetic in petitioning for the establishment of a hospital. On January 17, 1750, a demand was presented that passengers be given enough food aboard ship.

One unstudied aspect of the migration involves deaths at sea. Where were those who passed away at sea re-

The Reverend Philip Jacob Michael was pastor of several small congregations in eastern Berks County, and, when war came, he served as chaplain to German-speaking troops in the Continental Army. This old photograph depicts the farm on which he lived near Bowers, eastern Berks. *Taken by W. W. Dietrich, 1900*

of these put down in Pennsylvania, but those who did found themselves part of a Germanic culture fairly well established.

Now, how many Pennsylvania Dutch were there in early America?

In 1932 a committee on linguistic and national stocks in the United States, acting for the American Council of Learned Societies and using studies of the American Historical Association, came up with an estimate, which is the best that we have. It was based on analysis of the occurrence of distinctly Germanic names in the 1790 Census. Of the total white population of 3,172,444 persons in the entire country, 257,775 bore Germanic names. Of a population of 423,373 white persons in Pennsylvania, 140,983 were German. More than half of the Germans in America were in Pennsylvania.

This estimate needs a critique. We cannot always tell an englished name. Shelley may hide Schilling, Carpen-

corded? Was it in the records of the Anglican Christ Church in Philadelphia? The yearly report of the sexton, under the rubric "Burials in Strangers' Ground," lists 172 such strangers interred for the year from December 24, 1746, to December 24, 1747 (old style). For the year 1750–1751 there were 319 such "strangers, viz. Dutch, and other white people." Now this was far too large a figure of unattached Germans to be buried in Anglican ground, especially as there were 56 "Dutch Lutherans" and 40 "Dutch Calvinists" also listed. The suspicion therefore arises that the sea captains thus registered deaths at sea; further study might establish a hidden aspect of the migration.

When he put down, the Pennsylvania Dutchman had a good eye for fertile soil; soon the best lands were his. He knew that where hardwoods grew—oak, hickory, ash, walnut, cherry—there was good soil. When the soil was red and overgrown with cedars, it was not so good. Seeing thick vegetation, hardwoods, limestone underneath, and well-watered acres, the new settler said, in the *patois* he had brought from the old world, *Doh sin mer daheem!*

During the American Revolution migration took a curious turn. In the eight years of the war the British sent 30,067 German mercenaries to fight their American battles, of which 7,734 died in America. A total of 4,818 so-called Hessians remained as settlers in the New World, almost one-fifth of the surviving force. Of course, not all

Pennsylvania farm with rail fence using slate uprights. *From an old photograph*

ter Zimmermann, Hoover Huber, and Albright Albrecht. Listing names on a linguistic basis ignores the hidden Huguenot element within the Pennsylvania Dutch migration—the Levans, deTurks, and Bertolets, who spoke German.

Thus, to the 8.1 percent of German names we must add another full percent of hidden Germanic blood, englished names, and Huguenots who can be classed as Pennsylvania Dutch, making about nine percent of Americans in 1790 Pennsylvania Dutch. It is estimated that at that time seventy percent of the population was Anglo-American, 8.3 percent Scotch, 6 percent Ulster

Irish, 3.7 percent Free State Irish, with smaller percentages of Swedes, French, Dutch, and a few Spanish. Scotch and Irish were English-speaking.

At the time of the first American census, the Pennsylvania Dutch formed the largest minority in Anglo-Saxon America.

Fireplace tools and "Pennsylvania plain" in the kitchen of the Daniel Boone homestead, Exeter Township, Berks County. *Courtesy the Pennsylvania Historical and Museum Commission. Photograph by Rath*

Sitting-room in the Boone Homestead, Exeter Township,
Berks County. *Courtesy the Pennsylvania Historical and
Museum Commission. Photograph by Rath*

Springhouse near Weaversville, Northampton County, showing musket holes for defending against the Indians. *Photograph taken 1912 by John Baer Stoudt*

Fort Ralston, erected by Scotch-Irish neighbors of the Moravians during the Indian troubles of the 1760s. *Photograph taken October 1912*

North Franklin Street, Fleetwood, just before the advent of the automobile.

Siegfried's Dale, in Maxatawney, Berks, at the turn of
the century.

Early photograph of Siegfried's Dale in eastern Berks County, showing rail fences.

This is what an old tavern looked like. The Whitehorse tavern in Douglassville as it looked September 12, 1911.

A typical walled family cemetery.

Georg Krauss, Schwenkfelder, made this plan of "the City." *Courtesy the Schwenkfelder Library*

Here and there in the Dutch country were isolated settlements of other nationalities, islands in a Germanic region. Here is the Irish settlement in Northampton County, showing the stone barn where David Brainerd preached. *From an old photograph*

2

Pennsylvania Pietism

*D*uring the earlier period, issuing from William Penn's tolerance, Pennsylvania Dutch culture was dominated by the pietist spirit, marked by a special kind of religiosity, which came from the nature of the early settlers. Moved by William Penn's generosity, religious radicals found haven here, refuge from intolerance. Once they were here they had to learn how to get along.

This gave Pennsylvania pietism its special spirit, one known perhaps in Rhode Island but generally not present elsewhere in Colonial America. As Johann Adam Gruber (1694–1763) was to write: "In Pennsylvania we have many religious opinions, but only one religion—the 'Pennsylvania religion' of go a little, give a little, live and let live."

Even before he became Quaker, William Penn had learned tolerance from the Huguenot professor at Saumur, Moïse Amyraut; his doctrines were known by the Latin title *gratia universalis hypothetica sub conditione fidei,* which replaced the arrogant old Calvinist doctrine of election by grace.

The motive for the settlement of Pennsylvania, at least for the first half-century, was religious. Quakers sought freedom from persecution and they granted others the rights they claimed for themselves. However, Ernst Troeltsch's distinction between "church" and "sect" does not really apply to Pennsylvania, for before 1742 there were here no static way of life, no fixed patterns; during this earlier period things were fluid, coming to a crisis in that year. Only afterwards did the American pattern of denominational pluralism appear.

The first work published in the young province showed the intellectual mood that was to dominate Pennsylvania pietism: *The Temple of Wisdom,* published in 1688, which included part of Jacob Boehme's *Complexions,* wherein Boehme made analysis of man's "humors," to which were added passages from several British authors, George Wither, Francis Quarles, and Francis Bacon. The compiler of this work was Daniel Leeds, a not-too-regular member of the Society of Friends, a dissenter among the dissenters.

The full spiritual and intellectual stature of Francis Daniel Pastorius is not yet measured. Obviously he was not a systematic thinker, but we do know in what slot to file him, for in 1697 the Amsterdam bookseller, Jacob Claus, published *Ein Send-Brief an die Sogenannten Pietisten in Hoch-Deutschland.* This was dated the last day of December in Germantown. Still, Pastorius's verse offers suggestion of a deeper piety, for here appears a non-mystical rationalism, bred in the baroque, a mood that even played with *Buchstabspielerei.* Pastorius was an ingatherer of other ideas, something of an eclectic spirit, only partly pietist, and deeply concerned with ethical matters.

In Germantown, in spite of its name, beyond the immigrants from Crefeld there were also Dutch Quakers, a fact known and acknowledged by Professor Oswald Seidensticker. Pastorius wrote that in 1686 a Quaker meetinghouse had been built. After 1696 Mennonites had their own place of worship in Isaac van Bebber's house; in 1708 they erected their own meeting place. It was from the German-speaking Quakers that the first

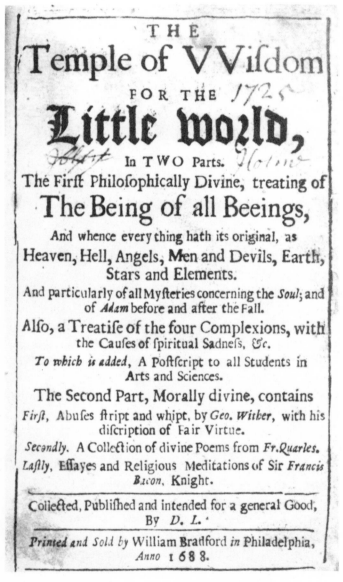

Title page of the first book published in Pennsylvania, which suggests the role that German culture will play in the life of Pennsylvania. Daniel Leeds, an errant Quaker, here reprinted English translations of some of the writings of Jacob Boehme, Silesian mystic of the seventeenth century. Other British works were added. Thus German culture was to enter America through translation. *Courtesy the Historical Society of Pennsylvania*

American protest against slavery came, directed—mark you—toward English Quakers! Only in 1755 were slaves excluded from Meeting.

"The Woman in the Wilderness"—as Johann Jakob Zimmermann's followers were named—presents much that is problematic. Actually they were not a typical sect, a fellowship of saintly folk cut off from the world and linked by a common spirit—a commune of refugees from an immoral Europe. The few sources that we have are confused; there is precious little accurate information; we do know that some sort of cloister life was followed, with celibacy, and that their religion was emotional and empirical. No thorough study of Zimmermann has yet come forward, and it is a necessity that this movement be better known. From Kelpius's *Letters,* his brief diary, and his poetry, we may gain only a meager bit of information about these chiliast dreamers who searched the heavens to learn when the new age would come.

They had fled Europe for an American new age, being both *Rosenkreutzer* (the seventeenth-century variety) and philadelphians, rebels against rotten morals who dreamed of an age of brother love. And they were aware of their niche in history, as Kelpius's *Letters,* which clearly define his pietism, show. Mystical contemplation and watching the stars for the dawn of the new age were expressions of hope.

It is said that Johann Kelpius's tract, *A Short Easy and Comprehensive Method of Prayer,* was brought out during the second decade of the eighteenth century. (It was reprinted in 1763 in a translation by Dr. Christopher DeWitt.) This work was dependent on similar books by Mme Guion and August Herman Francke.

Some members of "The Woman in the Wilderness" never lost interest in the more orthodox religions. Bernhard Köster inclined toward Lutheranism, as did Daniel Falckner also. Justis Falckner, one-time theological candidate at Halle, returned to Europe but came back to New York State where he served as pastor. Seelig bound books, wrote poetry, taught school, and pored over the writings of Jacob Boehme down to the year 1740. A Swiss, Conrad Matthei, remained a significant figure in Germantown until his death in 1748.

The surviving poetry, still posing many problems, shows its baroque themes: the soul controlled by Jesus' love, the cooing of the mateless dove, the bitter-sweet mood of the nightingale. Some of this verse shows noteworthy competence.

In 1710 an old Swiss warrior Samuel Guldin (1664–1745) came to Pennsylvania, fresh from the bitter wars of Swiss pietism, and he wrote here a *Short Apology or Defence,* which was a justification of his position in the old battles in Bern where he had been chief preacher and where, on June 9, 1699, he had been tried for pietism. This rare work was probably the first German book published in America and it bears the note, "Gedruckt zu Philadelphia im Jahr Christi, 1718." Does "Philadelphia" mean Berleberg?

In 1714 an interesting figure appeared in Oley, Mattheis Baumann (? –1727) of Lambsheim, a typical separatist. In 1701 he had had a religious experience wherein he felt called to ask the world to repent. Ridiculed by his Reformed pastor for arrogating spirituality to himself, he was haled before the church court, then shunted to the civil court. At his trial in 1705 he propounded the principle that magistrates had no authority in matters of conscience, an early instance of separation of church and state. Banshed from the Palatinate, he fled to Wittgenstein, then came to America with the Kocherthal colonists, and in 1714 bought land next to deTurk's in Oley. From here he spread his doctrines, winning some converts who were called "Newborns." Around 1723 he wrote *A Call from God to the Unregenerate World,* published in 1730 in the pietist periodical *Die Geistliche Fama.* Baumann had some success among his Oley neighbors, but the clerics opposed him with bitterness. Several tracts came out against him, including one by the Reverend Georg Michael Weiss, pastor at New Goshenhoppen.

Sometime around 1720 the awakenings that had been coursing through western Europe during the previous decades appeared in Pennsylvania, often led by the same persons. Extraordinary physical manifestations occurred —some quacked like ducks, some brayed like jackasses. The countryside was alive with charismatic manifestations; excitement lingered on the frontier. Perhaps the claim of the *Chronicon Ephratense* that the Pennsylvania awakening of the 1730s spread over the Anglo-Saxon parts of America during the 1740s needs to be balanced by the notion that revivalism marks all frontiers.

Among these early settlers a new ideal of religious fellowship manifested itself, tempered by the splintering tendency of dissenting religious groups, a curious form of religious primitivism expressed by the colorful phrase, *Die wahren Stille im Lande,* the true quiet in the land. In a world where intolerant state was joined to intransigent church, the point of view forced upon those who would be rid of religious strife was full separation. They wanted to remain passive before religious aggressiveness, to live

in stillness of spirit wherein mystical resignation had become objective—a quietism of life as well as spirit. The phrase, "the quiet in the land," does not quite explain their goal, for, much like the quietism of Mme Guion, they founded stillness upon inner serenity. Here is a definition of this point of view as given by Dr. Friedrich Carl in *Die Geistliche Fama,* Berleburg, 1733, the periodical of radical pietism (pp. x, 40):

> The true quiet in the land withdraw themselves from soiled spiritual works as well as from other sinful works of the flesh and church affairs. They penetrate into the hiddenness of spirit in which they experience the light of grace, praying to and listening to God, thus enjoying, like obedient children, the Fatherly will and counsel. They oppose the forms of holiness and meaningless church affairs, seeking to prevent formalism from again rising in worse aspects than before.

This nihilism led those hounded by European churches and their subservient magistrates, who had in truth been shown the gate by both magistrate and priest, to withdraw from society. First they had gathered in hilly Sayn-Wittgenstein, in quiet isolation.

Soon, however, this spirit showed in Pennsylvania. Already, in 1715, in some interior valleys sheltered settlers were living alone, without religious fellowship, apart from crowds. In 1721 four companions who had been together in Wittgenstein came to Lancaster: Conrad Beissel, Jacob Stuntz, Heinrich van Bebber, and Georg Stieffel. In 1723 came Isaac Friedrich and Jan Meiley. In 1724 came Sigmund Landert and the widow of Strassbourg pietist Michael Eckerlin with her four gifted sons. Others also came, including Michael Wohlfarth, who was a student of the mystic Tauler; Rudolf Nägele; and Christopher Saur I.

These people formed no sect. They were individuals fleeing a befouled church, seeking to get as far away from a corrupt culture as possible. Thus, long before Jean Jacques Rousseau, there was this religious primitivism which had a point of view implicit in Wittgenstein but which came to formal expression in a work that Conrad Beissel apparently wrote during this period: *Some Theosophical Sayings, or Rules for the Solitary Life.* These were later published at Ephrata on the Press of the Brotherhood. Here the solitary primitivist quietism of the early Pennsylvania frontier came to full-throated expression, a mystical nihilism both akin to quietism and strangely modern, where isolation of spirit—rugged individualism—had become a deep spiritual value. These were not rules for cloister living, like Benedict's rule, but guidelines for a strongly individualistic faith wherein

The restored buildings at Ephrata. *Courtesy the Pennsylvania Historical and Museum Commission*

the corrupted world is excluded with its corroding values. This point of view never wholly left Beissel.

This third decade of the eighteenth century, the 1720s, was a spiritually creative period. All of Pennsylvania—Germantown, Skippack, Falckner Swamp, Oley, Tulpehocken, Conestoga—was seeing a growth of religious individualism. This was a religious land, but not a church land. Things were fluid, in motion, and people were going back to fundamentals. In addition to serving as agent for the Berleberg Bible, the famous sectarian translation with mystical commentary, Christopher Saur I,

who had deserted the Conestoga solitary to establish a printing shop in Germantown, announced that he was going to print a Bible, and in 1743 he produced a volume of 995 (O.T.) and 277 (N.T.) pages, reprinting the thirty-second Halle edition, a massive accomplishment.

Yet something was still lacking in this philadelphian land—love! One does not live alone and still have love. Therefore, around 1736, a new idea came from out of the heart of this free-flowing separatism. Johann Adam Gruber (1684–1763), crown prince of German separatism who had known the solitary life, issued a "call"

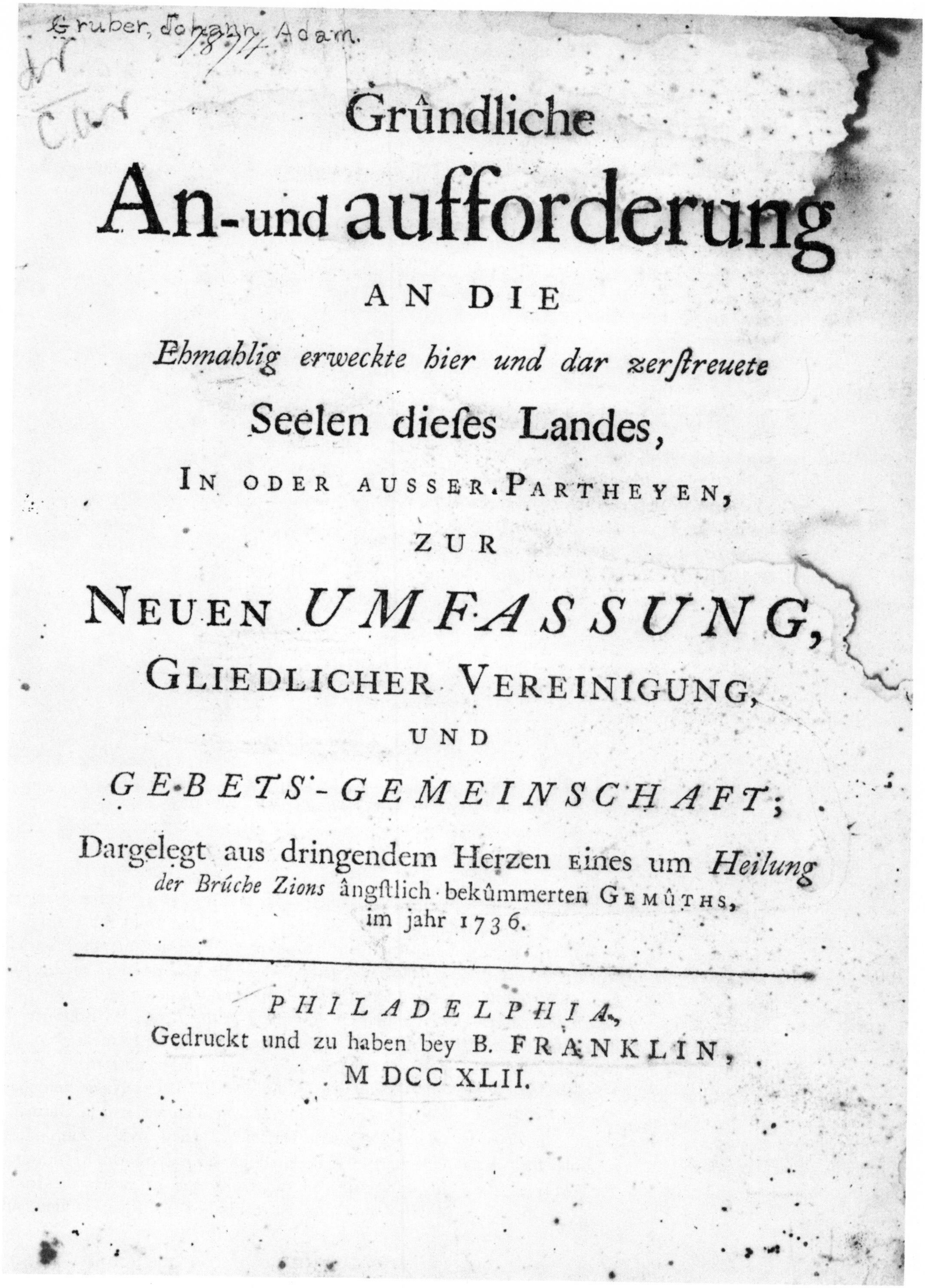

Gründliche
An- und aufforderung

AN DIE

Ehmahlig erweckte hier und dar zerstreuete

Seelen dieses Landes,

IN ODER AUSSER.PARTHEYEN,

ZUR

NEUEN *UMFASSUNG,*

GLIEDLICHER VEREINIGUNG,

UND

GEBETS-GEMEINSCHAFT;

Dargelegt aus dringendem Herzen EINES um *Heilung*
der Brüche Zions ängstlich bekümmerten GEMÜTHS,
im jahr 1736.

PHILADELPHIA,
Gedruckt und zu haben bey B. FRANKLIN,
MDCCXLII.

Benjamin Franklin's reprinting of Adam Gruber's *Call*
for an association of like-minded persons in a religious
fellowship, the end of radical individualism in religious
matters. This was the first ecumenical document in
America. *Courtesy the American Philosophical Society*

to Pennsylvania religious leaders to gather for fellowship and devotion. Having probed the lonely life of the solitary, Gruber yearned for love. He asked the "awakened" leaders of Pennsylvania pietism to gather at Christopher Wiegner's house in the Skippack, thirty miles from Philadelphia. Just as the Conestoga solitary were clustering around Conrad Beissel to form the Ephrata societies, so Wiegner's house became the center for another attempt to overcome religious isolation—the Associated Brethren of the Skippack. One of the members was August Gottlieb Spangenberg (1704–1792), formerly a university professor and now scout for the Moravian leader and later the director of the Bethlehem communal experiment. These "awakened" brethren of the Skippack met several times, with much blessing.

In 1740 Spangenberg returned to Germany. He told Count Zinzendorf of the lonely individuals in Pennsylvania, rich harvest indeed, for nowhere, he said, did the outer church contend so little. Zinzendorf listened. He construed this as *eine Vocation nach Pennsylvanien,* a call to Pennsylvania. At the Moravian Synod in Gotha in 1739, he broached his "plan" for Pennsylvania.

In all truth this was magnificent vision, worthy of a place among the great utopian dreams. He envisaged a state of Indians and Germans to be established in Pennsylvania, with its active center (Bethlehem ?) at some distance from the English settlements; also, he saw a league of "awakened" *tropes* within all groups, including the Anglo-Saxons. Here Spener's idea of the "little churches within the Church" was revived. Indians were given a proper role in this new society, the only instance of a precise plan for integrating the Indians into religious life.

His plan neatly outlined, Count Zinzendorf "invaded" Pennsylvania, renouncing his rank and traveling under the democratic name of "Brother Ludwig." He arrived late in 1741 and remained here for thirteen fateful months, proceeding to develop his plan without sensing the broader implications: what kind of religious fellowship shall replace the European-style established church in free Pennsylvania, an issue that could be neither posed nor solved in Anglo-Saxon America (with the possible exception of Rhode Island). Three answers to this broader question were being brought forward: Conrad Beissel's gathering of awakened people into a medieval-type monastery; Gruber's devotional association for cultivating the inner life; and Zinzendorf's league of the awakened.

Zinzendorf chose an interesting figure to issue his "call" for the Pennsylvania Congregation of God in the Spirit—Henrich Antes (1701–1755). Antes was the son of Baron Friedrich von Blume who, on turning monk, had changed his name to Antos, Greek for flower. Heinrich had married his cousin, the Baroness Katharina von

Obscure grave of Henry Antes, "King of the Germans." *From an old photograph by S. R. Fisher*

Blume, and, after experiencing bitter persecution in Europe, in 1722 they bought land from the Frankfurt Land Company. Coming to Pennsylvania they settled at Falckner Swamp, where he became elder in the Reformed congregation and became known as the "king of the Germans." Prominent in the Associated Brethren of the Skippack, Antes was a suitable instrument through whom Brother Ludwig's "call" might go forth.

Responding to Antes's "call," Pennsylvania religious leaders, including several from Ephrata, met in Germantown New Year's Day, 1742 (new style). Zinzendorf took charge. He declared that his purpose was to enthrone the universality of the Lamb and to gather the fruits of His fellowship. He envisaged no organic union, no merger of denominations—there were as yet no final ones—but simply the joining of awakened persons from various "opinions." Antes had a somewhat less doctrinaire approach; he was more practical, seeking to settle differences and to meet and recognize mutually the good within all groups, covenanting to work for the common good.

Three sessions took place. The result was withdrawal, first by Ephrata and then by each set of leaders, a retreat into denominational consciousness. The failure of these efforts to join the awakened resulted in the emergence of denominational pluralism.

Strong personalities clashed in Pennsylvania: Conrad Beissel with his nihilist, quietist mysticism, who was meeting his call and building his own fellowship along the Conestoga; Johann Adam Gruber—*Ein Geringer*—who had led the awakenings in southern Germany during the 1710s and was a fully charismatic personality; and Count Nicholas von Zinzendorf, imperious, commanding, dedicated, devout, and stubbornly loyal to his "plan" for Pennsylvania. In the end the failure may have come from this clash of personalities.

Between Zinzendorf and Beissel were parallels and contrasts. Both were uncommon religious poets, dynamic proponents of their ideas; both were creative personalities. Both were theological empiricists, advocates of *Wundencompassio,* concerned more with life than with doctrine. The differences were marked: Zinzendorf was a count, an aristocrat, imperious and hungry for affection; Beissel was a peasant, a baker's apprentice, sickly, aloof, misanthropic. Zinzendorf's marriage was happy; Beissel was an unhappy bachelor. Zinzendorf was wealthy, Beissel poor. Still, when the Count came to Ephrata, the Peaceful Father did not greet him.

Between Zinzendorf and Gruber also there were parallels and contrasts. Both were committed Christians, gifted, and of strong minds. Both were fine poets and competent writers. In their ways, both were world renouncing: Gruber called himself "a little one," Zinzendorf "Brother Ludwig." There were also differences. Zinzendorf had been raised by a doting grandmother at court. Gruber had shared the hard knocks of a deposed Swabian cleric. Gruber's marriage was stormy. Zinzendorf was a troubled extrovert, Gruber a melancholy introvert.

Beissel and Gruber do not seem to have clashed. They probably had known each other before in Berleburg, and Frau Gruber was a sister of Georg Stieffel, Beissel's friend.

Thus, in the fateful year 1742, Count Zinzendorf, driven by great vitality, became the catalyst that brought Pennsylvania's religious matters to a head. Previously

(33)

wenigen wahr. Und wan ja jemand mit Wahrheit seine göttliche Träume und Gesichter den stockblinden Menschen erzehlen würde, so solte mancher es nur verächtlich tractiren, oder gar lästern.

Man hört die blinde Welt auf die Gesichter schmähen ;
Wie nun? wan's des *Elisa* Knaben
Von GOtt dem HErrn geschahe,
Daß er den Berg voll Feuriger Roß und Wagen sahe
Was kont er dan davor, daß er so viel gesehen?
Es muß die blinde Welt etwas zu lästern haben.

Die Historie, wie man sie aus *Elisabeth* Joderin zu Oly ihrem eigenen Munde geschrieben Anno 1743, lautet wie folget :

IHr Vatter, Namens Jost Joder, welcher vor zwey Jahren und etlichen Monathen diese sichtbare Welt verlassen, hatte in seinem Hertzen noch einige Worte oder Erinnerung an seine Kinder, und sonderlich an seine obgemelte Tochter, welche er sehr liebete; sie hingegen war ihrem Vater mit gleicher Geneigtheit und Liebe zugethan. Er wurde aber wieder sein Vermuthen aus dem Zeitlichen geruffen, ehe er seine im Hertzen habende Rede an seine Kinder ausgesprochen hatte. Währender Zeit nach seinem
C   Abster-

The Pennsylvania Dutch matched the Quakers in seeing visions and having other ecstatic experiences. One of the more celebrated of these "ghost stories" was that of the return of Yost Yoder from the grave and his conversation with his daughter Elisabeth in 1743. Christopher Saur himself visited Oley and reported the incident. Here is the first half-page of his account, taken from a later edition of the work, which first appeared in 1744 but was reprinted in 1748, 1755, and 1792. *Courtesy the Historical Society of Pennsylvania*

things had been mobile. There were give and take, desire for fellowship. Now matters became fixed. Each group was forced back into itself and had to project its own reason for existence in rational terms. Thus was denominationalism born.

One old warrior of the pious, Samuel Güldin, returned for a moment to the wars, publishing his *Unsectarian Witness,* which dealt with Zinzendorf's efforts to remake Pennsylvania religions. This theoretical analysis was published by Christopher Saur in 1743.

Perhaps it is not fair to put all the blame on Zinzendorf, wide as his shoulders were. The first casualty had been the split between Conrad Beissel and the Dunkers of Peter Becker. Although this split had taken place two decades previously, literary reassertions did not come until 1743 when Saur published Hochman von Hohenau's *Glaubensbekentniss,* a Dunkard Confession. Next year the Dunkard hymnal came out, *Das Kleine Davidische Psalterspiel,* reprinted in 1760, 1764, 1777, 1797, 1812, and 1879. This contained the poetry of Angelus Silesius, Gerhard Tersteegen, and other European mystics, adding some materials from American authors. Thus the Dunkards became a "denomination."

Ephrata continued to gather in other awakenings— from Falckner Swamp, Tulpehocken, French Creek, Germantown, Amwell in New Jersey, and even from Gimbsheim in the Old World. Ephrata was a pietist cloister and we err when we call it medieval.

Conrad Beissel, its founder, who was born about 1690 in Eberbach near Heidelberg, had been mixed up in pietist affairs as early as 1715. He arrived in Germantown in 1720, hoping to join "The Woman in the Wilderness," but the death of Kelpius had made this impossible. So he fled to the Conestoga, erected his hut for the solitary life, grubbed his living in the wilderness, wrote mystical poetry in this situation as far from corrupt Europe as he could get, for he was then at the very edge of civilization.

The frontier was then hospitable to awakenings. In 1724 Beissel let himself be baptized again by Peter Becker, and he was now seen as leader of the Conestoga Baptists. Soon the old separatist spirit prevailed; sometime around 1727 a new sect began to appear. During these years Beissel's views held as a lonely solitary were expressed in four books, all published before there was an Ephrata.

The first was *Das Buchlein vom Sabbath,* privately published in 1725 by Andrew Bradford. No copy sur-

vives. It advocated the seventh day, Saturday, as the sabbath.

The second, of which no copy survives, was *Das Ehe das Zuchthaus Fleischlicher Menschen,* appearing probably from Franklin's press. Its views on marriage were discussed in later tracts and they became an issue with the Moravians. Beissel's view on this subject came from Hochmann von Hohenau and Jacob Boehme.

The third work was poetry, *Gottliche Liebes und Lobes-Gethöne*—not hymns in the usual sense. There was as yet no congregation to sing them! These were lyrical verses born out of the stillness of Beissel's Conestoga solitude, baroque in the then old-fashioned traditions of German poets like Friedrich Spee, Angelus Silesius, and Gottfried Arnold.

At the same time a poor work of ninety-nine mystical sayings came out, perhaps with other short pieces. This was on Franklin's press. All these were published before there was a community at Ephrata.

For Beissel was living as a "quiet in the land," a solitary among other individuals, refugees from corrupt Europe. By 1732, however, the land came to be somewhat cluttered with people. Beissel again withdrew deeper into the wilderness. But he was not to live alone; others followed him. A camp for solitary began to develop, much like that in the hills of Wittgenstein in Westphalia. In 1735 Beissel began to proselyte and he caught some important fish: the Reverend Peter Müller, the Reformed pastor in Tulpehocken, graduate in theology from Heidelberg, and one of the leaders in the awakening in that region, also Conrad Weiser, among others, who came to be associated with Ephrata, as this place came to be called.

The new community began to shape up. Beissel went forth to get more of the "awakened." Wherever an awakening occurred, Beissel appeared, to bring its members to Ephrata. The congregation that developed around Conrad Beissel was an offshoot of the German Baptist Brethren, but it incorporated three societies: Solitary Brethren, Single Sisters called "Roses of Sharon," and married Householders. This was the old Franciscan pattern. The two single orders were formally celibate, reflecting Beissel's views on sex; also they were self-governing, with elected officers and adopted rules. (The Rule Book of the Sisters survives in the Historical Society of Pennsylvania.) Surrounding the community were the third order, married Householders. Over all, as *Vorsteher,* was Conrad Beissel—unordained, depending

First page of Conrad Beissel's Preface to the *Turteltaube*
Manuscript, in the Library of Congress.

machet dem barir den obern e. und dem töner und baß a. der e machet dem barir und baß C. dem töner a. wie es zu heben wan der gesang gefallen kan oben aus den b. weisen geholt werden..

Nun sind uns die f weisen noch übrig, also f. a. C den schlüssel zu den 4. Stimmen ausmachen, die übrigen 4 bedinte, als g. b. d. e so machet der g. dem barir und baß den C und dem töner den e. der b macht dem barir den d. und dem töner und baß den g. der d. machet dem barir u. baß den b. und dem töner den g. der e. machet dem barir und baß C, dem töner a. auch zuweilen g. wan der gesang gefallen, so wird gethan, wie oben schon gemeldet, daß ich einen andern f mache, welches dann mit f. g as geschaffet wird, da ich dann meinen f nehme, und steige auf folgende weise.

auf und wann ich den as hab so nenne ich ihn f und setze meinen Gesang fort, die Prob ist richtig.

Nun wollen wir zu einem gründlichen unterricht die ganße Sach auf 6 Tafeln abmahlen, worinnen das ganße Werd enthalten da wir dann allemahl zuerst den schlüssel der 4 Stimmen. und dann hernach, wie die übrigen noten in 4 Stimmen Lassen wollen sehen lassen.

Last page of Conrad Beissel's Preface to the *Turteltaube* Manuscript, in the Library of Congress.

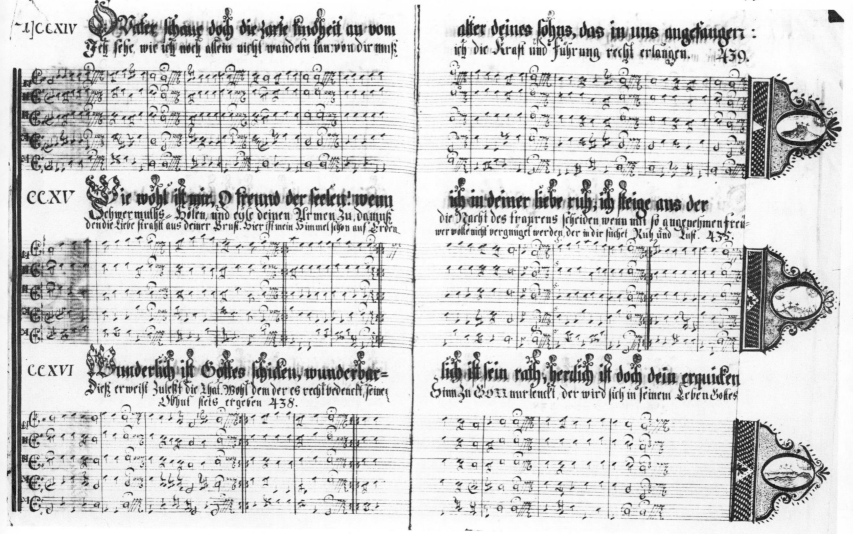

These pages from the Ephrata *Turteltaube* Manuscript in the Library of Congress are rare in that they use pictures of Calvary. *Courtesy the Library of Congress*

on the charisma of his personality.

In 1735 Kedar, the first building for the Solitary, was erected, put up without nails, for use of the Sisters. Three years later a Brothers' house was built. The first prior of the Brethren was Gabriel Eckerlin, a physician, who was succeeded in 1741 by his brother, Israel. In 1739 the *Saal* for worship was built, with cells on the third floor. In 1741 another prayer house was erected, and the same year a new cloister, Hebron, was erected for use of the Householders. In 1746 Bethania was built for the Brethren.

Outwardly Ephrata recalled a monastery: the Brothers wore long beards, were cowled, and wore white robes that fell to the ankles, a habit similar to that of the Capuchins in Europe. The Sisters also wore white robes, frocks underneath, with hoods to frame their faces—linen in summer and wool in winter. They took cloister names: Beissel was *Vater Friedsam* in spite of his contentious spirit; Peter Müller was Jabez; Israel Eckerlin Onesimus. Sisters were Euphemia, Mana, Phoebe, Rahel, Zenobia, and Anastasia, who was the chief folk artist. Hair was close cropped, except for beards. Meals were eaten in silence from wooden bowls (although archaeologists have found much china). Water was the drink. Sleeping was

Interior title page of the theory of music done by Conrad
Beissel, in a manuscript in the Library of Congress.

on unmattressed wooden benches with wood-block pillows. Schools for further disciplining the flesh by singing and writing were founded.

The inner spirit was preciously tender. Around 1735 Beissel ordered that on the Sixth Day everyone was to examine his heart before God, in his own cell, and then turn in a written statement about his spiritual condition. In 1752 some of these statements were published as *Lectiones*—sometimes mistakenly ascribed to Beissel— a remarkable achievement in group mysticism. Beissel as *Vorsteher* undertook to go over these reports and answer them at Seventh Day Meeting. After his death a selection of these answers was brought out as his *Geistliche Reden,* and while these are not direct answers to

specific statements, we can nonetheless gain some understanding of what the mood was like.

But we have much better evidence concerning the spirit of Ephrata. Beyond doubt the finest cultural achievement of Ephrata—and I believe of the entire eighteenth century among the Pennsylvania Dutch—was the poetry that was being continually composed, gathered in the *Wunderspiel* of 1766. Here we have important lyrical verse—and we must disabuse our minds of our modern notion of hymnody—which deserves to be better known in both German and American literature. As far as the former is concerned, the Ephrata *Wunderspiel* presents the best one-volume collection of verse by radical pietists, persons who lost no creativeness when

Conrad Weiser could not abide the lack of personal freedom among the Ephrata Brethren. So in September 1744, he sent this historic letter of resignation to the dear friends and Brethren there.

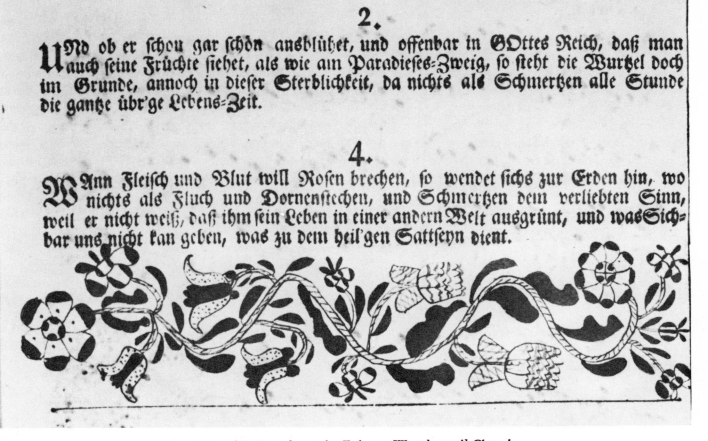

2.

UNd ob er schou gar schön ausblühet, und offenbar in GOttes Reich, daß man auch seine Früchte siehet, als wie ain Paradieses-Zweig, so steht die Wurtzel doch im Grunde, annoch in dieser Sterblichkeit, da nichts als Schmertzen alle Stunde die gantze übr'ge Lebens-Zeit.

4.

WAnn Fleisch und Blut will Rosen brechen, so wendet sichs zur Erden hin, wo nichts als Fluch und Dornenstechen, und Schmertzen dem verliebten Sinn, weil er nicht weiß, daß ihm sein Leben in einer andern Welt ausgrünt, und wasSichbar uns nicht kan geben, was zu dem heil'gen Sattseyn dient.

Here on this page from the Ephrata *Wunderspeil* Choral book in the Historical Society of Pennsylvania, we see the joining of design and words. Stanza two speaks of the Paradise-twig that bears fruit; stanza four speaks of roses cursed by thorns. Do not the designs depict what the hymnals say? Can there be any doubt that the meaning of Fraktur designs, and perhaps of all folk art, is to be found in this poetry?

they migrated to Pennsylvania; this work deserves to be recognized in German literary histories as one of the sources of the romantic spirit. As for American literature—and although the language is German, it was written in Lancaster, Pennsylvania—I have to suggest that together these poets form the most significant school in Colonial America and that Conrad Beissel wrote more verse than any other Colonial American, including Edward Taylor. The *Wunderspiel* does not include all of Beissel's Ephrata verse.

This was in truth strange hymnody, nearly paranoic in mystical intensity, joining pietist confession with objective praise. These "hymns" move from resignation to sexual boasting, from nihilist resignation to ego-assertion, from surrender of will to arrogant claims that one has hit the spiritual target. In spite of stylistic weaknesses and lame composition at times, Beissel's verse remains the most impressive Pennsylvania Dutch cultural achievement.

The work has four parts: I, pages 1 to 296, containing 441 poems by Beissel; II, pages 297 to 347 with 72 poems by Solitary Brethren and a communally composed *Bruderlied;* III, pages 348 to 403, has 99 poems by the Sisters and the communally composed *Schwesterlied;* IV, pages 404 to 473, has 111 poems by the Householders.

Paradisisches Wunder-Spiel,

Welches sich

In diesen letzten Zeiten und Tagen
In denen Abend-Ländischen Welt-Theilen als ein Vor-
spiel der neuen Welt hervor gethan. Bestehende
In einer gantz neuen und ungemeinen Sing-
Art auf Weise der Englischen und himm-
lischen Chören eingerichtet.

Da dann das Lied Mosis und des Lamms, wie auch das hohe Lied Salomo-
nis samt noch mehrern Zeugnüssen aus der Bibel und andern Heiligen
in liebliche Melodyen gebracht. Wobey nicht weniger der Zuruf der
Braut des Lamms, samt der Zubereitung auf den herrlichen
Hochzeit-Tag trefflich Præfigurirt wird.

Alles nach Englischen Chören Gesangs-Weise mit viel Mühe und grosem Fleiß
ausgefertiget von einem

Friedsamen,

Der sonst in dieser Welt weder Namen noch Titul suchet.

EPHRATÆ Sumptibus Societatis: 1 7 5 4.

Ephrata *Wunderspiel* choral book, partly printed, partly illuminated. *Courtesy the Henry Francis duPont Winterthur Museum*

Beissel's work ranges widely, passing from metrical paraphrases of Scripture to highly developed interpretations of sexual matters. He wrote of Sophia, *Ungrund,* and other mystical ideas strange to lyrical verse; he was full of *Wundencompassio* and an anxiety-rooted mysticism that in many ways anticipates Kierkegaard.

Michael Wohlfarth, student of Tauler, was the most prolific versifier of the Solitary, but about a dozen other Brethren wrote, including Peter Müller and Friedrich Gass. The brothers joined to produce a communal poem in celebration of filial love.

Sisters wrote more delicately and tenderly, lacking the robustness of the brothers, but where else were there so

many women writing verse in the Colonial period? Among these were Christina Lässle, Elizabeth Eckstein, and Maria Müller, among others. The sisters likewise wrote a communal work on sister love.

The chief Householder poet was Ludwig Höcker, community schoolmaster, an old pietist already well known in Germany. Others were Valentin Mack, Jacob Gass, and George Adam Martin.

It took about thirty years for the *Wunderspiel* to take form, a compilation of the poetical work of a community with at least fifty persons involved in its composition.

Beissel's prose was less dramatic, perhaps even less creative, although I suggest that, seen in its Boehmist context, it takes on special meaning. His *Wunderschrift,* apparently based on an earlier writing on marriage, was brought out in final form by the press of the Brotherhood in 1745. Here Beissel stood on the boundary between Boehme and Freud, looking backward toward the ascetic

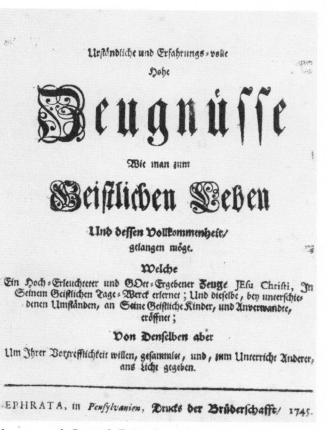

Umständliche und Erfahrungs-volle

Hohe

Zeugnüsse

Wie man zum

Geistlichen Leben

Und dessen Vollkommenheit/
gelangen möge.

Welche

Ein Hoch-Erleuchteter und GOtt-Ergebener Zeuge JEsu Christi, In
Seinem Geistlichen Tage-Werck erlernet; Und dieselbe, bey unterschie-
denen Umständen, an Seine Geistliche Kinder, und Anverwandte,
eröffnet;

Von Denselben aber

Um Ihrer Vortrefflichkeit willen, gesammlet, und, zum Unterricht Anderer,
ans Licht gegeben.

EPHRATA, in *Pensylvanien,* Druck der Brüderschafft/ 1745.

Title page of Conrad Beissel's important mystical tract printed on the press of the Brotherhood at Ephrata. *Courtesy the Historical Society of Pennsylvania*

Ephrata Press and wall chart. *Courtesy the Pennsylvania Historical and Museum Commission*

renunciation of carnality and forward toward the specula-tive realization of sexuality. Beissel, however, saw the sexual problem as religious. Original man, Adam, was androgynous, bisexual. He had both masculine and fem-inine "tinctures"—an alchemical word as good as any other—and Christ also was a man of dual sex. Separation into sexes arose with the Fall; mankind was divided into Adams and Eves. Eve replaced heavenly wisdom (Sophia), and fallen man now sported with Eve instead of with Sophia. Christ was wed to Sophia, and regenerate man the same. This doctrine, here summarized, came

from Boehme, Gichtel, and Gottfried Arnold, and was strengthened by Beissel's own sexual experiences and by his reading of the Song of Song. Some of his poems, with astonishing frankness, expose his peccadilloes with the daughters of Eve. Still we may ask, was Conrad Beissel anticipating Freud and Jung?

In the same year, 1745, there also appeared a work of superior mysticism, *Original Experiences and High Testimonies* (see title page). This collection of short meditations was highly regarded and considered to be his profoundest work. The first meditation, it is said, was

Johann Valentin Haidt: The First Fruits
Haidt painted the theology and people of the Moravian movement. Here in this Moravian heaven all races were embraced, all who were washed in the blood of the Lamb. This showed the pietist democracy inherent in the "little churches within the Church." One of these figures is Tschoop, the last of the Mohicans. *Copyright, 1955, by the Board of Elders of the Northern Diocese of the Church of the United Brethren in the United States of America, and used by their kind permission*

Anonymous: The Pennsylvania Blue Boy
Thomas Gainsborough in old England had painted the famous *Blue Boy* in 1770. Several years earlier an unknown Pennsylvania painter tried the same theme, but with different results. *Courtesy Mr. and Mrs. Walter C. Moser*

Two eighteenth-century paintings

German language metamorphosis

The changing symbols are described in the verses that accompany them. Here is strong evidence that the artists were aware of the complicated meanings of these symbols. How else could they express such elaborate symbolism? *From a private collection*

required reading for all who entered Ephrata. Its first printing contained a Foreword by Israel Eckerlin, which was deleted from subsequent editions when misunderstanding between Beissel and Eckerlin arose. These *Testimonies* were his finest writing, cryptic and aphoristic, with a mood of somewhat negative nihilism. They stressed the poverty of spirit and the emptied self of the old classical mysticism. In these Beissel may have anticipated the philosophy of the unconscious of Edward von Hartmann, which arose in the middle of the nineteenth century.

The Press of the brotherhood became the source for mystical and Anabaptist literature, a cohesive cultural force in early Lancaster county. In 1745 they printed *Göldene Apfeln in Silbernen Schallen,* which presented the writings of the Palatine Anabaptists. In 1748 a remarkable production was the *Martyrer Spiegel,* which was translated by Peter Müller and printed by fifteen of the Brethren. Other works continued to appear even after the Press was in private hands.

Conrad Beissel was not the only author at Ephrata. Michael Wohlfarth, Heinrich Kemper, and Israel Eckerlin also wrote. Eckerlin left a manuscript of considerable interest, a vindication of his views, called *Scriptures of the Zionitic Order;* this was sent back from the Allegheny wilderness.

When Conrad Beissel died in 1768, Ephrata lost spirit. The battle was over. For forty years his strong personality had inspired a remarkable phrase of American Colonial life. Almost three hundred persons, at one time or another, had been moved to accept his mystical and ascetic views. With all his intellectual acumen, Peter Müller, who succeeded Beissel, could not match Beissel's personal *magia.*

So, then, Ephrata and Conrad Beissel's views proved a stumbling block to Count Zinzendorf's Pennsylvania plans, and especially those on marriage, a theme much discussed at that time. In fact, Heinrich Antes wrote a brief tract on marriage.

The break of the Schwenkfelder sect with Count Zinzendorf had already taken place in Germany. After persecution, the sect fled from Harpersdorf to Herrnhut, Zinzendorf's estates, accepting the Count's generosity. But Pennsylvania beckoned them, and when the Count reminded them of their past obligations, they thanked him and refused to be drawn into his net.

Three important literary works gave character to the Schwenkfelder sect, marking its transition to a denomination: 1) the 1762 collection of their poetry; 2) the

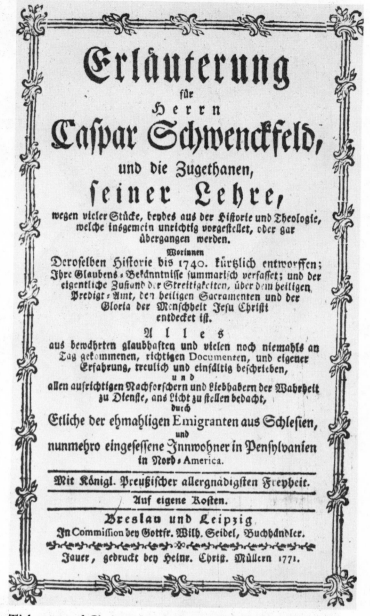

Title page of Christopher Schultz's *Vindication of Caspar Schwenkfeld,* one of the books written in Pennsylvania and printed in Europe. In typical fashion it was dedicated with long-windedness, to Frederick the Great of Prussia, with an appeal for tolerance. It touched the monarch, who invited the sect to return to their homeland. There is as yet no bibliography of works written in Pennsylvania and published in Europe. *Courtesy the Schwenkfelder Library*

Erläuterung or *Vindication,* first published in Europe in 1771; and 3) Christopher Schultz's *Compendium of Theology,* written during the grim years of the American

Schwenkfelder women in their sectarian garb. *Courtesy the Schwenkfelder Library*

Revolution, circulating in manuscript until its publication in Philadelphia in 1836. Taken together, these works are sufficient to establish the intellectual vigor of the sect.

The 1762 hymnal, *Neu-Eingerichtetes Gesang-Buch,* likewise carries us beyond narrow views of hymnody. Published in Germantown by Christopher Saur, it contains both European and American poetry by members of the Schwenkfelder sect or persons closely connected with it. As its basis it has the poetry of the Bohemian Brethren, and included among the European writers are some names otherwise unknown in German literature because, as members of a persecuted sect, they dared not publish—names like Adam Reisner, Georg Frell, Daniel Sudermann (who did escape into print), Georg Heydrich, and Martin John, Jr. American writers include: Abraham Wagner (1715–1763), Balthasar Hoffmann (1678–1775), Caspar Kriebel (*c.* 1700–1771), Christoph Kriebel (*c.* 1688–1741), David Seipt (1699–1765), Johannes Hübner (*c.* 1684–1745), and the prolific Georg Weiss (1687–1740). This collection was the result of many years' work on the part of the Schwenkfelder housefathers. Because they dared not print, they copied out their poetry in longhand, making fine manuscript collections, thus both preserving their sectarian verse and developing into poets themselves. A series of fine manuscripts is preserved in the Schwenkfelder library, among them Balthasar Hoffmann's magnificently written work.

The second significant Schwenkfeld work, the *Erläuterung,* or *Vindication of Caspar Schwenkfeld and his Adherents,* is an example of the (so far uncatalogued) works written in Pennsylvania and published in Germany, appearing in Berlin and Leipzig in 1771 and dedicated to Frederick the Great. This was an apology for Schwenkfeld and his doctrines, a justification of his theology, and a vindication of the historical events that surrounded the bitter persecution in Silesia. It looked backward to battles lost and won, and now, from the vantage point of a free Pennsylvania, it sought rational vindication. This was an able and sober apology, containing a brief doctrinal statement and emphasizing the doctrine of the sacraments, the point where the Schwenkfelders differed from the other sects most markedly.

While the outer world was aflame and political revolution was proceeding, the Schwenkfelder Christopher Schultz (1718–1789) produced the finest intellectual achievement of Pennsylvania sectarianism, his *Compendium of Dogmatic Theology,* a work whose text has not yet been translated. Although not published until 1836 (Philadelphia: Shelley and Lester), the work is dated, for it belongs to the pre-Schleiermacher period of theological writing. Schultz learned his lessons from pietist Johann Jakob Rambach's *Dogmatische Theologie,* discovering from this the rational content of religion. This shows that American Schwenkfelders were thinking in broader areas than the narrow confines of their sect. Schultz's work, in my opinion, is as fine as any Anglo-Saxon intellectual achievement of the Colonial period.

Schwenkfelders were largely a literary movement, self-taught farmers who kept precious traditions alive. They were spiritual, pacifist, biblicist, and bound together by the memory of common suffering and by the dedication of their leaders.

If the Schwenkfelders were small and untrained farmers, seeking only to dwell in peace, early American Moravians were a larger movement, led by university men from Leipzig, Jena, and Halle who were aggressive in seeking new converts. The literature that supports the Moravian work in Pennsylvania is not only difficult to

The Gemeinhaus, Bethlehem, from an old drawing.

separate from associated European materials, but also massive and exceptionally competent, an ignored chapter in American intellectual history. Most of the earlier material was written under the domination of Count Zinzendorf, and the rare *Verzeichniss der Schriften des Grafen Ludwig von Zinzendorf* (Stettin, 1834) lists his works written during his American visit of thirteen months. Included are his *Reden,* Latin and German; a commentary on Luther's catechism; a Latin apology directed at the free thinkers; two hymnals; several books of apologetic documents; plans for schools (which may be among the earliest pedagogical writings in Pennsylvania), and so on.

Moravian intellectual achievement passed from strong apologetic to practical Christianity expressed in economic patterns. Modern studies of Zinzendorf's theology, which dominated the movement, have brought understanding of the mental and psychological processes operating on

An die Brüder-Gemeinen.

Ihr Blut-Würmlein im Meer der Gnade!

Ich bin hier in der Wüsten, und laure auf Wilde, wie sie, auf die wilden Thiere.

Meine Seele handelt mehr mit dem Lamme, als mit den Menschen; und in dieser Gemüths-Fassung ist dieser Eilfte Anhang vollends zu stande kommen.

Einem von der Gemeine entfernten Cantor ist nicht zuzumuthen, daß er liefern soll, was er mitten in der Gemeine liefern würde: doch, damit ich den Zwölften Anhang, wovon inzwischen der meiste Theil wird zu stande gekommen seyn, vor meiner zweyten Entfernung aus Eurer Nähe, noch ausgehen lassen könne, will ich diesen nicht länger aufhalten.

Mein herzliches Lamm lasse Euch doch bey diesen Liedern fühlen, was bey den meisten kräftig empfunden hat

Aus dem Zelte vor Wayomick, in der grossen Ebene Skehantowáno, in Canada, am 15. Octob. 1742.

Euer unwürdiger

JOHANAN*.

_____

* Das ist der Name unsers Bruders LUDWIG, wie er unter den Heiden bekant ist.

Preface to the Eleventh Appendix of the Moravian hymnal written by Count Zinzendorf among the Indians in the Poconos, here erroneously called "Canada." He signed himself Jonathan.

his spirit, yet when all is said, he still remains the most significant figure in radical pietism, a man of great vitality whose genius was broad and empirical. His attitude toward mysticism was ambivalent: in 1740 he edited an edition of Mme Guion's *Spiritual Guide* wherein he opposed those Inspirationists who were "long dead and still living"—did he mean Johann Adam Gruber?—calling them false guides.

In America Zinzendorf's most significant bit of editing was the eleventh and twelfth appendices to the Görlitz Moravian hymnal. Its noteworthy preface is dated October 1742, "on the great plane Skehantowana" among the Indians in the Poconos. He was impressed by his own daring: "I am here in the wilds, and glare at the savages as they glare at wild beasts!" The court-bred German count faced the noble savages!

Moravians were even more prolific at writing verse than the members of the Ephrata societies and Bethlehem —and of course the larger Moravian community—and surpassed Ephrata in both the quality and quantity of its verse. Several collections survive beyond what was printed in several hymnals; a major work on American Moravian verse is much needed. In addition to Zinzendorf the following American Moravians wrote tolerable verse: Anna Caritas Nitschmann (1715–1760), Johann F. C. Cammerhof (1721–1751), Johannes de Watteville (1718–1789), Gottlob Büttner (1716–1745), Augustus Gottlieb Spangenberg (1709–1782), Matthias Stack (1711–1787), and Georg Neisser (1715–1785).

Early Moravian music remains a mystery. We do know that John Antes (1740–1811), American-born son of Heinrich Antes, wrote secular music as well as liturgical, graceful lyrical works that have been compared to Haydn's. Johann Frederik Peter (1744–1813) also wrote music during his Pennsylvania stay, although most of his composition was done in North Carolina. Other Moravians who composed music were: Johannes Herbst (1730–1812), Jeremiah Dencke (1720–1795), and David M. Michael (1751–1827).

An intriguing Moravian figure was John Tschoop, whose Mohican name was Wasemba and who lived along the Hudson. Converted by C. H. Rauch, baptized April 16, 1742, he became an evangelist to his people. In 1746 these Christian Indians from New York came to Bethlehem, where many caught the smallpox and died. Some writers claim that Tschoop was the prototype for the Indian hero of Cooper's *The Last of the Mohicans*. Tschoop died at Bethlehem in 1746 and lies buried next to a Saxon bishop.

There was also Andrew the Negro, the first convert from St. Thomas, whom Count Zinzendorf brought to Bethlehem.

The Moravians reacted to the failure of Zinzendorf's grand scheme by becoming energetic missionaries. They produced some romantic figures like Gottlob Büttner, who lived with his wife among the Indians at Shekomeko, where he died an unalterable pacifist.

However, gradually sectarian migration waned. Odd personalities appeared, such as Johann Franz Regnier, who had been born in Vivres in Switzerland and came to America in 1728, joining Ephrata in 1743. Next he showed up in Oley, where he lived three miles from deTurk's and where he wrote an autobiography with the (translated) title: *The Mystery of the Zinzendorfian Sect, or, The Autobiography of Johann Frantz Regnier*. A physician by profession, Regnier wandered with David Gemähle as evangelist, having some success among Jews in Pennsylvania and New York, going from sect to sect, seeking peace. His work, which had at least three German printings, was one of America's first works of its kind, reflecting the pietist spirit of self-examination.

Another interesting figure was George deBenneville (1703–1793), founder of American Universalism, onetime ward of Queen Anne of England, and a medical graduate of Padua, who joined pietism with medicine. (The relationship of pietism and medicine does not yet seem to have been studied.) When deBenneville's surviving manuscripts—theological, medical, and chemical—have been studied, they may illuminate a figure still shrouded in mystery. DeBenneville also made an impact on Oley, where his doctrines spread among the Bertolet family and others.

However, the most important and almost unknown figure in Colonial Pennsylvania sectarianism was the already-mentioned Johann Adam Gruber, who had issued his call for a gathering of the awakened. Gruber had written works in Germany dealing with the spirit of inspiration. The British Museum has several of his earlier works and it is said that some of his manuscripts are at Amana, Iowa. We do know that his *Kinderstimme,* a work of poetry far more sophisticated than any children's

"Jesus Call Thou me, from the world to Flee; . . . Not Jerusalem, but Bethlehem. . . ." Here the hymn sung when Bethlehem was founded is illuminated.

In 1747 Dr. George deBenneville wrote this prescription for the cough of Mr. Johannes Yoder of Oley. Dr. deBenneville was still living in this valley, spreading his peculiar brand of universalist pietism, which replaced with some settlers the Moravianism of the years immediately past. *Photograph by William B. Daub*

book, was published in 1717, probably at Ronneburg in Germany. Gruber wrote under several pseudonymns (he was retiring by nature), but his known works include the first discussion of educational theory in America; apologetic works against Zinzendorf; a long account of Pennsylvania religious conditions; an anthology of mystical literature between 1679 and 1750; and several volumes of verse. Unquestionably Johann Adam Gruber was the most important individual in Pennsylvania sectarianism.

Gruber lived next door to Christopher Saur I in Germantown. He was somehow related by marriage to this champion of sectarianism. In 1739 Saur began to publish his celebrated newspaper, *Der Hoch-Deutsch*

Pennsylvanische Geschichts-Schreiber, which changed its name several times during its long publication. At first it was only a small monthly; by 1775 it had become a weekly, and under Christopher Saur II a weapon of adroitness in the sectarian wars. Saur I and his son used the newspaper, the almanac, and the *Geistliche Magazien* as weapons in the dissenting cause. Between 1764 and 1770 the younger Saur published this give-away magazine, the first religious journal in America, wherein he reprinted mystical and dissenting materials. The Saur press—father and son—produced a steady stream of mystical, pietist, and sectarian works by George Whitefield, Gilbert Tennant, William Law, Thomas à Kempis, Gerhard Tersteegen, Christian Hoburg, Fénélon, Paul

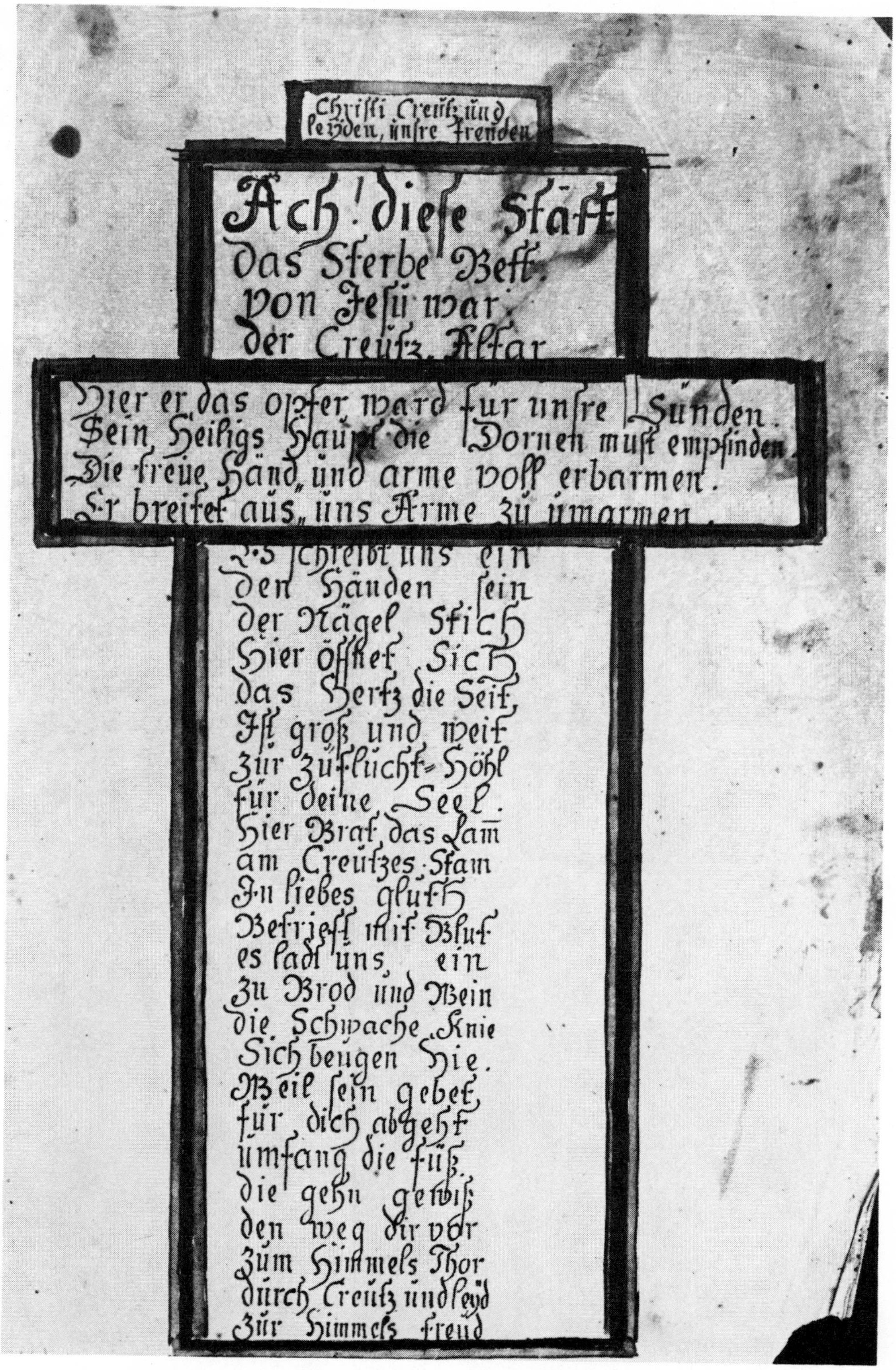

Baroque-style poem by the Reverend Daniel Schuhmacher.

Siegvolck, John Bunyan, Stephan Crisp, John Everard, Thomas Bromley, William Dell, and Johann Arndt. Its fare was cosmopolitan. Saur also imported books for sale, chiefly of dissenting and mystical traditions; his catalogue is revealing. He was the agent, too, for the famous Berleburg Bible, the great translation with mystical commentary done in Germany.

Hence, for the first seven or eight decades of its history, Pennsylvania was the land of dissenting religion, a haven for the oppressed, and a place where new values were emerging and where we may see the highway leading from the love-drunk religions of the seventeenth century to the democratic formulations of the eighteenth century.

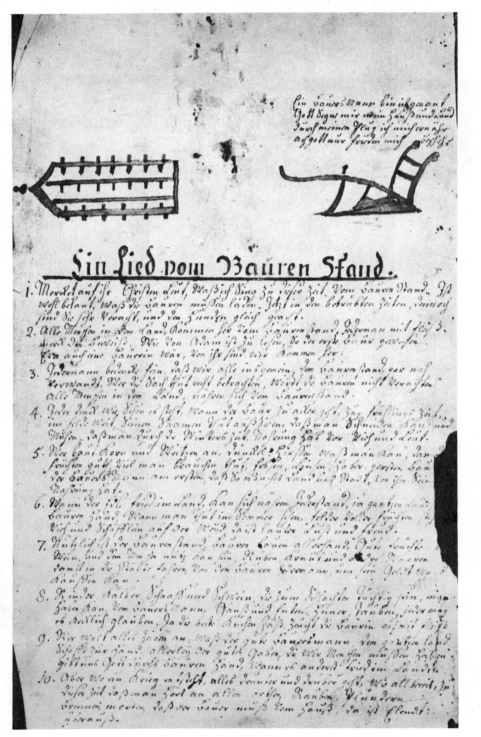

First page of the Reverend Daniel Schuhmacher's poem on the farming situation during the Revolution. There exists a second page of manuscript in his hand.

Goshenhoppen, 2 May, 1777

Whereas in the present time our land, because of the scorn for the demonstrated Grace of God, and because of other sins, has been brought to heavy oppressions by weighty circumstances, great unrest of war, and military ordinances;

Whereas on the First Day of this month we have declared our opposition to Militia affairs, that for conscience sake we cannot join in with such arrangements;

Whereas, at the same time, it is to be expected that many persons who refuse military service will be oppressed and because of refusal to perform such duties may expect to have fines and other punishments;

Therefore, as a consequence, we who follow the apostolic doctrines of the blessed Caspar Schwenkfeld, and who in open assembly and before the youth have promised to follow the same before each other and our own, and after having discussed this thoroughly, are herewith bound together that they will take such fines which the land may impose upon those who because of conscience reject military duty in which death-dealing weapons are employed, and are commanded to use the same, we, the said subscribers, shall commonly and together bear these fines and so as to keep one another in Christian character, and all those who are thus punished have the right to present a true account of the case and to expect reimbursement therefore.

Copy of one of the great documents of Pennsylvania pietism. *Courtesy the Schwenkfelder Library*

3

Developing Conflict

Slowly the character of the migration to Pennsylvania changed. The stage was set for a conflict that was to last for several decades and that altered the nature of Pennsylvania Dutch culture. For as the migration of sectarians waned, a flood of settlers came into Pennsylvania who were less interested in religion and more concerned with practical worldly affairs. Thus conflict between sectarian and churchman arose, a dispute that was to sear the sixth and seventh decades of the eighteenth century and ultimately to determine the nature of our life.

Two ideals were in conflict. Sectarians were seeking to build an ideal society, where moral perfection was possible, where there were no wars. Churchmen understood religion as part of the larger life. An old dichotomy thus lingered in Colonial Pennsylvania, coloring its culture and characterizing its history.

The first chuch to emerge as a formal denomination among the Pennsylvania Dutch was the Evangelical Lutheran. Of course, Swedish Lutherans had been in the Delaware Valley for many years and German Lutherans had a congregation at New Hanover (Falckner Swamp) in 1701, ministered to by Justus Falckner, who had been ordained by the Swedes. Still, frontier conditions were bad, and with the increasing number of Lutheran families coming into the province, congregations arose without ministers. In 1733 David Weisiger, the Rev. Johann Christian Schultze, and Johann Daniel Schöner were sent to England and Germany to acquaint authorities with

the spiritual destitution in America. They presented themselves to the court preacher in London, the Rev. Friedrich M. Ziegenhagen—King George was a Hanoverian Lutheran!—and he referred the petitioners to Germany with appropriate letters. On May 3, 1734, Weisiger's pamphlet, *Brief Report . . .* , a summary of religious conditions in the New World, appeared in Hildesheim, along with several descriptive letters. These came to the attention of August Herman Francke, pietist leader in Halle, who was to become the driving force behind the movement to supply Lutheran ministers to America. In September 1741, he presented a call to a young pietist minister, Heinrich M. Mühlenberg, in the name of the congregations in Pennsylvania: at New Hanover (Falckner Swamp), Providence (Trappe), and Philadelphia. Mühlenberg accepted this call and he arrived in England on April 17, 1742, spending several months learning the language, and, after a long, hard voyage, he landed on September 24, 1742, in Charleston, S. C., coming to Pennsylvania November 23, 1742, just as Count Zinzendorf was bringing his American affairs to a burning climax.

Mühlenberg was needed. His call was regular, even royally sanctioned, so there could be no question about his orthodoxy. The king's chaplain showed his support for the work by composing a hymn for use in instruction of Lutheran youth in Pennsylvania.

However, Mühlenberg had come to a land where dis-

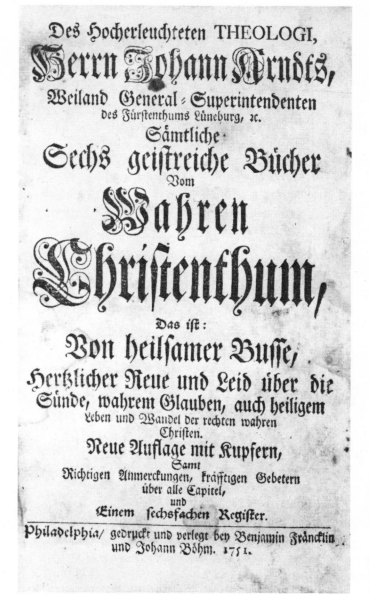

Des Hocherleuchteten THEOLOGI,
Herrn Johann Arndts,
Weiland General-Superintendenten
des Fürstenthums Lüneburg, ꝛc.
Sämtliche
Sechs geistreiche Bücher
Vom
Wahren
Christenthum,
Das ist:
Von heilsamer Busse,
Hertzlicher Reue und Leid über die
Sünde, wahrem Glauben, auch heiligem
Leben und Wandel der rechten wahren
Christen.
Neue Auflage mit Kupfern,
Samt
Richtigen Anmerckungen, kräfftigen Gebetern
über alle Capitel,
und
Einem sechsfachen Register.
Philadelphia, gedruckt und verlegt bey Benjamin Fräncklin
und Johann Böhm. 1751.

Title page of Benjamin Franklin's printing of the basic work of mystical piety: Johann Arndt's *True Christianity,* with a preface by Lutheran pastor, J. A. C. Hartwig, and containing a subscription list of 512 names, including prominent Lutheran and Reformed clergy. Arndt, kindly received by the sectarians, was also a favorite with pietist-minded church people. This was the largest book published in Philadelphia during the eighteenth century, having 1388 pages. The copperplates were of European origin. *Courtesy the Historical Society of Pennsylvania*

sent was dominant, where sectarianism molded the public press. No other American colony was so rich in journals, both English and German, and the conflicts between sectarian and "liberal" was reflected in these journals. From

the start of his ministry in Pennsylvania, Mühlenberg was opposed by Christopher Saur, self-appointed defender of sectarian principles, guardian of nonconforming views, who sought to hinder the ministerial office. Thus battle lines were drawn for a war that was to continue, albeit with changing focus, until the American Revolution. Saur railed against black-gowned clerics, and Mühlenberg in turn warned his people about purchasing the Bibles that Saur printed and sold; the Bibles might indeed contain unevangelical errors intended by Saur to deceive, for was not Saur agent for the heretical Berleburg Bible? Saur's newspaper, which unfortunately survives only in incomplete file, was an instrument of the printer's moods.

As helpers came for embattled ministers, the conflict between Saur and the Lutheran pastors grew; the printer understood that new verve had been added to the conflict. Among these helpers was the Reverend Johann C. Kunze, who was to become professor at the University of Pennsylvania, which Saur distrusted much, and also the Reverend Justus C. H. Helmuth. Early ministers itinerated, preaching in wide areas to scattered, loosely organized congregations meeting in poor buildings often shared with the Reformed. They adhered to the *Augsburg Confession,* with a great deal of Francke pietism added, and they often shared the Marburg hymnal with the Reformed, a work that included Lobwasser's metrical version of the Psalms and Neander's hymnal. This saved money in union churches, for the old Palatine custom of worshiping in the same building with others was followed.

The second formal denomination to come forward among Colonial Pennsylvania Germans was the Calvinist Reformed Church, which had been the state church of the Palatinate, Hesse, Wittgenstein, Switzerland, and Holland. The first Reformed worship services on the North American continent had been held even before John Calvin's death by French Reformed under Jean Ribaut in South Carolina. Dutch Reformed had followed the French Reformed to the New World.

The first Reformed settlers in Pennsylvania were Dutch in Bucks County, who spread to Whitemarsh. Some early Germans like Gabriel Schuler and Johannes Yoder of Oley became members of this congregation as early as 1711, although an actual German Reformed church did not appear until 1725. Congregations later arose in Falckner Swamp, Skippack, and somewhat later at Goshenhoppen where an entire congregation had put down under Friedrich Hillegas and pastor Georg Michael Weiss.

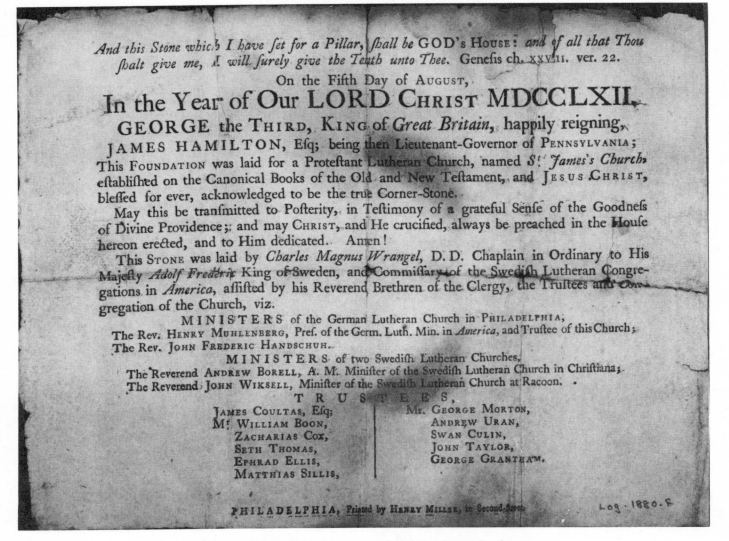

And this Stone which I have set for a Pillar, shall be GOD's HOUSE: and of all that Thou shalt give me, I will surely give the Tenth unto Thee. Genesis ch. XXVII. ver. 22.

On the Fifth Day of AUGUST,

In the Year of Our LORD CHRIST MDCCLXII,

GEORGE the THIRD, KING of *Great Britain*, happily reigning, JAMES HAMILTON, Esq; being then Lieutenant-Governor of PENNSYLVANIA; This FOUNDATION was laid for a Protestant Lutheran Church, named *St. James's Church,* established on the Canonical Books of the Old and New Testament, and JESUS CHRIST, blessed for ever, acknowledged to be the true Corner-Stone.

May this be transmitted to Posterity, in Testimony of a grateful Sense of the Goodness of Divine Providence; and may CHRIST, and He crucified, always be preached in the House hereon erected, and to Him dedicated. Amen!

This STONE was laid by *Charles Magnus Wrangel,* D.D. Chaplain in Ordinary to His Majesty *Adolf Frederic* King of Sweden, and Commissary of the Swedish Lutheran Congregations in *America,* assisted by his Reverend Brethren of the Clergy, the Trustees and Congregation of the Church, viz.

MINISTERS of the German Lutheran Church in PHILADELPHIA;
The Rev. HENRY MUHLENBERG, Pres. of the Germ. Luth. Min. in *America,* and Trustee of this Church; The Rev. JOHN FREDERIC HANDSCHUH.

MINISTERS of two Swedish Lutheran Churches,
The Reverend ANDREW BORELL, A. M. Minister of the Swedish Lutheran Church in Christiana; The Reverend JOHN WIKSELL, Minister of the Swedish Lutheran Church at Racoon.

TRUSTEES,

JAMES COULTAS, Esq;	Mr. GEORGE MORTON,
Mr. WILLIAM BOON,	ANDREW URAN,
ZACHARIAS COX,	SWAN CULIN,
SETH THOMAS,	JOHN TAYLOR,
EPHRAD ELLIS,	GEORGE GRANTHAM.
MATTHIAS SILLIS,	

PHILADELPHIA, Printed by HENRY MILLER, in Second-street.

Log. 1880. F

Bulletin for laying cornerstone for Saint James Lutheran Church, Philadelphia, August 5, 1762. Present were Swedish and German Lutherans. *Courtesy the Historical Society of Pennsylvania*

Early congregations had no formal ministers and they were served by men like Johann Philip Boehm (1683–1749), one-time schoolmaster whose father, a Marburg graduate in theology, had been a pastor in Germany. Later Philip Boehm was ordained by the Dutch Reformed in New York, after controversy had arisen about the regularity of his orders. To guard against sectarian aggression two tests were established: regularity of clerical orders and adherence to the *Heidelberg Catechism.*

Johann Philip Boehm was a zealous adherent of the *Heidelberg.* When Count Zinzendorf was seeking to draw Reformed persons into his Moravian net, he compiled a catechism which he gave out as Johann Bechtel's, a fervent but doctrinally colorless work which was never widely used outside of Bethlehem and Germantown. Regularity of doctrine was the issue, because both Lutheran and Reformed churches sought to maintain it, as, for example, did the Quittapahilla (Annville) congregation, where the agreement between the denominations worshiping there said:

No other doctrine shall be preached or the sacrament be

administered in any other way than only according to the pure and clear rule of God's word, to which is added on the part of the Lutheran the unaltered *Augsburg Confession* and its symbolical books, and on the part of the Reformed the *Heidelberg Catechism* with its Confessions.

On September 28, 1748, the newly formed Coetus of the Reformed Church, still under the dominion of the Dutch Reformed in New York, declared its devotion,

Gebhard, Ingold, and Rieger. From Marburg came energetic churchmen, defenders of orthodoxy, strugglers for correctness: Pomp, Rübel, Zufall, Bucher, Pick, Gross, Decker, Lapp, Giese. From Herborn came sentimental pietists: Frankenfield, Stoy, Otterbein, Waldschmidt, Müntz, Wissler. Several other universities were represented among Pennsylvania Reformed clergy: Helmstadt, Leyden, Francken, Rostock, Duisburg, Utrecht,

The Reverend Michael Schlatter imported Bibles printed in Basel for use of Pennsylvania congregations. Here is one of these Bibles, with collection sacks and pewter communion ware from the Egypt Reformed church, now in Lehigh County. *Photograph by W. W. Dietrich*

"heart and soul," to the *Heidelberg Catechism.* The irrational empiricism of the sects offended the denominational sense of order.

The character of Reformed piety was partly determined by the European universities from which its ministers came. From Heidelberg came the rationalists and traditionalists, the theological leaders: Georg Michael Weiss, Batholomai, Alsentz, Hendel, Henop, the Fabers (father and son), C. L. Böhme, Helfferich, Helffenstein,

Halle, Göttingen, Leipzig, and Groningen. No serious study of the influence of European universities on American life and thought has yet been made; it is known, however, that a son of Marburg, Johann Daniel Gross, student of the philosopher Wolff, wrote the first textbook on ethics published in the United States and, while teaching at Columbia University, instructed the second generation of American federalists.

The orthodox defense against Pennsylvania sectarian-

Front and rear of a Northampton County church, now
demolished, taken in 1901. This shows the Germanic style
of church architecture.

ism was the assertion of submission to doctrines expressed in the approved symbolical books and the *Heidelberg Catechism.* Between 1755 and 1849 at least thirty-five editions of the *Heidelberg Catechism* appeared and about fifteen English versions. In the time around the Revolutionary War there were half a dozen editions of the *Palatinate Catechism,* which was a shortened version of the *Heidelberg.*

Reformed clerics also asserted orthodoxy by fighting sectarian vagrancy with zest. Georg Michael Weiss wrote

The Anglicanization process is clear in this picture of Western Salisbury Church, Lehigh County. The German for Salisbury is *Salzburg,* and this is a typical rural church with balcony on three sides, a *Bordkaerrich. From an old photograph*

Communion tankard at Friedens Church, Wernersville, dated 1744. *From an old photograph*

an answer to the tract by Mattheis Baumann, leader of the Newborns. This came from Bradford's Philadelphia press in 1729. In 1742 Johann Philip Boehm published a *Warnungs-Brief* against the Moravians on Bradford's press, followed the next year by a second warning against them on Armbrüster's press. In 1748 Boehm's constitution for the Reformed church, then organized into Coetus, came out from the same press. Nicholas Pomp published a refutation of Paul Siegvolck's arguments for universal salvation, a doctrinal work against the main idea of the sects.

However, both Lutheran and Reformed were never quite able to gain the status they had enjoyed as established churches in the Old World; here they had to do battle with dissent.

Drawing of old Zion's church, Allentown, in which the Liberty Bell was hidden during the British occupation of Philadelphia.

Then, too, the first clerics, with a few notable exceptions, were not of highest quality, hence churches had to guard themselves against vagrancy and adventuring rascals. Questions of regularity of orders and orthodoxy arose. The sects had a vigilant watchdog in Christopher Saur I, whose father also had been a theological graduate of Marburg, and Saur's opposition to incompetent clerics

Organ from the Germantown Reformed Church.

may have been somewhat justified. Bitter fights marked early Pennsylvania church life. Here, for instance, are a few: between Georg Michael Weiss and Johann Philip Boehm, Michael Schlatter and Johann Conrad Steiner, and Mühlenberg and Nyberg in Lancaster. Lutherans fought Moravians in Tulpehocken. Controversy ruled.

Clerics were grossly underpaid. They had no legal status and were forced to fawn before their congregations—to beg. At first there was neither Ministerium nor

Coetus; some went straight from plough to pulpit, from schoolmaster's desk to chancel.

This conflict between sect and church was to dominate Pennsylvania history for three decades, perhaps longer, until it merged with a larger issue.

One area of deep conflict was the schools. Here the sects were supreme. Although the Anglo-Saxons accused Germans of being stupid (i.e., uneducated in English), we do know that seventy-five percent of those who entered the port of Philadelphia after 1727 could read and write. In Protestant Germany every church-village had its school. This was not so in England. Sectarian schools, attached to meetings, were well developed, some even becoming academies. This indicates that in Pennsylvania the sects took over the educational function. Pastorius was a schoolmaster, as was Kelpius. In 1718 Christopher Dock founded the Skippack school, which, however, did not have a continuous life. In 1769 Dock's pedagogical theories were so popular that Saur published them. Moravians began female education in 1742 and had Latin schools early. There was an academy in Nazareth before the Revolution, and soon thereafter a girls' school in Lititz. Sectarians were school-minded.

Likewise, Lutheran and Reformed schools were erected as early as 1720 and were kept by both laymen and clerics. Johann Philip Boehm, arriving in 1720, started school about the same time. By 1762 each Lutheran and/or Reformed congregation had its school, and in some instances where there was a union church there was a union school too.

Indeed, Germans, both sectarian and church, were education minded. But they taught lessons in German and were developing a culture based on values foreign to the Anglo-Saxon mind. German intellectuals, if they wanted to succeed in Pennsylvania, had to succeed in English. Most Germans were farmers, but there were some physicians, such as Casper Wistar, Abraham Wagner, Adam Kühn, and George deBenneville, who left a *Materia Medica* that is as yet unstudied. David Rittenhouse gained fame as an astronomer. But on the whole German intellectual life was meager.

Change in the character of the German migration to Pennsylvania, joined with the intrusion of larger events, spread the conflict between sectarian and churchman and so brought about the major crisis of the colonial period. Around 1746 this began to show itself in print. As the formal denominations took shape, the literature that came from the German presses began to change.

In 1760 Peter DeLong gave a piece of land just over five acres for a church which was to be Reformed "as long as sun and moon do shine, and the rivers run down to the sea." Here is the surveyor's draught.

The main plank in the sectarian platform, one shared by nearly all dissenting groups, was pacifism. Of this there were many kinds. Both Quakers and Germans, political allies at first, resisted every effort to establish military operations in the province.

In 1747 matters came to a head. A proposal was made for a voluntary militia. The opening shot in the literary war that followed (from the German side) was the translation of Benjamin Franklin's pamphlet *Plain Truth,* wherein he seems to have been writing with more knowledge of German history than of his Pennsylvania neighbors. For he spoke therein of a people "whose sons have ever since the time of Caesar maintained the character he gave their fathers, joining the most *obstinate courage* to all other military virtues." This writing, aimed at the "brave and steady" Germans, was marked by misunderstanding.

The militia matter was crucial; even Gilbert Tennant, fiery Presbyterian leader, allowed the militia to exercise in his church on rainy days.

But the old warrior of the sects, Christopher Saur I, was adamant. He wrote:

> Those who are strong in faith have no fear when war lifts itself against them. If the world is full of French and Spanish, and might overcome them, they would never fear for they shall persevere. If someone would build high fortresses, they say: a mighty fortress is our God, a bulwark never failing. If God should turn war to Pennsylvania, they say: Thy will be done, do Thou as thou wilt! They do not love their things so much that they fight over them. They do not love life so much that they would take another's life for it. For if God so ordains it that they shall die they know that they shall find a better place and a better life than the one they are losing.

Saur answered Franklin in *Ein Kurze Vermittlungs-*

82

January 24, 1764, after the failure of the Charity School movement was apparent, Andres Hauk and his wife Onnikinot, "having at divers times thought that it was necessary for the encouragement and promoting of learning and piety," gave land for a schoolhouse in Maxatawney Township, Berks County, under the trusteeship of Jacob Sheredon. *From an old photograph*

Schrift, a spirited defense of the pacifist position.

Saur did not remain unanswered for long. A "Philadelphia workman"—could it have been B. Franklin himself?—addressed *Ein Kurtze Verteidigungs-Schrift der Lauteren Wahrheit* to a "friend in the country," calculated to win support of the Dutch.

By 1748 fears of immediate war passed. Some measure of calm returned, marked, however, by an increasingly massive migration of Germans, of those who became Pennsylvania Dutch. By mid-century this had become a flood. Fears seized Anglo-Saxons. They were willing to admit that these Germans were hard-working, thrifty,

Benjamin West's portrait of the wizard of Philadelphia drawing electricity from the sky was still in classical tradition, with cherubs aiding the genius. *Courtesy the Philadelphia Museum of Art*

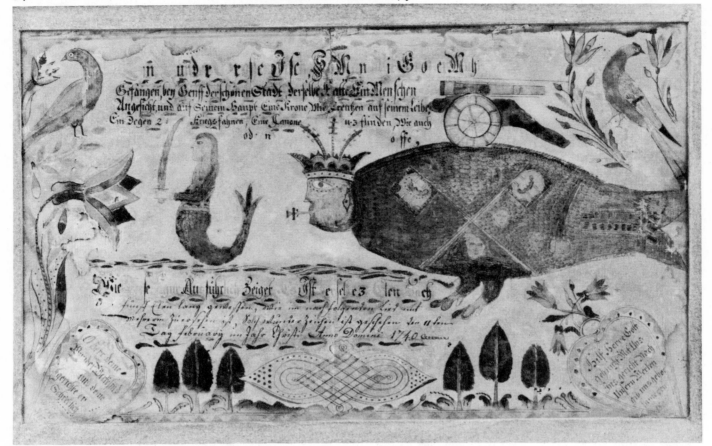

Illumination of an old Swiss pacifist ballad dealing with
the war-like Leviathan that was said to swim in Lake
Geneva. This theme was done several times. *Courtesy
the Henry Francis duPont Winterthur Museum*

solid; but they were disturbed by their politics and they
feared this "foreign" element that was not British. As
early as 1738, however, Governor Thomas had encouraged migration of Germans for economic reasons.

On the whole, however, Germans were culturally im-
poverished, seemingly wanting in those values and virtues
which British peoples cherished. Thus, they needed education. In 1751–1752 the Reformed minister, Michael
Schlatter (1718–1790) returned to Europe to get help
for establishing Reformed schools and churches in Pennsylvania. Schlatter was politically liberal, an able or-
ganizer, capable of doing for the Reformed what Mühlenberg had done for the Lutherans.

In Europe Schlatter described—and perhaps overstated
—the need; his account aroused much interest among
Reformed congregations in Holland, where he was able
to gather some money, for Pennsylvania churches and

schools. He wrote an *Appeal* wherein he pictured in bold
lines—he was, of course, begging—the dire Pennsylvania
situation. This work was translated into English and it
made a strong impression in England. King George II
was minded to contribute generously for these "poor
Palatines." Twenty thousand pounds sterling were gar-
nered for his province and given to the trustees of a newly
formed "Society for Propagating Knowledge of God
among Germans in Pennsylvania." The purpose—con-
cealed—was to anglicanize the Germans.

Meanwhile, back in Pennsylvania, Benjamin Franklin
began to publish a bilingual newspaper that was to
express his liberal mood. The English was taken from
his *Gazette* and the German was a poor translation. The
paper failed, for the time had not yet come for a liberal
German journal.

In 1753 another actor strode across the stage—we

may even want to call him the villain—the Reverend William Smith, eager anglophile and advocate of liberal policies, who saw the alliance of pacifist Quaker and German sectarian as dangerous. Smith developed a plan for English-language schools where German children would be taught free. There were therefore known as "Charity Schools."

By 1755 the dream of a land of peace was being shattered. Pacifism became impossible. Reality came in the form of Indian raids. Red men came from Shamokin and murdered settlers, taking some young persons prisoner. On November 25, 1755, five hundred landowners, mostly German, came down to Philadelphia, peaceably and in good order, to ask the governor for protection. After they left, the Assembly voted £50,000 for defense. Christopher Saur saw this as a deviation from faith.

Now, however, the pacifist issue changed focus. It became not just a religious but a national issue. Pacifists were looked on as being anti-British. This gave the Charity School movement *raison d'être*.

William Smith's plan to anglicanize German settlers by exposing their children to a British-style education conducted in the English language impressed English Archbishop Herring (who wished to keep the Colony both British and Protestant, not a prey for the papist French). On May 30, 1754, soon after having returned from England, Smith had written to the Reverend Samuel Chandler describing the dangers coming from the Ohio French and telling of a plan to send German aid to the French. This was so far from the truth that Lutheran and Reformed leaders were forced to protest their loyalty to the British king. The Reformed fathers turned back Smith's accusation with indignation. The effort to link being German with being anti-British failed.

In 1755 another German newspaper was started by the Society for Propagating Knowledge of God among the Germans in Pennsylvania, subsidized by the trustees of that Society: James Hamilton, William Allen, Richard Peters, Benjamin Franklin, Conrad Weiser, and the Reverend William Smith. The editor's job was first offered to Heinrich M. Mühlenberg, who wisely declined. The political purposes behind the Charity School movement now were out in the open, although Pastor Mühlenberg saw some good in them. Schools actually opened at Trappe, Upper Salford, Tulpehocken, Heidelberg, Easton, Lancaster, and one in Chester County.

The main opponent remained Christopher Saur, who had sensed the true purpose. When he announced the plan in September 1754, he had added that German

preachers were being advised to use English. However, Saur's opposition was not so much a matter of language as of pacifism. Even in May 1755, with Michael Schlatter as overseer of the Charity Schools, they had become a major political issue. B. Franklin, Saur's old foe, again entered the lists with his famous letter to Peter Colinson, published in *The Gentleman's Magazine* in London,

Naturalizing Foreigners, why pernicious. 485

pestilence, but cannot increase a people beyond the means provided for their subsistence.

16. Foreign luxuries and needless manufactures imported and used in a nation, do, by the same reasoning, increase the people of the nation that furnishes them, and diminish the people of the nation that uses them.—— Laws therefore that prevent such importations, and on the contrary promote the exportation of manufactures to be consumed in foreign countries, may be called *generative laws*, as by increasing subsistence they encourage marriage.

17. Some *European* nations prudently refuse to consume the manufactures of *East-India*:—They should likewise forbid them to their colonies; for the gain to the merchant is not to be compar'd with the loss, by this means, of people to the nation.

18. Home luxury in the Great, increases the nation's manufacturers employ'd by it, who are many, and only tends to diminish the families that indulge in it, who are few. The greater the common fashionable expence of any rank of people, the more cautious they are of marriage. Therefore luxury should never be suffered to become common.

13. The great increase of offspring in particular families, is not always owing to greater fecundity of nature, but sometimes to examples of industry in the heads, and industrious education; by which the children are enabled to provide better for themselves, and their marrying early is encouraged from the prospect of good subsistence.

19. If there be therefore, in our nation, that regards frugality and industry as religious duties, and educates their children therein, more than others commonly do; such sect must increase more than any other.

21. The importation of foreigners into a country that has as many inhabitants as the present employments and provisions will bear; will be in the end no encrease of people; unless the new comers have more industry and frugality than the natives, and then they will provide more subsistence, and increase in the country; but they will gradually eat the natives out.— Nor is it necessary to bring in foreigners to fill up any occasional vacancy in a country; for such vacancy (if the laws are good, § 14, 16) will soon be filled by natural generation. Who can now find the vacancy made in *Sweden* by the plague of heroism 40 years ago; in *France* by the expulsion of the protestants; in *England* by the settlement of her colonies; or in *Guinea* by 100 years exportation of slaves, that has blacken'd half *America?*

22. There is in short, no bound to the prolifick nature of plants or animals, but what is made by their crowding and interfering with each other's means of subsistence. Was the face of the earth vacant of other plants, it might be gradually sowed and overspread with one kind only; as, for instance, with fennel; and were it empty of other inhabitants, it might in a few ages be replenished from one nation only; as, for instance, with *Englishmen*. Thus there are supposed to be now upwards of one million *English* souls in *North-America*, (though it is thought scarce eighty thousand have been brought over sea) and yet, perhaps, there is not one the fewer in *Britain*, but rather many more, on account of the employment the colonies afford to manufacturers at home.—— This million doubling, suppose but once in twenty-five years, will in another century be more than the people of *England*, and the greatest number of *Englishmen* will be on this side the water. We have been here but little more than one hundred years, and yet the force of our privateers in the late war was greater, both in men and guns, than that of the whole *British* navy in queen *Elizabeth's* time.—How important an affair then to *Britain* is the present treaty for settling the bounds between her colonies and the *French*, and how careful should she be to secure room enough, since on the room depends so much the encrease of her people?

23. A nation well regulated is like a polypus; cut it in two, and each deficient part shall speedily grow out of the part remaining. Thus if you have room and subsistence enough, as you may by dividing, make ten polypuses out of one, you may of one make ten nations, equally populous and powerful.

And since detachments of *English* from *Britain* sent to *America*, will have their places at home so soon supplied, and increase so largely here; why should the *Palatine Boors* be suffered to swarm into our settlements, and by herding together establish their language and manners, to the exclusion of ours?

The most fateful page in Pennsylvania politics during the eighteenth century. Part of Benjamin Franklin's article in the November 1755 issue of *The Gentleman's Magazine*, London, wherein he called the Pennsylvania Germans "boors." *Courtesy the Haverford College Library*

wherein he called the Pennsylvania Germans "Palatine Boors, the most stupid of their nation." Saur's instinct foresaw the liberal trend.

Also, William Smith wrote a letter, wherein he said that the Germans, instead of being peaceful and hard-working as before, now had discovered their own importance and were making others agree with them. He argued that now Germans were in a position of being able to prescribe laws and languages for the English settlers, saying that the hated French were counting heavily on the Germans. "They know that the Germans were extraordinarily stupid and think that a big farm is the greatest blessing in the world."

Nor did Smith spare printer Saur. Smith said that Saur had been one of the French prophets in Germany and that he was a papist emissary of the Jesuit pope. Saur's paper, he wrote, was read only by Germans, and they even believed him! He had so deceived the Germans that they would rather serve as indentured servants than in the militia. (The incomplete file of Saur's paper that survives makes it impossible to delve deeper into these matters.)

On May 6, 1756, the *Philadelphia Zeitung* wrote: "Nine companies quickly appeared with their arms. And we had the pleasure of seeing that our German people made up a goodly portion of the personel."

Christopher Saur was of another opinion. He wrote:

On the 18th of May last the six companies of militia came together in Germantown from Philadelphia and exercised and trained, showing what they would do to the enemy were he to appear. Each company had something special in its flag, for example, an elephant, a sleeping lion. The most remarkable or strangest was that on one flag was the image of the prince of peace, the Lord Jesus, with 11 or 12 Apostles, precisely and knowingly painted. They brought four wagons and cannon from Philadelphia which they fired off left and right. There were a great many spectators who looked on approvingly. Some few were saddened that the long blessed, quiet and peaceful land of Pennsylvania should be and become a murderous land.

Conrad Weiser, who knew Indians at first hand in Tulpehocken, disowned Saur.

Old-style pacifism was dying, and in spite of the fact that William Smith was no match in literary affairs for pacifist Saur, the anti-military cause was doomed. In 1756 Smith edited H. Scougal's *Das Leben Gottes in der Seele,* calling himself "Wilhelm Schmidt." It did not work.

By 1757 the purpose of the Society for Propagating Knowledge of God among Germans in Pennsylvania came out in the open, since the Society's trustees spent their remaining monies to publish rules and articles of war for the American regiment in the German language. Was the Society a recruiting agent for the Royal Army?

In any event, the Royal American Regiment appeared, under General Montgomery. In June 1758, Christopher Saur, the grand old pacifist, was sent for and escorted under guard of kilted highlanders to the inn *Zum Hirschen,* where he was examined. He denied that he had done anything treasonable. He answered General Forbes, who was examining him, that for thirty-four years he had had only the welfare of this land in mind. In an interview of just over three minutes the old pacifist was cowed. Later Saur said that he had found the red-coated General more understanding, more astute, and more moderate, than many a black-gowned preacher.

By 1758, then, the first crisis of conscience produced by pacifism in Colonial Pennsylvania had passed. Danger from marauding Indians subsided, although bloody tales circulated about barbarities, such as *Die Erzählung von Maria LeRoy und Barbara Leiniger,* describing perils of white people among the Indians. Such tales became legendary among the Germans, expressing the still-latent fears among them. Pennsylvania was still a land of peace, but the Germans were beginning to understand that it was one thing to be a pacifist in the warm comfort of a Quaker home in Philadelphia and quite another thing to be a pacifist on the raw frontier in Northampton County.

On September 25, 1758, Christopher Saur I, who had been the great bulwark of German pacifism, died. He was succeeded by his churlish son, Christopher II (1721–1784), who tried to take up his father's torch but who did so without the old man's fire and verve. A new kind of literature began to appear in the German printshop, like formal prayer books, regional law books, and other less fervent materials.

Quakers sensed the change in mood, too. The *Epistle from Yearly Meeting* in 1760 marked a return to quietism, withdrawal from the holy commonwealth that they had been seeking to build. Franklin, in the New Year Verses for the printer's lads (whether composed by Franklin or not is insignificant) paraded a new mood of patriotism and self-adulation:

While with Joy I recite some Feats of last Year,
From which, I assure you, 'Twill plainly appear
Brave *Britons* and *Germans* of Protestant Turn,

Proper Times and Occasions can wisely discern
For convincing the French . . .

The poem was indeed jingoist and sword-rattling:

And *Amherst,* the Wise, advancing to fight
Red Indians and French in terrible Fright,
And therefore, with Speed they walk'd off in the Night,
And *Ticonderoga* and *Crown Point* became our's.

Finally it lamented that the "great Wolfe" was no more.

The year 1760 saw the death of Conrad Weiser (b. 1696), the one Pennsylvanian of the colonial period who had played a meaningful role in Pennsylvania politics. Weiser had once been one of the Ephrata brethren, but he turned from religion to politics after discovering that sectarianism denied freedom. Having lived among the Indians as a youth, knowing their languages, Weiser's counsel was followed by provincial authorities; governors did what he said. It was, then, not just Quaker tenderness or Moravian concern that kept good relations with the aborigines. Weiser's lasting achievement was that he kept the Iroquois Confederacy friendly to the government, preserving British dominion in America. Like Pastorius and Daniel Falckner, Weiser did not cheat Indians, sell them rum, or let them contract debts.

In 1760, prodded by Benjamin Franklin, Heinrich Müller (1702–1782) began to publish German materials in the city, opening his presses to new liberal views. Outwardly Moravian, Müller had met Zinzendorf as a young man and served as his traveling printer in several European centers, including London, Amsterdam, and Hamburg.

On January 16, 1762, the first issue of Müller's *Der Wochentliche Staatsbote* appeared. The new liberalism that this paper expressed replaced the pacifist sectarianism of Christopher Saur II. Here was a newspaper that welded liberal Germans behind Scotch-Irish Presbyterians, not only in Pennsylvania but throughout the Colonies. In the first issue of 1762 we get a clue to what kind of liberal party was emerging, for here Müller gave a list of the agents who sold his paper. The *Staatsbote* was found in taverns, as Saur's paper was not, where it was much read and discussed. Many agents were innkeepers like Georg Honig, host of the "King of Prussia" in Philadelphia, and Jacob Wentz of Methacton.

In 1763 Müller published a second list. Here the full political impact of the new alignment of forces is clear. In Goshenhoppen, for example, the agent was Daniel Hiester, who was the father of several revolutionary pa-

triots—Gabriel Hiester, Brigadier General Daniel Hiester, and Colonel John Hiester. Agents in Berks were Daniel Hunter (Jaeger) and Peter Spyker, both of them well known in patriot affairs, and in Northampton county the agents were Jacob Arndt and Christian Müller. These four were chosen delegates to the Provincial Conference, July 8, 1776, and were present when the province ratified the Declaration of Independence. Jacob Wentz, another agent, was keeper of a hotel that became Washington's headquarters when the patriot army was in the Perkiomen region. Other of Müller's agents for the *Staatsbote* included "Baron" Heinrich Wilhelm Stiegel, maker of "American" flint glass in defiance of British laws; Paul Hochstrasser, of Albany, New York; and Heinrich Fry, of Albany, both members of the Albany Convention; Heinrich Rinker of Winchester, Virginia, brother of Colonel Jacob Rinker; Dr. Bodo Otto, of Cohanse, New Jersey, later to become Surgeon in the Continental Army. In short, study of the character of the agents for Heinrich Müller's paper from Nova Scotia to Georgia shows that a new political party was emerging in American life, replacing the older sectarian pacifism that had dominated the first years of Pennsylvania history.

The calm that followed the repeal of the Stamp Act was specious. Confidence did not return. The pacifist principle, now in question, was still to be tested.

On December 14, 1763, moved by the hysteria then sweeping the frontier, a group of Scotch-Irish Presbyterians from Harris' Ferry butchered some harmless Susquehannocks. Other friendly Indians turned toward Philadelphia for safety, followed by enraged settlers. On February 5, 1764, confrontation came in Germantown, where the "invaders" were halted. Even some Quakers joined the hastily gathered militia. A conference was held and reason prevailed. Many pamphlets came out, including an "Address to the Germans," which reported unrest in town and country.

A crucial election for seats in the General Assembly was scheduled for the Fall of 1764. All sorts of electioneering broadsides appeared—*The Plot By Way of a Burlesk to Turn F----n Out of the Assembly.* This was followed by *An Answer to the Plot.* . . . Franklin was beaten, mainly by the Germans who voted against him, and Germans were regarded now as heroes by those who opposed Franklin. More broadsides came out, saying:

Drink a Health to the Boors
Who turn'd BEN out of Doors

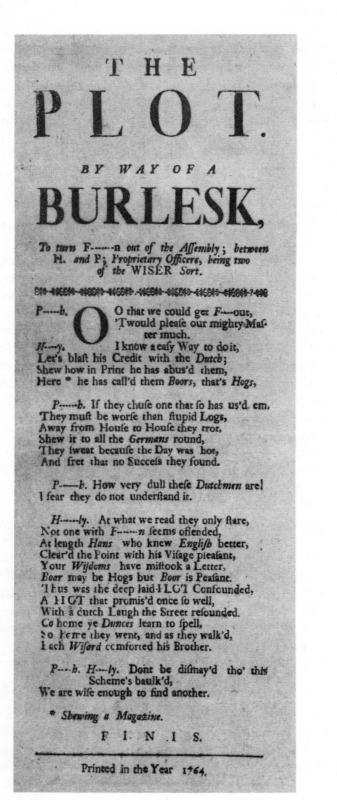

THE
PLOT.
BY WAY OF A
BURLESK,

To turn F——n out of the *Assembly*; between H. and P; *Proprietary Officers*, being two of the WISER *Sort*.

P——h. O O that we could get *F——* out,
'Twould please our mighty Master much.
H——y. I know a easy Way to do it,
Let's blast his Credit with the *Dutch*;
Shew how in Print he has abus'd them,
Here * he has call'd them *Boors*, that's *Hogs*,

P——h. If they chuse one that so has us'd em,
They must be worse than stupid *Logs*,
Away from House to House they trot,
Shew it to all the *Germans* round,
They sweat because the Day was hot,
And fret that no Success they found.

P——h. How very dull these *Dutchmen* are!
I fear they do not understand it.

H——ly. At what we read they only stare,
Not one with *F——n* seems offended,
At length *Hans* who knew *English* better,
Clear'd the Point with his Visage pleasant,
Your *Wisdoms* have mistook a Letter,
Boar may be *Hogs* but *Boor* is *Peasant*.
Thus was the deep laid PLOT Confounded,
A PLOT that promis'd once so well,
With a dutch Laugh the Street resounded.
Go home ye *Dunces* learn to spell,
So home they went, and as they walk'd,
Each *Wizard* comforted his Brother.

P——h. H——ly. Dont be dismay'd tho' this Scheme's baulk'd,
We are wise enough to find another.

* *Shewing a Magazine.*

F I N I S.

Printed in the Year 1764.

Anti-Franklin broadside poem, which helped to defeat the long-time member of the Pennsylvania Assembly. His unfortunate use of the word "Boors" is here capitalized on. Note, however, that they are called "Dutch." *Courtesy the Historical Society of Pennsylvania*

AN
ANSWER
TO THE
PLOT.

The silly Ass who wrote the Plot,
And wrack'd his Foolish Noddy,
Perhaps was drunk, just like a Sot,
O'er Cyder, Gin, or Toddy.   TOM THUMB.

I.
WHILST busy Cits neglect their Shop,
To turn State Politicians,
No human Arts on Earth can Stop
The Growth of our Divisions.

II.
Each Fool manures his Barren Head,
By Contradicting Papers,
When all the Nonsense that they read,
But turn to windy Vapours.

III.
Yet tutor'd by the Flying Post,
The Gazettes, and the Post-Man,
Each Fancies he can rule a host,
Or steer a Fleet with most Men.

IV.
When thus grown Wise in their Conceit,
And Skilful in State Matters,
They Charge their Fault, when Things don't hit,
Unjustly on their Betters.

V.
Thus every shallow Doat-Head vents,
Some groundless Exclamation,
And raises Feuds and Discontents,
To the Mischief of the Nation.

VI.
Therefore the Prudent *Dutch* should Use
All Female soft Perswasion,
To draw F———n from raising News.
To mind (his Occupation) *

VII.
Who then that knows his own Decay,
Would be so lewd a Letcher,
To teach the sprightly *Dutch* the Way
To crack his Head with a Pitcher.

VIII.
F———n, tho' plagu'd with fumbling Age,
Needs nothing to excite him,
But is too ready to engage,
When younger Arms envite him.

IX.
Who then that has a Dram of Brains
Wou'd prove so vain a Noddy,
To enflame the *Dutch's* more spightly Veins,
With Stories of his Daddy.

X.
Yet Pride in Age so oft prevails,
That Men turn Goats and Satyrs,
And, by their wicked idle Tales,
Debauch the *Dutchmen's* Daughters.

* *He has not only followed Electricity for many Years, but has brought it to a very great Perfection.——Is he not then a Philosopher?*

Answer to *The Plot*, wherein Franklin is further castigated, this time for his supposed morality. Note again the mid-eighteenth century use of "Dutch." *Courtesy the Historical Society of Pennsylvania*

And like Heroes erected their Banners,
For He said they were Swine
Who did *Herd* and Combine
To spread both their language and manners.

Then the writer added:

Go on, you brave Men!
Never chuse him again
Who GERMANS was always reviling,
If you till our Plains
We partake of the Gains
And rich industry ever is smiling.

Franklin did not go empty-handed; new horizons opened. The General Assembly appointed him their agent to plead with Parliament to do away with the proprietory government.

Many protests against Franklin's mission to London were made, especially by the churlish younger Saur, who was answered in a broadside published by Heinrich Müller that was addressed to the Germans who voted in Philadelphia, Bucks, and Berks Counties. This paper was witnessed by Daniel Hiester, Johannes Wistar, and Daniel Wistar, who said that Saur's accusations were false. It was subscribed by Philip Syng, Damiel Williams, Abel Jones, Thomas Wharton, and Thomas Say. It concludes by saying, "If it comes to this again, Christopher Saur shall be taken to task."

So the pacifist party, which had been led by Quakers, to whom the German sectarians were allied, was now thrust into the background and a new political alliance came forward. There can be no question that sectarian labels were also political labels. Scurrilous broadsides came out, like the sarcastic *The Quaker Grace, Prayer, and Thanksgiving, on Sunday sixth, Tenth Month, 1765, for the late Victory over the Rebels in the Province of Quylsylvania, in electing Law Makers for the Same.*

Not only was Pennsylvania now joined with other American colonies, but the issue that had arisen in provincial Pennsylvania had now become international in scope. At first the French had been the enemy—Gallic villains inciting red men. However, in 1765, to ease the financial burden of supporting troops in America, the British Parliament sought to pass the Stamp Act. If stubborn colonials, especially Pennsylvania pacifists, refused to vote funds for their common defence, then the British parliament would have to tax them, without quibbling about whether this was an "internal" or an "external" tax. The armies had to be paid, and there can be no question that the refusal of Pennsylvania pacifists to vote support for British arms in America was one cause that led to the Stamp Act. Even though its repeal brought thanksgiving from Pastor Mühlenberg and others, the idea was not unjust. It was, however, taxation without representation.

Matters became tense. With something of a defeatist mood the Pennsylvania presses, sensing the coming battles, turned to other matters, ignoring the conflict; they brought out catechisms, psalters, hymnals, and medical books. For a new breed had come into this peaceful land where political parties bore sectarian names: "Quaker," "Dutch Presbyterian," and the like. Heinrich Müller's *Staatsbote* continued to speak for the new liberals. He published an account of B. Franklin's reception by both houses of the British Parliament and his speech on how the Stamp Act was being received in Pennsylvania. He was asked: "How many Germans are there in Pennsylvania?"

Franklin's answer: "Perhaps a third of the population, but I cannot say exactly."

Question: "Have some served in the European military?"

Answer: "Yes, many; In Europe as well as America."

Question: "Are they just as dissatisfied with the Stamp Act as the British?"

Answer: "Yes, much more and with justice, for in every case they must pay double for stamped paper and parchments!"

Deep rumblings continued. In 1774 H. Müller appealed to Philadelphia to show sympathy for Bostonians, who were being oppressed. The next year he translated and printed William Pitt's speech on conciliation. When the Stamp Act was repealed jubilation followed, but distrust of British purposes still existed. Associations arose to protect provincial rights and freedom. In 1772 Philadelphia already had a "Patriotic Society of the City and County of Philadelphia." Some of these "associations" were semi-military; in the outlying areas, more so.

On June 18, 1774, a large gathering took place in Philadelphia to determine what ought to be done for the other colonies. In this Germans were active: Christopher Ludwig, Georg Schlosser, Adam Hubley, and Michael Hillegas. On July 16 a provincial convention met, with the following Germans in attendance: from Philadelphia Ludwig, Schlosser, Hubley, and Jacob Barge; from Lancaster Georg Ross, Joseph Ferree, Matthias Slough, Moses Erwin; from Berks Christopher Schultz, Jonathan Potts; from Northampton, Peter Küchlein, Jacob Arndt; from Northumberland Caspar Weitzel. A second meeting took place January 23, 1775, and some of those who participated were: F. Hasenclever, Isaac Melcher,

Melchior Wagner from the city; Sebastian Groff, Adam Simon Kühn from Lancaster; Georg Eichelberger, Michael Smyser from York; Sebastian Levan and Balthasar Gehr from Berks. It was this convention which declared that Parliament's claims to power were unconstitutional and that Massachusetts was to be defended. They called for a continental congress. The rebellion had begun.

German churches in Philadelphia now took a significant step that shows the relationship of religious affiliation to politics during this time and establishes that a new political party had emerged. Under the leadership of Ludwig Weiss, an officer in the German Society of Pennsylvania, a broadside was issued with the (translated) title: *Letter of the Evangelical-Lutheran and Reformed Church Councils, as well as of the German Society in the City of Philadelphia, to the German citizens of the Provinces of New York and North Carolina* (Philadelphia, 1775). This work commiserated with German patriots in those colonies for their political sufferings, and for their problems with the British authorities. In 1775 the New York Provincial Council ordered that five hundred copies of the acts of the Continental Congress be printed in German. Müller's newspaper had forged a new political faction among Germans in all the colonies; he reminded these patriots of their former services in Germany.

In the city, men like Christopher Ludwig assumed leadership in patriot affairs. Ludwig had seen military service in Europe in Austria and Prussia, and for a time in the British army. He had arrived in Philadelphia in 1754 and became an energetic partisan for freedom, ultimately becoming baker-general of the Continental Army and friend of General Washington. In up-country regions Germans were equally energetic; preparations for conflict mounted. On July 4, 1776, Lancaster, it is said, had fifty-three battalions, a large number for that time (battalions were much smaller then.) On May 22, 1776, even before they had passed the Declaration of Independence, Congress decided to form a German regiment for its Continental Army with Nicholas Haussager commanding. Of this regiment the first, third, fifth, seventh, and ninth companies were from Pennsylvania. Their officers were:

1. Daniel Burckhardt, Friedrich Rollwegen, Georg Rohbacker
3. Georg Hubley, Peter Boyer, Johann Landenberger
5. Jacob Bunner, Wilhelm Rice, Georg Schäffer
7. Benjamin Weiser, Jacob Bower, Friedrich Weiser

9. David Wölpper, Bernhard Hubley, Wilhelm Ritter

This regiment participated in the battles of Trenton, Princeton, Middlebrook, Brandywine, and Germantown, and wintered with the Continentals at Valley Forge. Other Pennsylvania regiments contained many Germans, especially the Second, Third, Fifth, Sixth, and Eighth. The Second Pennsylvania Regiment was commanded by (later) General Philip de Haas. Some Virginia outfits had many Germans, and there were German troops, mostly militia, under General Herkeimer in New York State. Together, the Germans, who made up one-twelfth of the American population, formed one-eighth of the Continental army. Many were also in the associated militia. Even a few pacifists caught the martial fever and drilled for a while.

Disaffection among Hessian mercenaries was great. Had General Washington been agreeable to it, hundreds of Hessians could have been enlisted in the Continental service. Desertions were many. The *Philadelphia Zeitung* for July 2, 1782, late in the war, said: "Desertion among British troops are extraordinarily large; most of those who come over to us are Germans who assert that the whole German army would come over if they had the chance."

I also must make mention of Michael Hillegas and Peter Mühlenberg. The former was one of the financiers of the Revolution, while the exploits of the son of the Lutheran patriot are legendary. Friedrich Augustus Mühlenberg later became first speaker of the American House of Representatives.

However, in spite of the fervent patriotism that surged in Colonial Pennsylvania, as is well known in American affairs, sectarian pacifists were still around. Christopher Saur II still was the prime example of the special breed of Tory that appeared in pacifist Pennsylvania. Saur opposed, not the American cause, but war. He may not have been pro-British. In this he differed from anglophile Jonathan Odell, who was siding with the mother country and castigating patriots. Saur saw war as a consequence of human sin, of divine wrath, of man's pride. He wrote a strong poem, *Anrede eines nachdenkenden Amerikaners an seine Mittbürger,* in which he suggested that the female desire for fancy clothes, for silks and laces, and for fine manners, led to war. If women would be quiet housekeepers, virtuous and industrious, rather than sitting around tea tables in lazy indolence, there would be no need for war.

Nor was Saur alone in opposing war. These Pennsylvania Tories—if indeed they may be called so—opposed war; but they were not anti-American. Ephrata became a hospital for patriot wounded. General Lafayette went to the Bethlehem Moravians to recover from wounds he received at Brandywine. Dunkards, Mennonites, and Schwenkfelders were at first simply against war, but the harsh treatment they got from the patriots turned many of them. The Schwenkfelders composed a common agreement by which they compacted to assume the fines for those drafted who would not serve. Quakers, on the contrary, were often anglophile and so were sent to Winchester, Virginia.

Patriots were not always gentle in suppressing Tories. They did not distinguish between religious pacifists and anglophiles. On June 13, 1777, the Legislature passed a law that adults had to renounce allegiance to King George and declare loyalty to Pennsylvania. This hit hard, especially those who would not swear oaths. Additional laws were enacted April 1, 1778, and December 5, 1778. A *Hetzjagd* began against those who would not take the oath of allegiance. After the Battle of Brandywine, lost by the Americans, when the City (Philadelphia) opened up to the British troops, many pacifists were sent to Winchester in Virginia.

On May 8, 1778, just as news of the French Alliance was breaking, a proclamation was issued that named recalcitrant Tories. This was an open invitation to patriots. On May 21 a similar proclamation closed with the names of C. Saur II and his son, giving Tories until July 6 to put

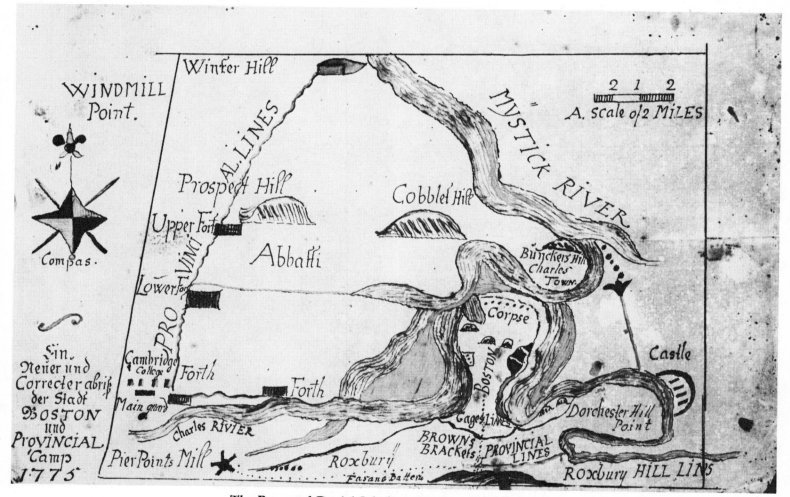

The Reverend Daniel Schuhmacher was chaplain to some Pennsylvania troops who went to Boston to join the Continental Army. Here is the military situation around Boston just before the battle of Bunker Hill. Note the English and German captions.

Eleanor Barba painted Lafayette recuperating from
wounds received at Brandywine among the Moravians
in Bethlehem. The Sisters' garb is authentic.

themselves right before magistrates. Stubbornly, however, Saur had anticipated this, for just about the time of the Battle of Germantown during the previous fall, he had taken off, forsaking his print shop. His two sons became pro-British. On May 22, 1778, C. Saur II was arrested by patriots, taken to Valley Forge, tried before General Washington, and released upon the cognizance of General Peter Mühlenberg. As with his father before him, his pacifism brought him before the military.

Christopher Saur's fate was an example for many Pennsylvanians. They sensed that the pacifist battle was lost. The dream of a land of peace, which had brought so many Germans to America, gave way before stark realities. After the war many sectarians left Pennsylvania, following the trail of the black walnut to Ontario, to live contentedly under British rule.

The holy experiment died from its own inner conflicts.

4

Economic Patterns

While politics and religion were thus projecting conflicts between pacifist sectarians and church people, new economic patterns were also seeking to come forth in German Pennsylvania, wherein both negative and positive factors were interacting. Pietist impulses in economic affairs emerged, clashed with rising mercantilism, only to be overshadowed by it in the end.

The first and negative factor that acted on Pennsylvania economic life was the failure of the European guild system to transplant itself in America. Craftsmen who were trained in the finest European work traditions, who were exceptionally competent, now were freed from restrictive work-patterns. No longer did they have to listen at guild meetings to long-winded speeches that described how they had to work. Thrown upon a demanding frontier and leaving their tools behind them, they began anew. Then, too, the European land system, with its feudally oriented agricultural village and strip-farming, was done away by the availability of cheap land from Penn and his heirs. Some settlers bought more land than they needed.

Such freedom from guild control, from feudal patterns of land ownership, made for economic vitality in the form of an agricultural-craft economy. This was no one-crop slave-holding economy, as in the Chesapeake basin.

To these changes in environmental influences must be added a theoretical attitude toward work, which came from pietism and replaced the Lutheran-Calvinist doctrine of the calling. Lutherans and Reformed—the formal churches—saw work as the duty of the Christian, God-given and obligatory, however obnoxious it might be. For Lutherans the performance of worldly duties was an act of worship; the Calvinist was somewhat more ascetic, although he sought by vigorous energy to prove his election. Both attitudes implied acceptance of bourgeois values and the ideology of capitalism.

Daniel Falckner's *Curieuse Nachrist,* an early description of the province, presented another attitude, which suggested that the value of a task comes from the degree to which it advances an earth-bound kingdom of God. The puritan worked for the glory of God and, by learning how to die blessedly, he awaited the day of doom; Lutherans worked hard even though their work could have but passing value; the pietist-Anabaptist view was founded on the view that they were building a permanent ideal society, a lasting earthly holy order, and that all deeds done shared in this purpose. The world in which Lutherans and Calvinists worked was a fallen one; the sectarian kingdom, on the other hand, would last the full thousand years. To wait for the new age, and to last out its life, the Anabaptist built his rugged barns and stone houses. Thus there was a theology of work behind Pennsylvania sectarianism that gave impetus to new, mundane, patterns of work and of economics and that, especially at Ephrata and Bethlehem, began to emerge as a new

Hewing tools used in making log cabins and other works in wood. *Courtesy the Pennsylvania Farm Museum, Landis Valley*

economic pattern, only to be overwhelmed by emerging capitalism.

This conflict also marked the Colonial period.

First settlements were grubby and scratchy; prosperity was not immediate. Germans usually followed other nationalities, letting the Scotch-Irish be first, or, in some cases, the Quakers. Presbyterians usually girdled the trees, planting between the stumps, which were left to foul. When the pietist-minded German came, the stumps were pulled out, stones piled, and the land readied for permanent use. At this time a primitive one-room cabin was built from logs and sometimes a log barn was at-tached. In these earlier years there was as yet no full dependence on agriculture, because hunting, fishing, and foraging added to the meager crops put out.

Once survival was assured, a second, larger, log cabin was erected, generally with attached barn in the European mode, with a chimney of stone in the middle of the structure, and with several rooms and a loft. Some second-generation log houses are still in use. With this second dwelling came expanded farming and less dependence on forest and stream. Cattle and other animals began to appear.

The third, more permanent, stage came when the log

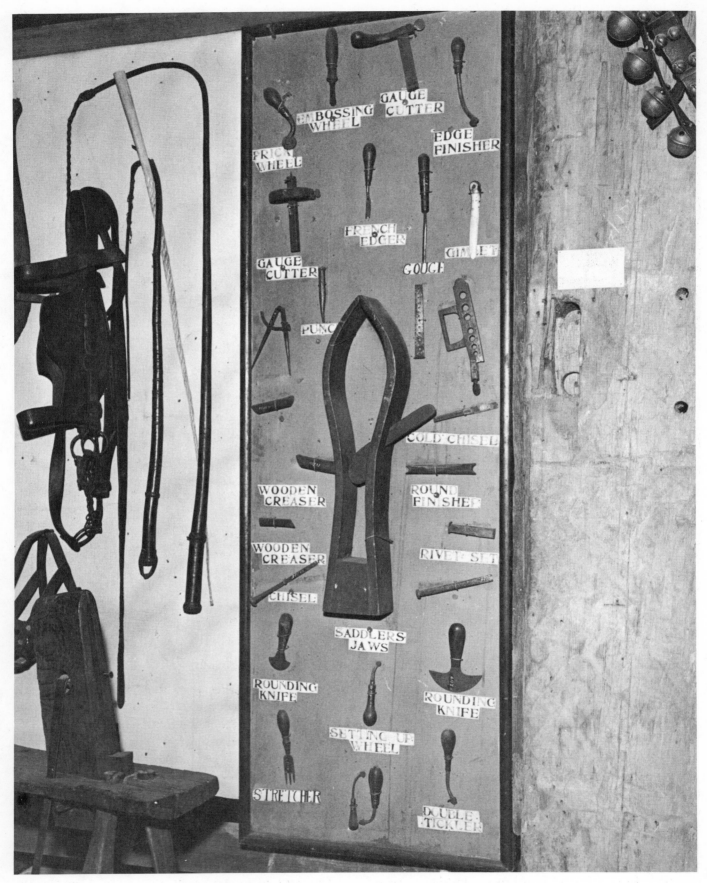

Tools of the saddlers' trade displayed at the Pennsylvania
Farm Museum, Landis Valley.

Cutout, 1784, from a private collection

From a private collection

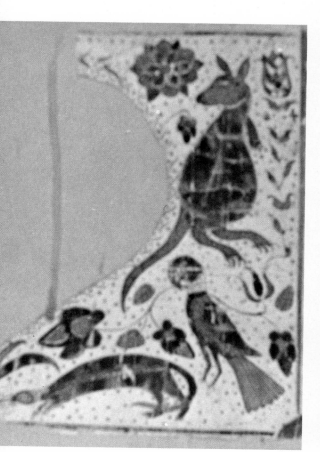

Fragment of a *Taufschein*

Valentine cutout, 1783

The range of the art of illumination

Taufschein from a private collection

Courtesy the Schwenkfelder Library

From a private collection

Fraktur designs

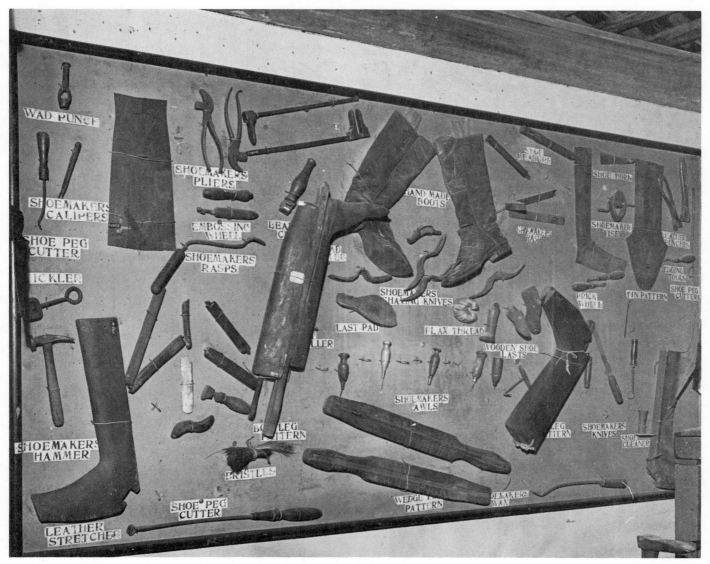

**Bootmakers' tools displayed in the Pennsylvania Farm
Museum at Landis Valley.**

cabin was surrounded by the Pennsylvania plantation, which was patterned on the *Freiherr*'s estate in Germany. Here was a stone house, a barn with separated *Vorbay,* and with *Vorhof* and *Hinterhof,* somewhat like the seats of the nobility in Germany. These new patterns suited a free man living on his generous acres.

The first barns were not massive. They were of logs, and were generally attached to the log houses. The first separated barn was small, made of stone, about forty meters long, fifteen to eighteen meters deep, with a high shingled roof. On the ground level were stalls, protected by the *Vorbay;* above, approached by a bridge of earth, was a floor for hay and straw. The stalls were covered and kept the animals warm in winter.

After the animals had thus been taken care of, the first stone house could be built. This was about 1740. At first these were in the European tradition, much like the stone houses of Alsace and the Palatinate. After the American Revolution, influenced by the Carpenters' Company of Philadelphia, Georgian-style houses in the English mode appeared. Most had shingle roofs.

The difference between German-style houses and English-style houses was seen in the number and position of the chimneys. Germans had only one chimney, centrally placed; English houses had two, one at each gable end. This reflected differences in heating methods; the Germans heated with stoves, iron or tile, while the English heated with open fireplaces. The German method used less wood.

Inside, houses were simply furnished. In the center was a huge stove, with simple wooden benches along the walls, and a table in one corner. The Germans did not put the table in the center of a formal dining room as did the English. There were no bedsteads at first. Husband and wife slept on straw pallets downstairs, in the *Kammer,* while the children, also on pallets, slept upstairs. Some upstairs rooms were for storage. As in southern Germany, the most important downstairs room was the *Spinnstube* where, in winter, there was a great deal of activity, mostly by females—weaving, spinning, quilting, nursing.

Outside of this stone house were several smaller build-

The gunmaking room in the Pennsylvania Farm Museum, Landis Valley. The machine for rifling barrels was a prominent part of the gunsmith's equipment.

ings, all functional. The spring house—sometimes the first permanent structure—was the domain of house-wife, where she kept butter, vegetables, and some sausages. Also there was the *Schnitzhaus,* generally wooden, for storing dried fruit. As in southern Germany, outdoor ovens and cider-presses were built, also a distillery for making vinegars and liquors. And finally, perhaps most important, were the craft shops, generally differing from farm to farm: for pottery making, cabinet making, and weaving, and the smithy, and the all-important gun-smithy.

Before 1750 life was frugal. Unlike their English neighbors, early Germans ate little white bread; rye and black breads were the fare. Meat was not much used, except pork. The national dish was sauerkraut. This frugality was in part religious. No ostentation! Both sectarian and pietist made a religion of frugality. Eventually good-sized and well-cared-for gardens were established: near the city the supplies were marketed. They introduced many new dishes to their Anglo-Saxon neighbors: *Panhaas,* which became Philadelphia scrapple, tripe, souse, and, of course, when molasses was imported, the classic pastry, Shoofly Pie.

The Pennsylvania Dutch were basically agricultural people, and for the first century their life-patterns were rural. Towns and cities did not appear in any strength until the end of the eighteenth century. Hence there developed what may perhaps be called an agricultural-craft economy, a form of economic life wherein crafts were joined with vigorous farming. Reading the *Journal* of Theophile Cazenove, French traveler who passed through Pennsylvania in 1794, we sense that agricultural life was well advanced while town life was just then beginning to emerge.

In the middle of the eighteenth century, however, two centers of economic activity emerged where pietist principles were attempted—Ephrata and Bethlehem. Here unusual patterns revealed themselves, only to become submerged beneath the capitalism then beginning to appear.

Ephrata had become a community of three orders; we are fairly well informed about its economic life from the *Chronicon Ephratense.* At first poverty was shared. One theme in Beissel's early writings was world-renunciation, which included, he said, private property. Of this the *Chronicon* says:

First of all, property was declared sinful, and everything was brought together in common, in support of a fund, out

of which everything needed for the sustenance of the Brethren was bought. This same also was the case for the Sisters' convent. It was therefore a great reproach for any-one to be accused of ownership. This lasted many years. . . . A common table was also introduced in both convents, during the first hour of the evening.

As late as 1786 there still was a commune at Ephrata.

When the Eckerlin brothers emerged as leaders, new

Baskets like these used at Ephrata were for storage of many different kinds of things. *Courtesy the Pennsylvania Historical and Museum Commission*

verve was given to Ephrata's economy. First Gabriel, a physician, was prior, then in 1740 his older brother, Israel, followed. Israel was extraordinarily gifted in business affairs and during the few years when he was prior, from 1740 to 1745, there was remarkable economic achievement. A "hot suitor of the Virgin Sophia," he joined mysticism with common sense, thus changing the brotherhood from an association of contemplatives who shared poverty of spirit to a hard-working guild of craftsmen—almost slaves—who aimed at creating a rich and prosperous order. Israel Eckerlin did not share Beissel's ideal of spiritual poverty. Agriculturally, more produce was raised than the community needed; surpluses were planned. An orchard of a thousand young trees was planted. In 1741 the brethren built a gristmill along the Cocalico, from which excellent flour was obtained. A saw mill and oil press were soon established, the last two to support the printing establishment, a press having been brought from Europe in 1742. In truth, Ephrata maintained the only self-sustaining printing establishment in the colonies, with paper, inks, and tannery for binding, all their own products. While the brothers followed the crafts, the sisters kept house and tended garden, raising more vegetables than the community needed. Israel Eckerlin kept an agent in Philadelphia, Wilhelm Jung (Young), who served also as purchasing agent and salesman. The restless prior advanced his plans vigorously, treating the brothers as workmen and seeking to forge a community of productive wealth.

The strength of Israel Eckerlin's dream was his undoing. His vision of a pietist community where wealth was shared conflicted with Conrad Beissel's idea of sharing poverty. Although at first highly regarded, on September 4, 1745, the blow fell. Beissel sacked Eckerlin. The mills were shut down. Orchards were uprooted. One night there was a big fire and Eckerlin's dream of a rich and thriving community along the Cocalico went up in smoke.

There was no chance to work out pietist economic theory at Ephrata.

Moravian experiments in communal pietism, however, were more fortunate and aggressive. Here pietist economics came to full bloom. The Moravians made at least a dozen settlements in early Pennsylvania where utopian vision joined economic experimentation. These communities were organized in choirs, which does not quite translate the German *Chor,* groups or members divided by sex and age: infants, small boys, small girls, larger boys, larger girls, single brethren, single sisters, married folk, widowers, widows. Each *Chor* had its own organization, leaders, and rules, with even separate liturgies for worship. Their clothes distinguished them.

The *Chor* system, taken over from European Moravianism, formed the basis of all phases of Moravian life. The whole village was a commune; economic activity was shared; all was administered by the congregation, for there was here no distinction between church and state.

Bethlehem was a Moravian economy. Goods were held in common and all work and property were shared. As at Ephrata, private ownership did not exist; the treasury was common. We cannot say whether all had to forgo private possessions, but we do know that Bishop Spangenberg, whose genius ruled the commune, gave up his personal inheritance. Nor was there private housing: the *Chors* lived separately, with only a few married families living alone. Individual security was won for the whole fellowship and property belonged to the congregation.

Far more than Ephrata, Bethlehem was a center for crafts. Most agricultural activity was centered at Nazareth, a few miles to the north, and also at Meierhüte and Christianbrunn, although some fruit and vegetables were grown in Bethlehem. As early as 1743, a year after its founding, a grist mill was erected, then enlarged in 1751. There were also a fulling mill, a dye house, and a cloth manufactory. In 1747, just five years after the founding, thirty-two crafts were operative in the village: gristmill, sawmill, oilmill, tannery, smithy, locksmith, pottery, joiner, glass house, turner, wagon shop, six linen weavers who were directed by Eva Maria Spangenberg, stocking and fulling mill, rope maker, cooper, distillery (for use of the community and not for Indians), cabinetmaker, tailor, furrier, chairmaker, button maker, mason, carpenter, stone-setter for the graveyard, baker, butcher, soap-maker, chimney sweep, boot cleaner, cultivator of medicinal herbs for the pharmacist, innkeeper, and cable ferryman for the river.

Some of these crafts produced more than the commune could consume. Products were sold outside for profit and in 1747 the profit derived from external business amounted to £211, 14s, 4d. At that time Bethlehem had three hundred inhabitants.

The community grew and soon supported large missionary work. By 1765 Bethlehem had 510 residents, a number that may be increased to 952 if we count all the Moravians on detached service as missionaries and itinerants. Accurate records were kept; we know how much wheat, meat, and eggs, how many shirts, stockings, and shoes were used, how much travel along the wilderness trail cost, how much missionaries needed, how large the surpluses were that were sent to the Philadelphia markets. One of the Bethlehem specialties was buckwheat flour, much sought for in city markets.

New methods of work were started. In 1754 Hans Christopher Christiansen originated an unusual water-pumping system, by which waters were pumped into

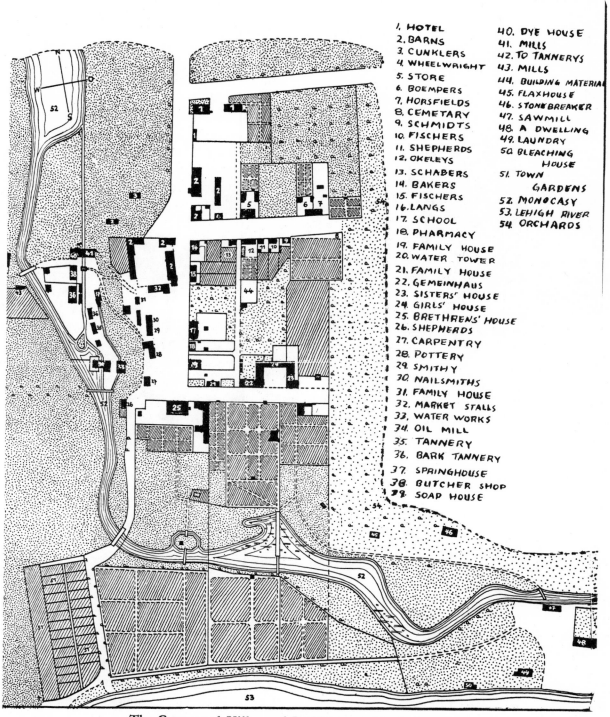

1. HOTEL
2. BARNS
3. CUNKLERS
4. WHEELWRIGHT
5. STORE
6. BOEMPERS
7. HORSFIELDS
8. CEMETARY
9. SCHMIDTS
10. FISCHERS
11. SHEPHERDS
12. OKELEYS
13. SCHABERS
14. BAKERS
15. FISCHERS
16. LANGS
17. SCHOOL
18. PHARMACY
19. FAMILY HOUSE
20. WATER TOWER
21. FAMILY HOUSE
22. GEMEINHAUS
23. SISTERS' HOUSE
24. GIRLS' HOUSE
25. BRETHRENS' HOUSE
26. SHEPHERDS
27. CARPENTRY
28. POTTERY
29. SMITHY
30. NAILSMITHS
31. FAMILY HOUSE
32. MARKET STALLS
33. WATER WORKS
34. OIL MILL
35. TANNERY
36. BARK TANNERY
37. SPRINGHOUSE
38. BUTCHER SHOP
39. SOAP HOUSE
40. DYE HOUSE
41. MILLS
42. TO TANNERYS
43. MILLS
44. BUILDING MATERIAL
45. FLAXHOUSE
46. STONEBREAKER
47. SAWMILL
48. A DWELLING
49. LAUNDRY
50. BLEACHING HOUSE
51. TOWN GARDENS
52. MONOCASY
53. LEHIGH RIVER
54. ORCHARDS

The Communal Village of Bethlehem, with the location of the craft shops. *Courtesy the Archives in Herrnhut, Germany*

Shocked wheat, cornfields, fruit trees, rail fences. . . . The Pennsylvania countryside photographed by **W. W.** Dietrich at the start of the twentieth century.

leather (later metal) pipes for the larger buildings. Bethlehem had two fine inns: The Crown and The Sun. In 1763 the first fire engine, with pumps, came in from London.

Bishop Spangenberg's vision of communal pietism can hardly be overvalued. He takes his proper place among utopian dreamers. For twenty years he guided the Bethlehem economy and made it into America's finest experiment in democratic living, worthy of being classed among the social experiments of the earlier period, perhaps the most successful of them all. Gradually, however, Bethlehem was drawn into the developing capitalist society that surrounded it. Dissatisfaction arose; not all Indians were willing converts. The older workers grumbled when they had to carry weaker brethren along. Still, while it lasted, it was an astonishing society, inte-

grated, without social security, medicare, or pensions—an interesting noncapitalist version of communal pietism. Bethlehem was overcome by mercantilism and the rising middle-class scheme of values as expressed by *Poor Richard's Almanac.*

By about 1760 the rigors of colonization were moderating. European influences were receding and during a period that has not yet been properly studied a more or less homogeneous culture was being formed in the fertile limestone bottoms of southeastern Pennsylvania. Patterns of life were emerging, languages firmed; it was now said that if one stood on limestone soil and spoke Pennsylvania Dutch, he would be answered in the same dialect. Included in this linguistic region were parts of Montgomery, Chester, Northampton, Lancaster, York, and Dauphin counties, and most of Lehigh, Berks, and Lebanon counties. And as the West opened, this heartland expanded to several fertile valleys beyond the Blue Mountains and down into Virginia.

Thus the Pennsylvania Dutch area remained, in the main, the Pennsylvania piedmont, where fertile fields were blessed by good water and temperate climate, an area situated between the "fall line" of the Delaware and Susquehanna rivers and the Blue Mountains, and as large as Connecticut, Massachusetts, and Rhode Island together.

In this region, then, a distinctive German-language culture arose with an economic pattern somewhat different from the mercantile capitalism then developing in Anglo-Saxon America. Basically agricultural, this economy was still rather aggressive in its methods. Germans introduced fourfold crop rotation: of wheat, of oats, corn or buckheat, clover; of clover; and of clover with ploughing. Fertilization was with organic manures and lime, generally burned in home lime kilns from native limestone and applied at the rate of forty bushels per acre. Plaster of Paris was good, but too expensive for the frugal Dutch. Manuring was done at the rate of four bushels per acre; most ploughing was by two-horse teams. Each farm had two or three such teams.

The main crop was wheat, apex of an interesting agricultural-craft economy. Many gristmills were needed to grind grain. We do know that by 1770 gristmills were extensive along the Skippack, Perkiomen, Pequea, Conestoga, Codorus, and Conewago, as well as along the smaller streams. (George Merkel of Richmond township, Berks, named the small stream that powered his mill the "Mosel"; he was a native of Metz.) The mill system was so well developed that grain harvested in Virginia and Maryland was brought to Pennsylvania and milled there. It is reported that around 1770 Lancaster County had at least a hundred gristmills and York County about two hundred and fifty. Carl Bridenbaugh, in that excellent work *The Colonial Craftsman,* reports that Philadelphia County had 107 gristmills with centers in Roxborough, and the Brandywine-Wilmington area was exceptional. These so-called merchant-mills were sometimes owned in tandem: Jacob Greisemer of Oley, former officer in the Revolution, owned six mills when he died in 1790.

Two other early industries are known: iron and glass. By the time of the Revolution there were about eighty bloomeries, forges, silting mills in Penn's colony, although not all were run by Germans. Associated with these operations was extensive forest work, because one forge consumed 840 bushels of coals every 24 hours, for

Montgomery County corn crib with scalloped eaves. *Photograph courtesy Mr. Edward W. Schlechter*

which about twenty-two cords of wood were needed. (Estimate 400 bushels of coals for one ton of iron.) Therefore if one man chopped two-and-a-half to four cords of wood per day, six men could produce two to three hundred tons per year. We know little about Colonial glass works. Caspar Wistar (d. 1752) made some lovely pieces; "Baron Stiegel" is more famous; but the traces of other glass houses have not been followed. In the 1760s there was a glass house in Bethlehem.

Generally speaking, however, the mercantile policies of the British government that dealt with Colonial manufacture hindered the development of American industry. By the time of the Revolution the Pennsylvania heartland was still chiefly agricultural, giving wheat prime place in the Colonial economy. Much was exported.

In 1795 Theophile Cazenove (1740–1811) journeyed through New Jersey and parts of Pennsylvania and kept a lively *Journal* of his travels, which gives a brilliant picture of life in the Pennsylvania piedmont, a cross-section of this region after major migration had ceased. Cazenove entered Pennsylvania at Easton, traveled west-

At the center of the farm-craft economy of early Pennsylvania, as in the center of this picture, was wheat. Grown in fertile acres, ground in the many gristmills that dotted our landscape, transported in the sturdy Conestogas to market and port, this staple was exported in quantity before the American Revolution. *Photograph by Robert Walch*

ward to Carlisle, then returned to Philadelphia by way of York and Lancaster. His comments are detailed and revealing.

Cazenove found Easton to be a pretty little town, well laid out with main square and rows of streets partly lined with good houses of limestone. The inhabitants were Germans, with one church used jointly by "Lutherans and Presbyterians." There also was a courthouse and prison,

a vaulted building for county records, and a printing establishment that brought out a paper every Wednesday, sold at a dollar a year and circulating about six hundred copies. It was in German. The printer was at the same time printer, poet, and compositor.

Next Cazenove found good lodging among the Moravians in Nazareth. This village, begun in 1763, had thirty houses, plain but well built, all associated with the Moravian congregation. Its water was piped underground and gardens were irrigated by gutters. The boys' college taught German, English, Latin, and French to thirty-six students, with twenty-two on the waiting list. The school did not impress Cazenove. He did say that the Nazareth church had a good organ.

Bethlehem was a town where the Moravians were merged into a common family; individuals had worked

farms, a brewery, a seminary for men, one for widows, and one for girls, a bakery, a tanyard, a store where all kinds of merchandise from England and from Germany are sold at retail, a large inn, shoemaker, tailor, locksmith, and carpenter. (p. 25)

In 1794 there were still supervisors appointed by the congregation. Twelve sisters did the laundry. In the girls' school the following subjects were taught: needlework,

Jim Hill's painting of Merkle's Mill near Moselem Springs, done around 1925. *Courtesy Mr. Richard C. Adam*

for the community and had been in turn supported by it. The old communal pietism was over.

Full surrender of fortune no longer occurs. Each one of the brothers and sisters keeps his property and is paid for his work. But the land and buildings and mills, etc.—everything is the property of the community. (p. 24)

The community also owned farms, supply mills, store, tanyard, bakery, school, and furnaces for the common good.

There are in Bethlehem one large flour-mill, one large lumber mill, one large oil press, one large tobacco factory, one large factory to full cloth, a boarding school . . . 4 large

painting, music, reading, writing, arithmetic.

Next Cazenove came to "Allen's Town," and found fair lodging at "Egler's." This was a pretty town of about one hundred houses and two German churches.

Ealer's Tavern (now in Whitehall Township, Lehigh County) was the center of an agricultural area where much clover was sown but where much land was still not cultivated.

They are all German farmers in this district; they are diligent and thrifty and become rich; few vegetables besides cabbage, potatoes, and turnips.

Trexler's tavern, isolated, afforded him "bad lodging."

With this kind of machinery, Pennsylvania wheat was ground for export to Britain and the Indies. Methods of milling changed little during the centuries. *Courtesy Mr. Stephan Kindig, Lobachsville*

Lime was burned in kilns like these in many locations in eastern Pennsylvania. This old photograph, taken by W. W. Dietrich in 1901, shows an unusual stone fence near the Guth homestead in Lehigh County.

a large church where union services were held. There were about 50 houses, with five taverns along the old King's Highway, which was followed by those who were migrating from the east. Used to the European agricultural village, this traveler noted that there is

not a farmer in this village, where, by asking from door to door, I found that there were: 1 turner, 1 carpenter, 1 joiner, 2 hatmakers making poor hats, 1 saddle-maker, 1 baker, 1 shoemaker, 2 tailors, 1 locksmith, 1 wheelwright, 1 minister, 1 school for learning to read and write German and English, 1 jeweller who also fixes watches, 1 weaver, 1 tobacco factory, 2 stores, 1 builder, 1 place where women spin cotton and wool, 1 gingerbread vender, 1 carpenter for

Page from the church record of the First Reformed Church in Easton, of the year 1787, showing the list of those who partook of the Lord's Supper at spring communion. This was just a few years before Cazenove went through the town.

Decorated door lintel in Allentown.

Soon he was in Berks County, where the ground was good, nearly all cultivated, and there were many farms. "These German farmers take very good care of their farms." Houses were either of stone or of logs.

Next he came to "Coots Town" in Berks County, where he stopped with "John Stauht . . . a Frenchman from Lorraine"—at the sign of Washington. He found "good lodging" here with this native of Wolfersweiler, in the Palatinate, a few miles from the French border. In 1780 Mr. G. Coots had laid out the town and it acquired

homes, 1 potter, 1 tanyard, 5 taverns, 2 of which are very good. (p. 31)

He noted that the houses were log cabins, or log beams with mortar between, and that the best ones were painted on the outside to look like bricks. The farmers, he reported, took their wheat to Germantown mills. By so doing they got 11s, 9d per bushel, while those who had their wheat milled locally were paid only 10s.

Datestone on the Abraham Knabb house, Oley. *Photograph courtesy Mr. Edward W. Schlechter*

Maxatawney had good land, with farms averaging 150 to 200 acres. Here one acre produced 25 bushels of barley, 20 bushels of wheat, 30 bushels of buckwheat, 2 tons of hay from both cuttings. Here, too, were many remarkable springs, which gave power to the mills. The German farmers manufactured coarse woolens for coats and skirts,

and there were also linen weavers. Only better cloths had to be purchased.

> They deny themselves everything costly, and when there is snow they haunt the taverns. They are remarkably obstinate and ignorant. (p. 34)

Farms had sufficient flax, hemp, and wool; gardens had cabbages and carrots. Everyone had bee hives. The charming countryside, he felt, was spoiled by the inhabitants who lacked education.

> All these farmers talk politics, and because they read the papers, they think they know a good deal about the government; they think that government officers are too many and overpaid. (p. 35)

He found only "fair lodging" at Nicholas Schaeffer's tavern in Maiden Creek.

Next Cazenove came to Reading, which had a court house and four to five hundred houses for about 3,000 inhabitants. Of these, fifty or so were of brick, "neatly decorated like the Philadelphia houses with a stoop of white marble." The town had two markets, "very clean"; streets were wide although not paved. The only manufacture was of hats, of wool and selling for a dollar; forty thousand were made for export in one year. A carpenter made river boats, flat and without keel, which carried five-ton loads to Philadelphia when the river was low, and twelve when the river was high. Inland trade was important: farm produce was sent to the city on flat boats. A German newspaper came out every Wednesday.

Womelsdorf gave Cazenove pretty good lodging. It had about fifty houses, some stone, a few new ones of brick, the rest of logs and mortar. The road to Meyerstown was bad.

At Meyerstown he stopped with Godfrey Keener. On the way there he saw a church letting out.

> The sermon ended just as I passed. It seemed to me I saw people coming out of church in Westphalia, so much have all these farmers kept their ancestor's costumes, only most young farmers have given up the straw hat for the cap of black silk . . . but for the men, the green coats, light blue ones, and large pulled-down hats, boots extending above the knees, etc. As in Germany. (p. 45)

He passed by part of the Susquehanna-Schuylkill Canal from Harrisburg to Reading, engineered by an Englishman, William Weston. (The whole canal was not opened until 1817.)

Lebanon was a pleasant little town, dividing Tulpehocken from Quitapahilla and Swatara, having 170

A variety of lamps. It is not always possible to separate those from Pennsylvania from the others. *Courtesy Miss Lottie Moyer*

Various kinds of lanterns, not all of which are distinctly Pennsylvanian. *Courtesy Miss Lottie Moyer*

houses and two cross-streets. All inhabitants were Germans, with two churches—union Lutheran-Reformed and Moravian. In this region the rotation of crops was: wheat; wheat again; oats; fallow; wheat, fallow. The cattle were in stables from December to April.

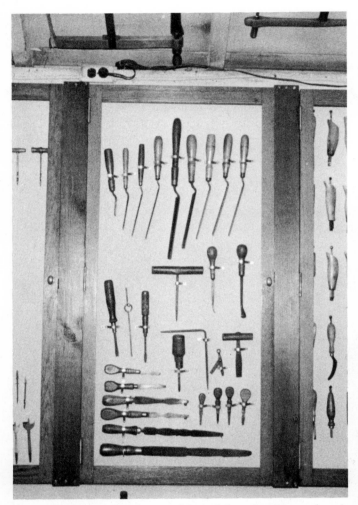

Screwdrivers and other tools used by the Pennsylvania Dutch. There was little difference after the earlier years in the tools used here. *Courtesy Mr. Wallace Wetzel*

Hummelstown, a village along the highway, had about fifty small houses of logs and mortar, with no English windows; a large retail store; and four taverns.

Harrisburg was one of America's little phenomena in the speed of its development. In 1785 it had only one house, Mr. Harris's. In 1794 there were about 300 houses neatly built of brick or logs and mortar, generally two

stories high with English windows. The inhabitants were chiefly mechanics who manufactured hats and tobacco. There were, astonishingly, thirty-two taverns. The Susquehanna was a traffic artery and in 1793 two hundred thousand bushels of wheat were sent down by two or three merchant millers. The printing plant brought out an English newspaper every Monday.

Cazenove visited Carlisle, where there was a small college with shabby buildings and 70 students, who were taught English, Latin, Greek, mathematics, history, and philosophy. Wheat from western Pennsylvania was sent to Baltimore because of the higher cartage costs to Philadelphia.

Next was Chambersburg, where he lunched with Henry Shryock, tavern keeper. From here he turned back

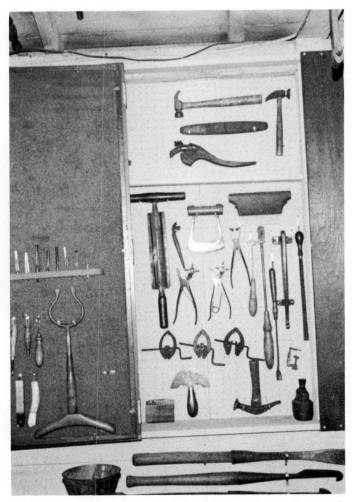

Leather-working tools used during the late nineteenth century. *Courtesy Mr. Wallace Wetzel*

In one-room schoolhouses like these, classes were held in the German language. Later they became soundly English. This schoolhouse stood in eastern Berks county, 1900.

Dutch heartland had become one of the richest areas in America and that its agriculture was prosperous. A traveler like Cazenove found an area where developing culture was replacing Colonial provincialism, where a new breed was emerging—democratic man, as that other French observer of the time, Crèvecoeur, was to see. German skills were not political, although growing interest in such matters was apparent.

The change from Colonial to democratic economy was visible in architecture. While European influences still appeared, they now were mixed. Old Germanic structures, erected in Old-World styles, gave way before the march of the English Georgian, in stone or brick. Now farmers could afford to bring in members of the Carpenter's Company from the City; places like the French-style Levan House in Oley were succeeded by the Fisher House with its classic lines. Or clockmaker Daniel Oyster could make a walnut clock case with classical fluted corners and inlaid with the ever-present Pennsylvania lily.

By the end of the eighteenth century, then, the heartland expressed, even in the names of the smaller towns and villages, its fundamental Germanic character. Of course, Lancaster, York, Reading, and Allentown were English names. There were, however, several Heidelberg Townships. Towns with German names were frequent:

toward York, noting that millers here sent their flour to Baltimore.

At "Abbot's Town" he dined with Jones at the sign of the Indian Queen—"fair lodging." This was a village of 25 houses and one inn, all inhabited by Germans.

At York he stayed at Spangler's "very good inn." The Codorus, he reported, is a little river rich in water, allowing several mills to operate.

As the traveler reached Lancaster he found the countryside well cultivated and the forests that remained were stocked with chestnut, locust, walnut, maple, and white oak, all useful trees. He stopped here with Christian Stake, but he should have stayed at the White Swan with Matthias Slough, where he would have been very comfortable. Three-quarters of the inhabitants were German. It had some brick houses, small and large, and many log houses for one thousand inhabitants, "mainly mechanics." Along the Conestoga there were many flour mills where "much flour" was made for the Philadelphia market.

New prosperity had come to the once-poor Colonial outposts. All travelers agreed that the Pennsylvania

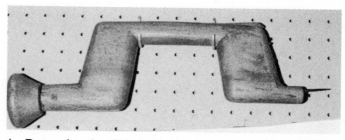

A Pennsylvania Dutch brace. *Courtesy Mr. Wallace Wetzel*

Hanover, Manheim, Berlin, Hamburg, Strassburg. Many a Dutch pioneer had a name made permanent in a village: Bechtelsville, Boyertown, Fogelsville, Gettysburg, Groffdale, Hellertown, Hummelstown, Kutztown, Meyersdale, Meyerstown, Orwigsburg, Schaefferstown, Selinsgrove, Strausstown, Stoverstown, Trexlertown, Weissport, Womelsdorf.

The Germans had settled in eastern Pennsylvania. But

Mercantilism came to the newly established Pennsylvania towns quite early. Here is Reading merchant Sebastian Algaier at his ledger. *Courtesy the Historical Society of Berks County*

Folk portrait of Jacob Meinsel of Womelsdorf, Berks County, dated April 20, 1825.

Around the turn of the nineteenth century eastern Pennsylvania was a center of hat manufacturing. Here is John
Mays of Schaefferstown, Lebanon County, a hatter. *Courtesy the Historical Society of Berks County*

they spread westward too. This migration is much harder to document.

We do know that three basic tools emerged in the Pennsylvania Dutch area to become symbols of the frontier: the long rifle, sometimes called "the Kentucky" because that is where it was used; the broad axe, which was used to fell trees for building the log cabins; and the Conestoga wagon, which carried the name of a Lancaster valley and bore the nation to the Pacific. All three tools were hybrids, the result of an assimilation of Old-World objects and their application to the frontier. But they did the job. The rifle provided the game. The broad axe hewed the trees to make the cabins. And the wagon took wheat to the port cities and people to the west.

In these three tools the Pennsylvania influence on the American west can be seen.

On the sturdy Conestogas goods and wares were shipped from inland areas to the port city, and, in the following century, this wagon bore the pioneers across the prairies to the Pacific. *Courtesy the Pennsylvania Farm Museum, Landis Valley*

Jacob Oberholtzer's illumination of the Bible of master gunsmith Hermann Rupp, with record of birth and marriage. *Courtesy of Reverend William Rupp*

Goose-wing broad axe made in Pennsylvania during the
eighteenth century, constructed of iron with a steel edge
welded. While later they were made throughout the
country, the early center of production was Pennsylvania.
Courtesy Mr. Henry J. Kauffman

Rifle made by Hermann Rupp, whose illuminated Bible is
pictured across. *Photograph of a rifle in the collection
of Wes White by Donald Wendling*

5

Americanization

*E*ven before the American Revolution had parted
pacifist from patriot forcing some aspects of Pennsylvania Dutch culture to withdraw into isolation, and
sending many sectarians to Canada, life in the Pennsylvania heartland came under the dominion of the environ-
ing Anglo-Saxon culture.

Older settlers found themselves buttressed by newer
immigrants, the beginning of a political migration that
was to become a flood. Sectarians had become politically
reactionary; their pacifism and perfectionism did not fit
the raw frontier with its robust realities. The denominations were more socially active and shared public life more
willingly, although surely not so eagerly as the Scotch-
Irish.

Many Pennsylvania Dutch sons and daughters moved
west, south, and north; they came into regions where
German languages were not spoken, into racially mixed
communities. Even the continuing migration from Germany, which did not come out of the same pietism, could
infuse only meager new life into a culture already well
established. Here we face a difficult area of study, for the
endeavor to chart a transition of cultural values is not
easy. Herder's solution was far too simple; no folk is an
island. His view was based on language and it ignored the
common Indo-Germanic sources of all languages. Early
travelers like Dr. Schoepff ridiculed the language spoken
as a mixture of Swabian, English, and Indian.

One untried method of studying the migration of the
Pennsylvania Dutch westward is through the establishment of Reformed Churches before 1830. The old Reformed churches founded before that date were essentially
Palatine in origin, spread by Pennsylvania Dutch. There
were at least fifty such congregations in Ohio before this
date; the one in Marietta dates from 1796. Of course,
these churches were mixed with Congregationalist ones,
for Yankees, like the Pennsylvania Dutch, brought their
religion with them.

Anglicanization—which is what is meant by Americanization—was a process that varied by regions. In country areas things remained conservative and the bastions of
Germanic culture were schools and churches. In the beginning things were still written in German and then
translated. "Baron" Friedrich von Steuben arrived at Valley Forge on February 23, 1778, full of plans for ordering
the American army. The fruit of his thought was a manuscript in German for disciplining troops, the first drill
regulations for an American army. In the spring of 1778
these regulations, duly translated, became standard operating procedure for the Continentals, changing a rabble
into a well-disciplined force. Some German preachers,
impressed by Anglicanization, moved over to English
churches, notably two sons of the Lutheran patriarch
Mühlenberg, Peter and Friedrich.

The dearth of trained clerics, frontier emotionalism,
and reaction against formalized religion produced many
evangelical sects. This was a general manifestation of a

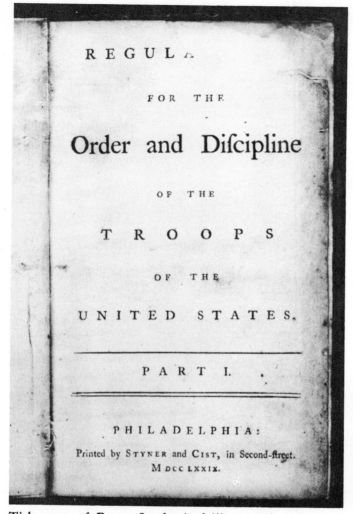

REGUL A

FOR THE

Order and Discipline

OF THE

T R O O P S

OF THE

U N I T E D   S T A T E S.

PART I.

PHILADELPHIA:

Printed by STYNER and CIST, in Second-street.
M DCC LXXIX.

Title page of Baron Steuben's drill manual, written at Valley Forge in German and here translated for use of the American Army. *Courtesy the Valley Forge Park Commission*

migration of Germans out of Pennsylvania increased. Also, about this time Philadelphia lost its place as the center of Germanic culture. After the Revolution Germantown—and, of course, Ephrata, which was in decline —no longer were centers of printing; newly established towns had their presses: Reading in 1786, 1789; Lancaster in 1797; York in 1795; and at the turn of the century, Carlisle, Chambersburg, Hanover, Harrisburg, Somerset, New Berlin, Allentown, Selinsgrove, Bath, Sumneytown. With this movement of the press to the provinces, the character of what was being printed also changed, although old-fashioned religious books still dominated. Most important was the weekly newspaper. In 1800 there were the following German newspapers:

Baltimore	*Deutsche Zeitung*
Easton	*Unparteyische Easton Bothe*
Germantown	*Die Germantauner Zeitung*
Hanover	*Die Pennsylvanische Wochenschrift*
Harrisburg	*Die Harrisburger Morgenröthe*

Stylized decorations on a house in Allentown.

trend visible elsewhere, showing sometimes as a splintering of denominations, divisions of established churches. It also expressed the impact of the British type of Methodism on pietist forms. A Lancaster Dutchman, Heinrich Boehm, is considered to be the forerunner of German Methodism, while a one-time Reformed preacher, William Otterbein, and Martin Boehm, a layman, were involved in Methodist meetings held in the German language. Similarly, the Evangelical fellowship, which was founded by Jacob Albright (Albrecht), stressed the conflict of penitence in Methodist style.

German migration into Pennsylvania declined as the

Lancaster	*Die Amerikanische Staatsbote*
	Der Lancaster Correspondent
Philadelphia	*Die Philadelphische Correspondenz*
Reading	*Neu Unpartheyisch Readinger Zeitung*
	Der Unpartheyische Readinger Adler
York	*Der Wochenberichter*
	York Gazette

Of these, *Der Readinger Adler,* whose first number appeared November 29, 1796, was essentially democratic, and it lasted as a German paper until 1913. In addition, an important printed work was the almanac produced by nearly every printing house. The materials in the almanacs have not yet been thoroughly studied.

Along with the provincializing of Pennsylvania Dutch culture, which set up conflict between "the city" and the hinterland, there went revived independence. The

furnace in Pittsburgh, and with associates in 1804 he erected one in Huntington. Economic freedom also was appearing.

German schools were everywhere in the heartland of Eastern Pennsylvania. Their problems were many, not the least of which was that of textbooks. Of course hymnal, Testament, and devotional works like Arndt's *True Christianity* formed the basis of reading. Textbooks as such were first either imported by schoolmasters or

"I herewith certify that Samuel Hoch, a son of Philip Hoch of Richmond Township, Berks County, and Sara Herbein, a daughter of Johann Herbein of Richmond Township, Berks County, in the State of Pennsylvania, were legally married on the 19th Day of November, 1820. Johann Knoske, Preacher of the Gospel." *Courtesy Mr. John Adam*

churches of formal character, Lutheran and Reformed, now cut themselves off from European controls; in 1786 the former cut away from Halle and in 1792 the latter from the Holland fathers. In 1796 a daughter society of Ephrata was erected at Snowhill, and soon buildings arose where the spirit of Conrad Beissel was followed. In 1793 Georg Ausschütz from Strassburg built an iron

improvised. Some were reprints, the more popular one being J. J. Bachmaier's *A Complete German Grammar in Two Parts,* which first appeared in 1772 with a preface by Heinrich Müller and which was reprinted as late as 1828. In 1789 Carl Cist published *Neu-Eingerichtetes Schul-Büchlein,* which reproduced the European Ebersdorf edition of 1784. In 1791 Samuel Saur, in Chestnut

Although outside of the heartland of the Pennsylvania Dutch in eastern Pennsylvania, Old Economy, the third and last home settlement of the Harmony Society, is related to Pennsylvania Dutch culture by its association with religious and poetical traditions. They arrived in the beginning of the nineteenth century, before the 48ers, and so find their place in an America wherein the Pennsylvania Dutch had already spread their culture to Ohio. *Courtesy the Pennsylvania Historical and Museum Commission*

Hill, brought out *Ein gantz Neu-Eingerichtetes Lutherisches ABC Buchstabir- und Namenbuch zum nutzlichen Gebrauch deutsche Schulen,* with a Philadelphia imprint. Several times reprinted, this work contained translations from the *New England Primer,* as in

Uriahs schöne Eheweib	Uriah's beauteous wife
War der Davids Zeitvertreib	Made David seek his life.

In 1795 the *New England Primer* was brought out by Cist. It is to be noted that these church schools taught students to read both the German and English languages.

Soon the pastors who were charged with educational tasks began to bring out their own textbooks for schools. In 1795 G. G. Otterbein published his *Lesebuch für Deutsche Schulkinder,* probably a Moravian work. In

1809 Christian Becker brought out *Der Deutscher algegenwärtiger Sprachlehrer* in Easton and the next year, *Der Deutschen Kinder Englischen und Deutschen ABC Buchstabier- Lese- und Sprechbüchlein.* This work sought to teach students to read and write both languages. Ambrosius Henkel published *Das Kleine ABC Buch* in Lebanon, 1818; C. L. Waley, *Die Elemente der deutschen Sprache,* 1819; and in this same year Ebner in Allentown published *Neu Englische Sprachlehre.* This was a noble effort to make the Pennsylvania Dutch bilingually literate.

Reformed pastors further asserted their independence from European controls by compiling "private" catechisms. This, however, was not universal, for from 1755 to 1847 at least forty German and seventeen English printings of the old *Heidelberg Catechism* were made by Philadelphia print shops while six editions of a rarer work, the *Palatinate Catechism,* were made. An independent catechism had appeared by Johann Bechtel in 1742, but its Moravian slant was suspected. Several Reformed catechisms came out that expressed independent views by pastors Lampe, Hermann, Ludwig Becker, Jacob Becker. Other important ones were by Samuel Helffenstein, Jonathan Rathnaur, the so-called Allentown, and Johann Heinrich Helfferich's, which was widely used and probably the best.

Anglicanization was in nothing more painful than in the language question that plagued the churches. At the time the American union was being formed (most established churches did their preaching in the German language). There were some exceptions. From 1784 on, the Germantown Lutheran church worshipped in English. A split showed in Zion's church in Philadelphia, leading to the founding of a congregation where English was used. Pastor Helmuth called for retention of German in church, school, and home. In 1812 the Harrisburg Reformed church held English services. Soon after 1815 the Lancaster Lutherans held German worship only on alternate Sundays. Easton went over to English in 1831, but Reading did not move to English worship until 1842.

If German churches fought the language question, the Commonwealth of Pennsylvania did not. From 1784 to 1840 the *Tagebuch* (Minutes) of both Senate and General Assembly were published in the German language. This was, however, simple expediency, for many citizens could read only German. Still, languages were problematic: English dominated the work of David Zeisberger among the converted Indians, for in 1803 he published *Hymns for Use of Christian Indians of the Moravian Mission.* The linguistic chaos of the period was further evident in the appearance of a trilingual newspaper, *Der Pelican,* on June 17, 1800, which was published in Philadelphia in German, French, and English. In 1812 the most significant linguistic achievement of

Datestone on the Kaufmann house on the road from Blandon to Fleetwood, Berks County. *Photograph courtesy Mr. Edward W. Schlechter*

early Pennsylvania appeared, the dictionary edited by Mühlenberg and Schiffer. This was a work of fifteen hundred pages and contained German-English and English-German sections. It gave words in then-current Pennsylvania usage, either of English origin, like *Fens* and *Flour,* or else words that had acquired special Pennsylvania connotations, as *gleichen* (to like), and *ausfallen* (to quarrel). In this same year Schiffer also published a grammar.

The first German-language magazine had been Christopher Saur's *Ein Geistliche Magazien,* which had appeared between 1764 and 1770 and was not sold but was given away with the newspaper in order to advance the kingdom. In 1812 an *Evangelisches Magazin* sponsored by the Lutherans began to be published in Philadelphia and it lasted until 1817. In 1824 a German magazine tried to establish itself in Reading and Philadelphia, but it was short-lived—*Readinger Magazien für Freunden der Deutschen Literatur in Amerika.* The editor is not known, and his purposes remain mysterious. Not to

Datestone on the George and Christina Krauss house,
Krausdale, Lower Milford Township, Lehigh County.

be outdone by the Lutherans, Professor Mayer brought out the *Magazin der deutsch-reformirte Kirche,* which appeared from 1827 to 1829 in Carlisle. In 1828 *Die Evangelische Zeitung* was published in York and in 1829–1830 the Reverend Samuel Helffenstein edited *Evangelisches Magazin der Hoch Deutschen Reformirte Kirche in der Vereinigten Staaten Nord Amerika,* Philadelphia. Competition was keen among the well-established denominations in the heartland.

Datestone on a house in Schwenksville near the State game farm. *Photograph courtesy Mr. Edward S. Schlechter*

While settlers in eastern Pennsylvania were bickering and feuding over old religious questions, Georg Rapp, Swabian pietist, brought his followers to western Pennsylvania. In 1803 he bought some five thousand acres along the Conoquenessing Creek north of Pittsburgh and the next year his adopted son, Friedrich, came with a

colony of five hundred and fifty persons. They formed a community of pietists—the Harmony Society—who shared property and followed the doctrines of Jacob Boehme, Jung-Stilling, and Swedenborg, and were stirred by chiliast expectations of a new age. They gave their members houses, bread, and clothes, and in return received work and obedience. During the first year forty wooden houses were erected for members, various mills, and a huge vegetable plot. In 1807 celibacy was introduced, and by 1810 twenty looms were busy weaving textiles. In spite of celibacy, each family lived apart, even though only as brother and sister. Their surpluses were sent to Pittsburgh and even to Philadelphia. Land was held commonly. They wrote considerable poetry, which is contained in their hymnal, *Harmonisches Gesangbuch,* printed on their own press in 1827, which was done in the sentimental flowery imagery of Ephrata. Some of these poems were addressed to the Virgin Sophia, some extolled the beauties of nature, and others the pleasures of the philadelphian spirit. Thus there was here a combination of mysticism, romanticism, and democracy.

While all this cultural activity was taking place and while all this new settlement was being attempted, the old economy in the heartland prospered. Great wheat harvests were being reaped. Threshed by hand with flail, milled in many gristmills now dotting the landscape, contained in casks made by local coopers, and transported by the great Conestoga wagons, this staple remained the basis of the economy. In 1810 Lancaster country had 171 gristmills, 105 saw mills, 20 hemp mills, 25 fulling mills, 11 oil mills, and 5 carding mills, while its neighbor York county had 108 gristmills, 101 saw mills, 20 hemp mills, 16 fulling mills, 11 oil mills, and one carding mill. In 1810 Lancaster city had 191 distilleries for making brandy, and York had as many. As early as 1809 David Heimbach of Shimersville, Lehigh county, started to operate a furnace, and in 1812 Clemens Rentgen opened two forges in Chester county. In 1814 one each was opened in Clearfield and Beaver counties.

Philadelphia Germans were pathbreakers in industrial development. In 1816 Wilhelm J. Horstman founded a silk mill. In 1819 Friedrich Lening started a chemical factory. In 1725 Joseph Rippon erected a factory in Manayunk. J. A. Roebling was one of America's most famous engineers, and is credited with inventing the suspension bridge, building one in 1844 over the Allegheny River and later one over the East River in New York.

Migration slowed considerably. Some Germans still continued their interest in their homeland. In 1814 Lutheran churches made substantial contributions to the orphan houses in Halle and in 1815 Schwenkfelders sent some money to Görlitz to repay debts their fathers had contracted.

The redemption system, unfortunately, continued until the 1820s. After 1785 indentures had to be registered and while the migration slowed, the percentage of indentured immigrants increased. Treatment aboard ships grew worse after the Revolution and in 1810 a law was passed concerning educational requirements, and in 1819 the German Society of Pennsylvania further regulated importation of passengers. These laws were incorporated into a national statute because troubles had spread to other ports. In 1818 Conrad Zentler published *An Act for Regulating the Importation of German and Other Passengers.*

Churches continued to prosper from the population surge: in 1813 the Lutheran Synod of Pennsylvania had fifty-two congregations with one hundred sixty-three schools. Except for Franklin College, higher education was lacking, or was to be had only in other places Churches splintered. In 1820 John Winebrenner of Harrisburg founded a sect that had a methodist character. Tensions continued within groups and sects like the River Brethren appeared along the Susquehanna and the Reformed Mennonites in Lancaster.

Music was well developed among the Germans. In 1818 Bethlehem had a musical organization led by

Datestone of a house near Friedensburg, Oley, Berks County, Pennsylvania. *Photograph courtesy Mr. Edward W. Schlechter*

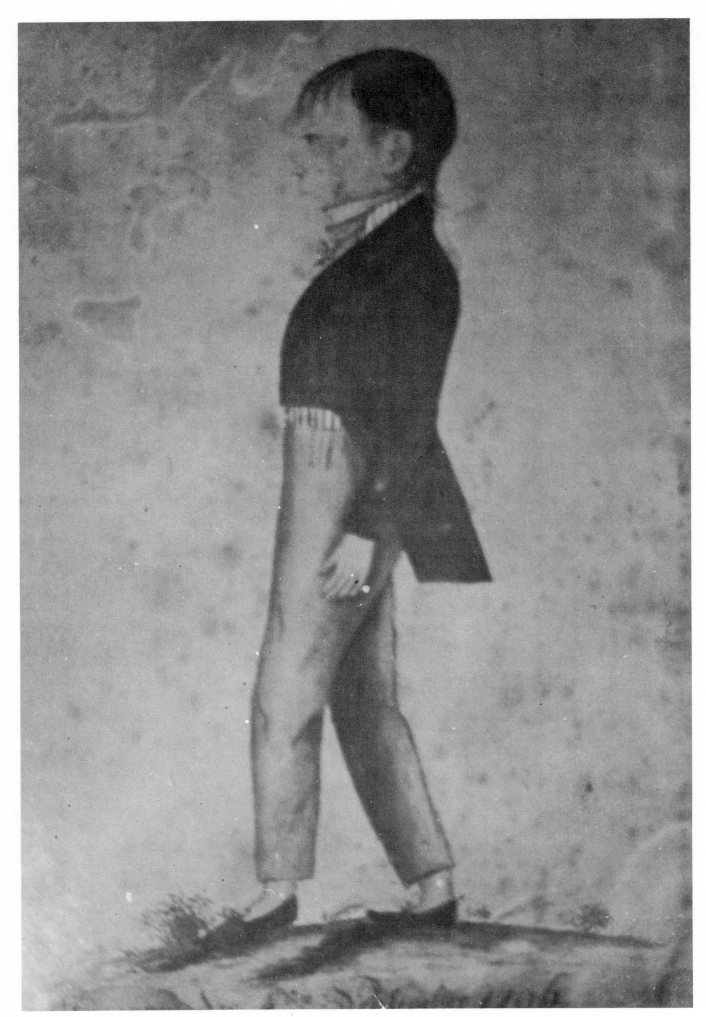

Dr. Isaac Hottenstein, born September 4, 1796, painted
by an itinerating but unknown Pennsylvania artist in the
early nineteenth century. *Courtesy Dr. David Hottenstein*

Interior doorway in the hallway of the Hottenstein house in Maxatawney, Berks County, showing woodwork over the door leading into the drawing room. *Courtesy Dr. David Hottenstein*

Germans, and after 1823 Bach, Handel, and Mozart were performed. In 1820 Philadelphia had a musical school of quality. Pittsburgh had one with a German leader as early as 1818.

The manufacture of musical instruments was a German monopoly. The Krause family of Perkiomen stopped making organs in 1790, probably because of the competition from men like David Tannenberg. Pianos were made in Philadelphia.

Thus, by the year 1830, a solid and basic Germanic culture was domiciled in eastern Pennsylvania that extended from Easton even into Ohio. The range of this language-island has never been charted, although the extent of German tombstones might prove how widespread this was. Nonetheless, we can gather some idea of its extent from the range of the German newspapers. Here is an alphabetical listing of major newspapers in the year 1830:

Allentown	*Der Friedensbote*
	Der Unabhängige Republikaner
	Der Lecha Patriot
Canton, Ohio	*Vaterlandsfreund und Geist der Zeit*
Chambersburg	*Chambersburg Correspondent*
Doylestown	*Bucks County Express*
Easton	*Der Northampton Correspondent*
	Republikanischer Presse
Germantown, Ohio	*Die National Zeitung*
Hanover	*Die Hanover Gazette*

The doorway to the Fisher mansion in Oley represents
a late triumph of Philadelphia Georgian in the piedmont
region. The exquisite detail of this entrance way and the
lovely use of undressed stone mark this structure as
classic.

Taufschein, circa 1795

Schwenkfelder design

TAUFSCHEINE by father and son

These two interesting certificates of birth and baptism were made by Heinrich Otto (above) and Wilhelm Otto. The father's was printed on the Ephrata press and then hand decorated, while the one by the son was done by hand, although the lettering was no longer in *fractura* style. Examination of the designs shows dependence. Moreover, the lower piece, done in the Mahatonga Valley, may be the link between the folk art of the eighteenth century and the painted furniture of the middle of the nineteenth century.

This fine *Vorschrift* in the Rare Book Room of the Philadelphia Free Library illuminates an old hymn that has rich symbolic meaning. It begins:

Wie siehet man zur Frühlings Zeit   How one sees in springtime
Manch schönes Blümlein auf der Heyd   Many lovely flowers on the mead . . .

And here are the flowers in gaudy array, guarded by the life-giving pelicans who pluck their breasts to feed their young. Below, the double eagle spreads his wings, with the proper Scriptures to describe his act. He speaks of the protection that the shield of his wings may bring. Above the eagle is the Virgin Wisdom surrounded by lilies. When this piece is compared with similar Shaker drawings, which are captioned, the symbolism becomes clear. *Courtesy of the Philadelphia Free Library, Rare Book Room*

Crewel sampler

Gros point cushion top

Sampler. *Courtesy Mrs. Walter C. Moser*

Cross-stitch fire screen

Sampler.
Cross-stitch pieces

Pinprick picture. *Courtesy Mrs. Walter C. Moser*

Fancy needlework

Harrisburg	*Der Harrisburger Morgenröthe*
	Der Unabhängige Beobachter
Lancaster	*Der Volksfreund*
	Der Wahre Amerikaner
	Der Lancaster Adler
Lancaster, Ohio	*Der Ohio Adler*
Lebanon	*Pennsylvanische Beobachter*
Marietta, Ohio	*Der Frölicher Botschafter*
Philadelphia	*Philadelphischer Correspondent*
Pittsburgh	*Pittsburg Beobachter*
Reading	*Der Readinger Adler*
	Readinger Democrat und Anti-Frei-maurer Herald
Somerset	*Somerset Republikaner*
Sumneytaun	*Der Bauern Freund*
York	*Die York Gazette*
	Der Republikanischer Herald

These newspapers, whose materials are largely unstudied,

Corner in the Hottenstein House, Maxatawney, showing built-in fireplace and Georgian paneling. *Courtesy Dr. David Hottenstein*

First page of the church record of the Reformed Congregation in Lowhill, now Lehigh County, from a photograph taken March 1916.

were in part edited by newer German immigrants, political refugees who then were escaping to America. Most were weekly sheets, generally, by modern standards, tamely edited, giving European news sometimes a year late. Still, their professionalism compared favorably with that of English-language journals of the same period, while as far as printing is concerned they were far superior. The newer Germans were better printers. *Die Alte und Neue Welt* ran in Philadelphia from 1834 to 1844 with materials mainly addressed to newer arrivals. About 1836 the *Philadelphia Demokrat* appeared, running until about 1842, edited by Ludwig A. Wollenweber, a former German bookseller who was a political refugee.

In 1831 a young scholar, Friedrich Augustus Rauch (1816–1841) arrived in Pennsylvania with credentials from Heidelberg and Marburg universities. After a short period of teaching in the college in Easton, and later in York, he became president of Marshall College at Mercersburg and eventually a professor in the theological seminary there. He was a well-trained student of Hegelian philosophy, having studied with Professor Carl Daub in Heidelberg, and he was a strong anti-rationalist who was engaged in writing a history of theology in Germany, never published. In 1834 he concocted a plan, in conjunction with a Lancaster printer, of publishing a library of German literature, which was to consist of choice re-

"Peter and the Apostles answered, We must obey God rather than man. . . ." A school exercise in penmanship using scriptural quotation, showing the lingering of the Vorschrift tradition. Four schoolboys had been sent to fetch slates: Daniel Edleman, Peter Breitigam, Moses Herbein, and Samuel Harburger. *Courtesy Mr. John Adam*

printing of distinguished German authors and which was to come out weekly in issues of forty-eight pages. The first and only issue appeared January, 1834, and it reprinted about one-third of Goethe's *Italienische Reise* (Travels in Italy) in German. Obviously Pennsylvania Dutch farmers were flattered but not educated enough to appreciate the favor that Rauch was doing for them. In 1840, however, he did bring forth, this time in English, an important publication, *Psychology, or a View of the Human Soul, Including Anthropology,* New York. This was the first truly Hegelian work in America. Rauch died a young man, not fulfilling his promise, leaving much literary work, including manuscripts on both Schelling and Hegel that have not been integrated into histories of American philosophy. Among his other printed works are studies on Goethe's *Faust* and works in comparative religion and philology.

In the period around 1840 agriculture was still

dominant in the Pennsylvania Dutch heartland and unparalleled prosperity was attained, especially in the older areas. Many mills that had been established during the Colonial period were now expanded. Threshing machines, reapers, better ploughs, and many new contraptions for farming appeared. Servicing farm machinery came to be a big business. New crops were added to the always-dominant wheat, mainly in Lancaster, where tobacco now appeared. Unsuccessful efforts to start silk culture continued and vineyards were tried. Cattle now were matured in the wheat fields and some farmers began to specialize in raising draught horses, fateening beeves, and then butchering beeves grown elsewhere.

As the steam engine became more widely used, the old crafts that had flourished during the period of the agriculture-craft economy began to wane. The isolation of rural areas now was broken by canals and railroads. Distilling of spirits prospered, but taxes were high! Brewing, earlier a province of the Anglo-Saxons, now became a German craft.

Discovery of the commercial use of anthracite coal was the work of a Pennsylvania Dutchman. In 1825, Friedrich List, who had been an outspoken critic of political faults in Germany, came to Pennsylvania and first settled on a small farm near Harrisburg. In 1827 he published in English *Outlines of American Political Economy in a Series of Letters,* wherein he opposed the liberalism of Adam Smith. Leaving his farm because of ill health, he went to the Blue Mountains where he became agitator for a railroad to connect Tamaqua with Port Clinton, whereby coal could be brought and loaded on the barges of the Schuylkill Canal. This railroad was built in 1831. For several years previously, 1828 to 1830, List had served as editor of *Der Reading Adler,* giving that paper its political character. Later he returned to Europe.

In 1840 the Pennsylvania branch of the American Tract Society, an organization for printing and circulating religious materials, was opened, with offices at Fourth and Arch Streets, Philadelphia, and rural Pennsylvania churches were flooded with German-language religious tracts. Many denominations used these evangelical pieces.

About 1848 new verve was given Germanic cultural affairs by the coming to Pennsylvania of the energetic

Lilies growing out of a star on this dower chest are certainly not put there to scare the witches away. This dower chest top is of another mood.

Pennsylvania plain from the Conrad Weiser home, Berks
County. *Photograph by Owen C. Sout*

theologian, Philipp Schaff, Berlin-trained scholar who became professor of church history at Mercersburg. Not only did Schaff enrich regional affairs by his depth, but he also gave American scholarship new zest. In this year he started to publish the finest German-language journal yet produced in Pennsylvania, *Der Kirchenfreund,* which, in spite of its excellence, enjoyed only meager success. Lasting about six years, and well edited, containing a goodly variety of theological, devotional, and literary articles, this journal could not succeed because there were not enough educated people who still read German. The youth were learning English. Even the poetry of "Meta," Schaff's wife, was of little help.

Some students believe that wagon sheds were the first structures decorated.

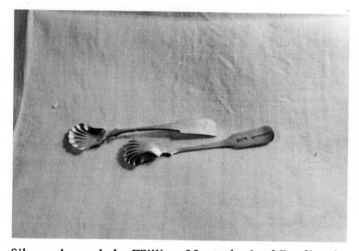

Silver salts made by William Mannerbach of Reading in early decades of the nineteenth century. This provincial silver has not yet been studied.

Interests of Young Men and Women. A monthly, it appeared until 1862, when the Civil War killed it. In *The Guardian* Harbaugh printed some dialect verse, as well as other scattered German materials, but the editor knew that English was the language of the future and his verse in dialect was already of battles lost, nostalgic pieces looking backward to the old home and to the schoolhouse by the creek where he had learned a language now passing. Perhaps the failure of Schaff's *Kirchenfreund* was in his mind.

Meanwhile, a regional historian came on the scene, whose interests, while not so catholic as Schaff's, were nonetheless intense. By 1835 I. Daniel Rupp had published some translations of Menno Simons; in 1837 he brought out an English edition of the *Martyr's Mirror;* and in 1846 he began to publish his remarkable series of histories of the Pennsylvania Dutch counties, the first reliable regional works. Rupp can be called, with accuracy, the father of Pennsylvania regional history.

Actually, the future was not to be with the German tongue, now decidedly starting to wane. In 1850 Henry Harbaugh, sensing the failure of German literature as a mass vehicle for communication among the Pennsylvania Dutch, began to publish his celebrated journal, *The Guardian: Devoted to the Social, Literary, and Religious*

Tavern sign outside of the Washington House, Siegfrieds, Northampton, from a photograph taken in 1904.

Much of the prosperity of nineteenth-century Pennsylvania came from commerce, which crossed from the coal mines in the north to the port cities in the south. Here a canal boat passes beneath Staudt's Ferry bridge, then the longest single-span wooden bridge in America. The towpath passed over the bridge. *Photograph, 1901, by John Baer Stoudt*

However, in 1853 circulation of German-language materials had not stopped. Religious groups were still reading this language. In this year Johann Bär, Lancaster bookseller and printer, published a catalogue for his circulating library of German books, which he was housing at his print shop on *Nord Quienstrasse* in that city.

German newspapers were still prospering Almost every crossroads printing office brought out its sheet. Largely ignored by modern scholars, these journals still offered an astonishingly competent number of feature articles, generally in addition to news items. In these pieces they brought out a mass of historical, religious, and moral pieces. There were, for example, some fine pieces,

freshly researched, on Ephrata, on General Peter Mühlenberg, and other folk-oriented themes. Dialect poetry from Pennsylvania was rarer, but it was printed, along with German poetry from the midwest and Ontario. Little of it dates before 1850.

The Civil War was the dividing point. People who had studied German in the older church schools were passing. The newer generation had been raised in English-language state schools, and this was bringing forth a new world with a unified culture. Hybrid Americanization, north or south, was dead. From now on, except for a few pieces, little German was printed. In 1865 Lancaster County had but one German newspaper and

Mr. Seem established his cigar factory in this building in Bath, Northampton County, where earlier several physicians had founded a school of homeopathic medicine. This was just about two decades after Dr. Hahnemann had projected the theory that like cures like. *From an old photograph*

one German almanac, and in 1871 the only addition was *Der Waffenlose Waechter,* a minor pacifist sheet.

Relentless indeed was the march of Americanization.

A new age was dawning. A new kind of immigrant was coming, the 48ers, from whom the descendents of the Colonial Germans were separated by a wide gulf. Johann Georg Wesselhöft, who had started a weekly newspaper in 1834 with the title *Old and New World,* was planning to establish a colony in Missouri. This was in 1838, when he purchased twelve thousand acres in Gasconde County, Missouri. In 1846 similar efforts were made in Wisconsin, and Pittsburgh Germans went there to form a town.

However, the flood-tide of immigration brought in the main political refugees, and tensions between descendents of Colonial German settlers and these newer groups were evident. The 48ers were more liberal than older colonials. The latter were no longer German-language conscious and the gap that separated these groups was the index of how far Americanization had gone. Some 48ers did succeed in becoming part of the older established culture.

So the new American synthesis, won in the blood of the bloodiest of wars, triumphed over regionalism; the southerner, the Yankee, the Hoosier, and the Pennsylvania Dutchman could no longer resist the process that was taking the tired and hungry and persecuted inhabitants of the Old World and making them citizens of a new one.

The symbolic climax of the Americanization process was reflected in an event that is still unstudied, perhaps

A piece of so-called Shenandoah pottery, made near Waynesboro, Virginia, in the middle of the nineteenth century.

Traditional folk designs inlaid on this clockcase made in Reading shows the dependence on motifs from the older culture. *Courtesy Dr. David Hoffman*

This inlaid eagle on the door of a grandfather's clock, made in Reading just about the time the new nation was being created, expresses the patriotic spirit. *Courtesy Dr. David Hoffman*

even scorned, by formal historians. In 1868, three years after the Civil War, Jim Hill, then still a teen-age Pennsylvania boy, made a self-propelling machine. This was at least three years before similar ones appeared in Europe. In 1885 the borough council of Fleetwood warned Hill about driving his contraption about the town's streets. In 1887, two years later, Daimler is credited with having made the first automobile in Germany. For the next fifteen years Hill stored his "car," while inventors in the rest of the world built their self-propelled autos. In 1900, when Hill saw a Reo pass by on the road, he got his car out and rebuilt it. He studied the new gasolene engine, replaced his old steam engine with one with opposed cylinders and cam mechanism, spark plugs, and thermo-syphon cooling system. This new engine was installed in the old chassis, which still survives, and with his neighbor, Oliver Laudenslager, Hill made cars to sell.

The significance of these events was that the old Pennsylvania craft economy was able to produce the earliest American automobile.

Americanization was here.

In an affidavit before Magistrate Charles V. Glynn of
Fleetwood, Berks County, Jim Hill swore that he made
this car in 1868, just several years after the Civil War.
With Oliver J. Laudenslager, Hill drove this car around
the town, becoming such a nuisance that in 1885 the
Borough Council passed an ordinance forbidding them
to run their contraption on the streets. Hill's first engine was steam-powered, the second gasoline. The chief
defect of the Hill car was that its makers had not solved
the differential, and when they went around a corner the
driving chain tended to break. *Courtesy Mr. William
Shade*

6

Problems of Pennsylvania Folk Art

Although Pennsylvania Dutch folk art has become the most appreciated aspect of our culture, being much admired, avidly collected, and widely exhibited—most museums now show Pennsylvania Dutch stuff in their collections of American decoration—serious problems of interpretation persist. In spite of much writing there still is much that we do not know and many interpretive questions pass unanswered. However deep our longing to have a room full of these pieces, we soon understand that possession does not make us expert on their significance.

The main theoretical problem is the relation of Pennsylvania Dutch folk art to German folk art, and especially to the folk arts of the Rhineland, from which most came. We dare not say, with cavalier superficiality, that our art was a "memory art," meaning thereby that methods of work were inherited and thus passed from generation to generation. This just does not explain how things came to be—how, for example, things like the Pennsylvania long rifle were made. Moreover, how does German art relate to the Pennsylvania barn sign, which did not appear until 1885, long after the settlers had forgotten about Palatine decoration? No foundation grants are necessary to study so American a product. Also why is slip-ware and incised Pennsylvania pottery of 1780 like similar European pottery of the 1830s? We need not claim that Pennsylvania folk art was Swedish in derivation; no Swedish-language inscription appears on any

genuine piece. So, in any genetic theory basic problems persist and we cannot accurately say what kind of influences lingered.

Some might want to suggest that ways of working were continued and that folk art means inherited patterns, habitual acts. This view ignores the truth that in Colonial Pennsylvania the guilds, the custodians of tradition, did not survive. While much that was European continued, also much changed, especially under the pressures of the American frontier environment. Dower chests, decorated pottery, small furniture pieces, and the like remained in the European tradition, while new creations like the Pennsylvania long rifle appeared. Methods of milling wheat did not change but methods of hauling flour did. The truth is that some old forms were so changed that their products were new.

Others may suggest that folk art is art unaffected by cosmopolitan influences, the art of unsophisticated country people who oppose the culture of cities. They see it as crude, boorish, peasant art against the culturally sophisticated arts of the towns. This view takes sustenance from the tensions between city and country. Although there was fundamental tension between "the City" and its hinterland, this view can be overworked.

It is my contention that the difference between folk art and formal art is that the former used a commonly held fund of images and symbols, while the latter expresses the individualism of modern society. For what

Front view and shadow of a hook of wrought iron. *Courtesy Mr. Stephan Kindig*

seems to be inherited is an iconography that expresses itself in many ways, that is re-created, or reprojected whenever something is made.

Pennsylvania folk art did not emerge full blown, all at one time; it passed through patterns and uncovered new forms, moving, it seems, from traditional but still individually made pieces to more traditional patterns. It grew and developed.

The first two of its forms, stove-plates and glass, were soundly European in style and technique. The earliest manifestation was plates for five-sided stoves, which the Germans used in their houses. At first stove-plates were imported; several of these have survived from 1710 to 1730, clearly European. However, once furnaces began to make stoves, these plates began to appear, with American themes: Durham furnace was established in 1727, Warwick in 1738, Cornwall in 1743, Oley in 1745,

Elizabeth in 1750. After these dates American plates, less elaborate than European ones, began to appear, sometimes with such distinctly American themes as the arms of the city of Philadelphia.

In design the stove-plate moved from representational scenes to folk motifs. The earliest have Biblical scenes: the woman of Samaria, the miracle of the widow's oil, the tenth commandment, Cain and Abel, David and Goliath, the molten calf, Abraham and Isaac, Adam and Eve, the rider on the white horse. These were done representationally, and the figures were dressed in common eighteenth-century styles. Next came symbols like the motifs in ordinary folk art, nonrepresentational in style, which were symbolic in mood. Thus, after 1750, a broader basis of design came into being, wherein communally conceived "folk" designs were used: hearts, rosettes, flowers, colonnades, and, of course, the ubiqui-

Early decorated box in the Historical Society of Berks County.

tous tulip, also broad-brim-hatted farmers and Shenandoah valley hunting scenes. As Henry Chapman Mercer said, this was the Bible in iron, both as representationally presented themes and as folk design.

May I here suggest that folk art, rather than involving common ways of working, implies commonly conceived images? This is of course philosophical idealism, out of favor in our more realistic age.

Folk designs were religious. The motifs that replaced representational biblical scenes on the stove-plates were religious in the same sense that medieval art was religious. This mood was not that of Catholic Germany, where peasant forms (like oil painting, reverse portraiture on glass, carved wood, copper, etc.) presented various pictures of Christ, the Virgin Mary, and the saints for devotional use. Protestant folk art arose in Europe just after 1750 and continued until about 1820, dates that roughly parallel Pennsylvania folk art. This new European *Bauernkunst* was another kind of art than that exhibited by Pieter Bruegel, whose Dutch peasants went to market without accompaniment of symbolism. Protestant *Bauern-kunst* was basically iconoclastic, and what made Pennsylvania folk art medieval was its employment of a common fund of images. Calvinist Dutch painters of the seventeenth century were strictly representational; all images were destroyed save that of the strong personality.

The left-wing sects that flooded into Pennsylvania were not so iconoclastic as the Lutheran and Reformed. In these sects images lingered, refurbished by their use in the German "metaphysical" poets of the seventeenth century. These poets, avoiding the stark iconoclasm of the early years of the Reformation, revived ancient symbols. There is no essential difference between the symbolism of medieval Christian art and Pennsylvania folk art. Both rest on an allegorical interpretation of Scripture, a tradition that was well established; the poets revived it, and from poetry it escaped to folk art. Therefore, if we read the Pennsylvania hymnals, we will find these same images. Conrad Beissel and other Ephrata solitary were not only writing these poems; they were also using choral books in which these designs were expressed. Did they not name their hymnal *Die Turteltaube* (the Turtle-dove)? Why, then, should we call it a "distelfink"? If they called it a lily, what should we call it?

One thing is sure: they were not depicting what their

Collection of stove plates in the Mercer Museum, Doylestown. *Courtesy the Historical Society of Bucks County.*

eyes were seeing. They were picturing what their hearts were longing for.

Symbols may die, but they cannot change meaning. And some can even be created, like those of the griffin and unicorn. The significance of symbols was already apparent in the *Physiologus,* a fourth-century bestiary, wherein religious meaning was given to animals. Not only were living creatures like the pelican, the lion, the dove, and the lily matched with meaning, but some creatures were either taken over from old legend or else constructed. Thus the unicorn, which is not natural, was said to be a small animal like the kid, but very keen; it thrusts about with its single horn. The hunter can catch it only by trickery. When we take a virgin and put her in the forest where a unicorn is feeding, as soon as he sees her he loses his fierceness, runs to her, and if she is a true virgin, chaste and pure, he falls asleep in her lap. This originally classical legend was applied to Christ. In Pennsylvania folk art the unicorn appeared on birth certificates and dower chests. Sometimes symbols were created, like the griffin, an eagle with a lion's body. This is a rational construction, joining the Lord of Heaven with the lord of earth, the eagle with the lion, a proper symbol for the God-man.

Thus, when I suggest that Pennsylvania folk art is religious, and that it involves commonly conceived images that derive from Scripture and that found literary expression in seventeenth-century poetry, I am giving an

These three types of Stiegel glass were made in the later glass houses of Baron Stiegel. These pieces are genuine, because they came from an Oley family in 1900, before glass was imported from Bohemia and passed off as Stiegel.

opinion that suits the character of the people who made this art. This theory "fits." The same person who drew symbolic designs at Ephrata, Sister Anastasia, helped to compose the communally written sisters' hymn that used these symbols in literary fashion. There can be no question that these folk artists knew the meaning of these designs; they were writing poetry with the same imagery.

Recent confirmation of this view has come from an unexpected source: a study of Shaker illuminated writings bears this out. Shakers, who were related historically to the Inspirationists, and so to Ephrata, also made drawings in which the same images were used, albeit with somewhat different mood and style. While there is changed emphasis, there is also concurrence in the matter of imagery; the Shaker art is labeled. The artists tell us what the designs mean. And these labels are the same as old Christian art and as Pennsylvania folk art.

In its main forms, then—dower chest, *Vorschrift, Taufschein*—Pennsylvania folk art was religious in that it employed traditional Christian images that may in the end prove to be universal archetypes, both as designs and as symbols of psychic integration. Some symbols may antedate Christianity, existing in pagan form before they were adapted to Christian interpretation.

Stove plate depicting Samson and Delilah.

Stove plate depicting Elijah and the Ravens, made in the Oley Furnace. The initials "B. S." and "D. W." stand for Bendict Swope and Dieterich Welcker, the men who designed the plates.

In Pennsylvania Dutch folk art does not, then, differ markedly from medieval art in its use of symbols, I shall have to suggest that, except for the highly developed art of manuscript illumination, it differs little from the folk arts of other lands. A Roumanian sampler and a Pennsylvania one are much the same; pottery from Sweden can be, and has been taken for Pennsylvanian; modern ceramics cannot be told, except for age marks, from the old; Bohemian glass, which has been imported, makes us now say "Stiegel type." Only when a piece can be authenticated as coming from a Pennsylvania family before 1900 can we be sure that it is native. While Pennsylvania art differs in style, it is also much like the arts of other lands.

Still, in coming to America, something happened that gave new verve and zest to the old peasant arts. This new frontier made new demands. People who had been trained in the best European guild system were here forced to work as primitives again; they were forced to go back to older ways and to repeat the work history of the race.

This is clear in the field of architecture. People who in Europe had been building stone houses had here first to erect log houses. However, the regionalism that had marked European architecture did not last here, even though Professor Wertenbaker professes to see regional-

Unidentified interpretation of a biblical story on a Pennsylvania German stove plate made by the Oley Furnace.
Photograph by W. W. Dietrich

This faint *Vorschrift* is important because it illuminates a medieval religious poem, one of the oldest bits of German poetry: "Ich weiss mir ein Ewiges Himmelreich. . . ." Other verses on it date from the seventeenth century. We must therefore assume that the persons who made these pieces knew this poetry, either from hymnals or other collections.

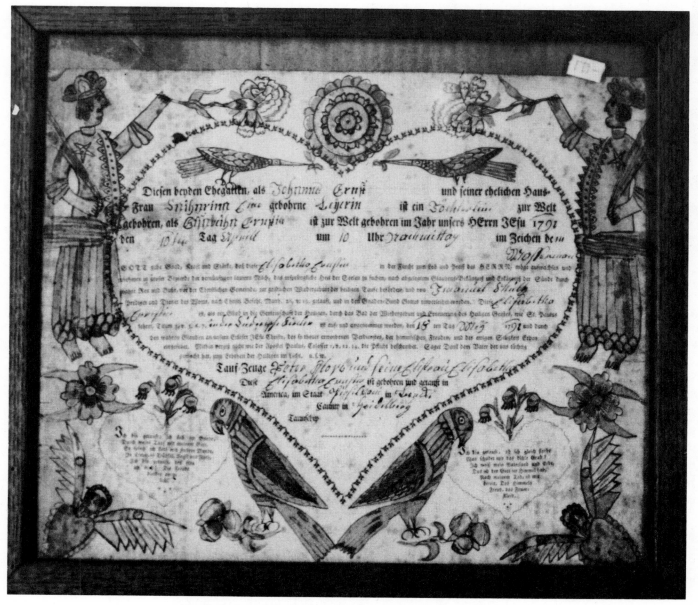

Vorschrift made in 1803 by Christian Strange, Lancaster county schoolmaster.

Symbolically interesting *Taufschein* with pelican on the left plucking its breast and the "beloved" on the right "feeding among the lilies."

Taufschein with Arab-style figures and other oriental designs.

ism in Pennsylvania methods of notching logs. There was rather, I believe, a hybridization of styles. Wood was the first material used, either as log house or *Fachwerk;* the fine stone houses still standing in Oley, Tulpehocken, and Maxatawney appeared later. Generally speaking, the

A true sampler, with examples of letters and designs for use of ambitious stitchers. *Photograph courtesy Mr. Edward W. Schlechter*

first 'stone houses came in the 1760s, like Fort Deshler and Fort Ralston in the Lehigh region, while the Georgian mansion, with a classic exterior like the Fisher House in Oley or an interior like the Hottenstein house in Maxatawney, resulted from expert supervision by English carpenters attached to the Carpenters' Company of Philadelphia.

A revolution was also taking place in furniture. Before the middle of the eighteenth century furniture was built in, like the closets in Maxatawney houses. Bedsteads, where they existed, went European fashion, from ceiling to floor, built in. Even in log cabins, tables and beds were attached. Moreover, Dutch houses were frugally furnished; the only movable pieces were blanket chests, wardrobes, and smaller pieces, and, of course, the blanket chests for the hopeful young girls. Much storage took place in baskets. The carpenter was what his name suggests, a *Zimmermann,* a room man, who made built-in cupboards. Traveling through Pennsylvania, Cazenove started to compare the furniture in France with that in Pennsylvania:

> In France everywhere I saw the farmers had 4 times as much furniture as the farmers in America generally have; above all there is no comparison between the keeping of the outside and inside of the farm.
> In France you see the farms having first, several large wardrobes, filled with clothes and linens, more or less, silver spoons, knives and forks, large silver drinking cups for each member of the family . . . much linen underwear, and table linen, good wines and brandy in the cellar, each farm has a well-kept garden with plenty of vegetables, cabbage, lettuce, turnips. (p. 42)

He did not finish the comparison but the meaning is plain, for even after the Revolution the meager life-conditions of the frontier had not much eased. While Philadelphia was an international city, capital of the new nation, with foreign ambassadors walking its streets and with fine halls and *soirées* in its elegant homes, the hinterland was just beginning to emerge from primitive frontier ways. There were, however, many smaller items of furniture, *Kleinmöbel,* like spice boxes, candleboxes, Bible boxes, spoon racks, and painted shelves.

One culturally interesting piece of furniture was the dower-chest (*Aussteyerkischt*), called *Truhe* in Germany. In this piece the young girl who was hoping to establish a family of her own someday put those things which she made in anticipation of that day. Most chests were given to daughters by parents or grandparents. The unicorn was an appropriate symbol for this piece.

Clearly the most distinctive aspect of Pennsylvania Dutch folk art, the most extensive in time and certainly the most closely related to other cultural forms, is the art of *Fraktur,* about which very little accurate information is known. This art of illuminating manuscripts still remains somewhat mysterious, as much so as when Henry Chapman Mercer discovered it. The name tells what it is, a broken style of lettering wherein the several strokes of the letters are fractured. This style of lettering was popular in seventeenth-century Germany, where it was used for religious works and prayerbooks. In Pennsylvania it passed through stages of development, going far beyond its more limited range in Germany. Why this happened is not quite clear.

The expansion of the art of *Fraktur* that took place in Pennsylvania has not yet received adequate historical explanation. We do not know why, except for the obvious point, the presence of the frontier. There were illuminators like Christopher Dock, Abraham Cassel, and others, began to make simpler pieces. The growth that ensued is apparent when we study these writings in chronological order, so far as this can be established. The earliest were simpler and less ornate, truer to the symbolic sense; later pieces were more elaborate. At the same time that these early schoolmasters were making their copy-pieces for use of their scholars, itinerant writers were beginning to make certificates of birth and baptism.

Decorated doll's benches, late nineteenth century. *Courtesy Mr. and Mrs. Walter Moser*

neither textbooks in sufficient quantity nor legal forms, so schoolmasters improvised pattern pieces and itinerant writers made *Taufscheine*. The close relationship between text and what was being illuminated proves that *Fraktur* was dependent upon the hymnals.

Fraktur first appeared at Ephrata, where magnificent choral books were made, a fine *Vorschriftsbuch* in one color, probably the work of Sister Anastasia, Anna Thomme, of a Swiss family. Ephrata work was highly developed, symbolically and imaginatively realized. It expressed in image the same moods as their music and poetry.

Just before the American Revolution, several scattered These earlier pieces were subdued in color.

After the Revolution *Fraktur* exploded. Due to peculiar sociological conditions that are not yet fully understood, a vast development of this art form took place. Still related to school and church, it obviously was religious art. Schoolmasters made patterns for scholars to use, showing them the forms of all the letters; we have several pieces with notations like the one illustrated, which says that it is for the best scholar in the second class. However, we cannot generalize about this for Susanna Hübner, the queen of Schwenkfelder illuminators, was not a school mistress and she did not make her pieces for pedagogical purposes. The *Taufschein* was a

Unretouched dower chest in the Boone Homestead. *Courtesy the Pennsylvania Historical and Museum Commission. Photograph by Rath*

From this dower chest it can be seen that many chest painters also illuminated their writings.

certificate of birth and baptism in a land where there was no bureau of vital statistics and no established churches. This certificate was usually made either by the local minister or by an itinerating writer like Heinrich Otto. But not always. Some were done by families. Contrary to the *Vorschrift*, which was free and fluid, the *Taufschein* was fixed, with given text and given hymns.

Likewise, Pennsylvania Dutch pottery presents grave problems of interpretation. It moved through stages. Most pottery was plain, simply in decoration. But gift pieces were highly decorated. Knowledge of the existence of Pennsylvania Dutch pottery came in 1891 when Edwin Atlee Barber found a piece with an inscription in Pennsylvania Dutch dialect. Language was the clue to identifi-

Esther Stevens Frazer discovered the Jonestown school of chest painters, led by Christian Seltzer. Only the rare chest was decorated. The young girl put her trousseau in it.

It needed only to be filled in. It could therefore be easily printed.

The art of manuscript illumination was basically Pennsylvania Dutch, although the art was known among both Quakers and Shakers, not to mention other Colonial groups. It took many forms; copy-pieces, certificates of birth, certificates of birth and baptism, marriage certificates, memorial pieces, bookplates, labyrinths, metamorphoses, and even representational drawings. Abstract symbolic drawings also were made. Taken together, the art of manuscript illumination is the most distinctive aspect of Pennsylvania folk art.

cation. In 1893 he published a *Catalogue of American Potteries and Porcelain* (Philadelphia) wherein he said:

> such ware was extensively made for a century and a half, but the old potteries where it was produced have long since entirely disappeared.

Barber claimed that this style of pottery was not confined to German settlements, citing as his proof an early plate, dated 1767, with an inscription in the English language and with fine slip decoration. Later work has identified the plate as made by Abraham Staudt, born in Wolfersweiler, Palatinate, a Perkasie potter who had studied

Late use of the broken style of lettering to spell out "Susan." This was long after the migration from Germany had taken place.

at the William Penn Charter School. What is significant in the Barber catalogue is his statement that he had found these pieces in the families of the potters who made them.

Pottery, unlike *Fraktur,* appeared fully developed. While there was a primitive period when the traditional pieces like roof tiles were made, its forms varied. Here are the forms as they appear in the early catalogues: flat bottomed vegetable dishes, pie plates, jars, crocks, deep dishes, flower vases, small and large plates, coffee pots, teapots, sand boxes for drying ink, umbrella handles (after 1870), large kegs, tubs, pottery toys especially whistles, sugar bowls, shaving basins, ink bottles, roof tiles, stove tiles, and floor tiles. These were the commonest forms. One interesting one was the making of clay tobacco pipes in the shape of Indian heads, like those by John Gibble of Manheim, by the Sturgis pottery in Lititz, and by Henry Gast in Lancaster. Glazed racks to store tobacco pipes were also made.

Three aspects of the craft of pottery have aesthetic interest: slip, scratching, and molding. The slip method was the tracing of sometimes crude, sometimes more elaborate, designs on red clay in variously colored clays, which were poured by quill and later covered by a transparent glaze. Scratching or engraving was at first done by covering the red biscuit or unglazed ware with a layer of white slip and then scratching designs in it, allow the darker red to show through. Molded pottery shaped the pieces in representational forms.

Later in the nineteenth century, as settlements expanded to the western valleys, new centers of pottery arose, one brand of which became known as "Shenandoah," appearing around Winchester, Virginia, chiefly the product of the Bell family of potters. This work is noted for its fine glaze.

Actually, we do not have much accurate knowledge about the potter's craft. Only about two-dozen early nineteenth-century potters are known by name and work; we have only guesses about eighteenth-century work. It is a sad commentary that Dr. Barber's *Tulipware,* published in 1903, remains the currently standard work in the field. Nor do we have solid information about other aspects of pottery and porcelain and the relationship of these crafts to Pennsylvania Dutch culture; I refer to Tucker ware and Hemphill ware. Moreover, in spite of declaimers to the contrary, it seems that some soft-paste porcelain was made in New Jersey and New York around 1830, that the pottery of Bonnin and Morris in Southwark (Philadelphia) produced cream work, and that in 1833 the Philadelphia China Manufactory was depicting Pennsylvania scenes in porcelain. Phoenixville majolica became popular and stoneware was also made in Philadelphia. The whole field is undercultivated.

Textiles likewise produce many problems. Before the invention of the cotton gin and several looms, the *Spinnstube* was the heart of the home. Here thread was spun, linen woven, ribbons made. Work here never stopped, for families were large and needed many clothes.

We can not say that there was a distinctive style to Pennsylvania Dutch textiles, only that they made textiles in goodly quantity and quality.

Samplers were made during the eighteenth century. The wheat-dominated agricultural economy used many flour bags, which needed to have the initials of their owners stitched in them; samplers showed how to make these letters. However, it is extremely rare to find a sampler with words in a language other than English; they are block-style, not *fractura*. German seems never to have been used, as far as we know, even by Catherine Hoch and Mary Yoder and Mary Bernhard. German farm girls were sent to "select schools" in the summertime, where they were taught by Quakeresses and other English-speaking ladies how to live graciously.

Pennsylvania Dutch weaving was no different from that of other peoples in America and Europe. At first looms were simple two-harness affairs; when the Jacquard loom came, having been invented in France, the weaving

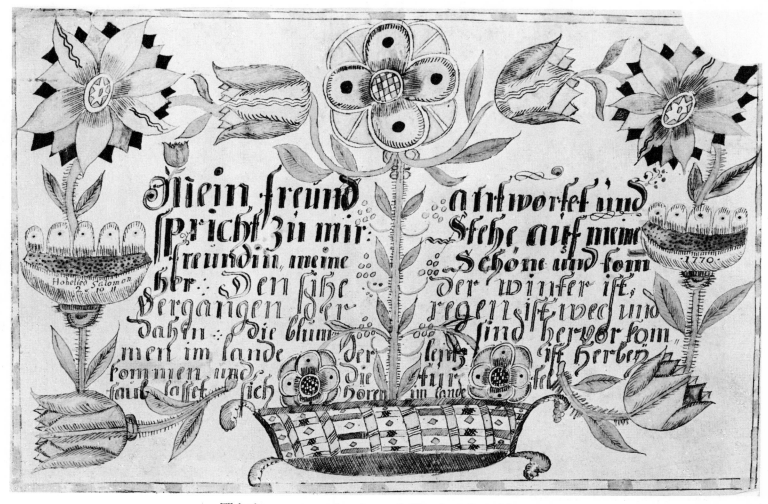

This important early piece of illuminated writing was done by the Reverend Daniel Schuhmacher in 1770. It presents an important biblical passage from Song of Songs, 2: 10-11, which speaks of the new age that is to come.

Lower-case letters, Ephrata ABC Book. *Courtesy the Pennsylvania Historical and Museum Commission*

Multicolored *Vorschrift* written by William Yerges for his sister "Margred Yerges," 17 April, 1806.

"Jacob Landis, December 13, 1830, a present for good behavior in school, on December 15th." Here, perhaps, is a clue to the social significance of the *Vorschrift*.

Hand-done certificate of birth and baptism of Jacob Fischer, who was baptized by Pastor Helferich in Upper Milford Township, Northampton (now Lehigh) County, on August 19, 1795.

Drawn-work "show towel." *Photograph by Mr. Edward W. Schlechter*

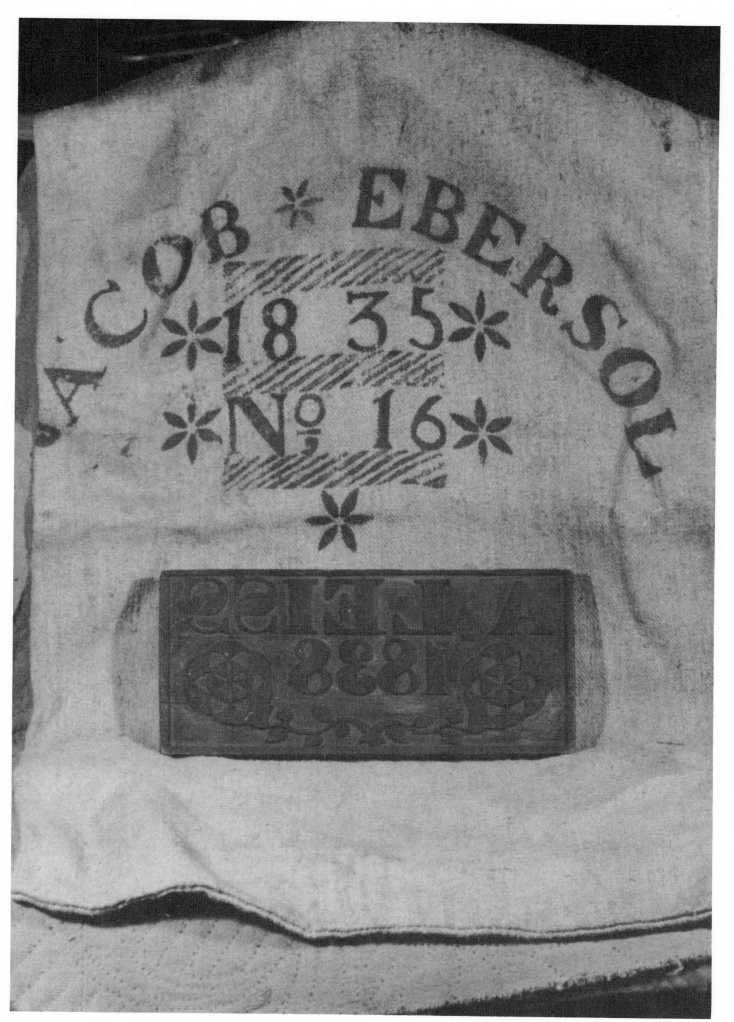

Here is a grain bag in which farmers carried their flour.
They were decorated with stencils. The stencil illustrated,
dated 1838, has flowers with the six-lobed star design.
Courtesy Mr. Joseph Kindig and Mr. Stephan Kindig

Cross-stitched "show towel." *Photograph courtesy Mr. Edward W. Schlechter*

more productive than bridge clubs. One quilt was set up in a room and it could take care of twelve garrulous quilters at one time who, as the sides were rolled, were reduced in number. The ladies made a day of it, doing one quilt, with, of course, much conversation and good food. Quilting bees later were moved to the churches.

The triumph of Pennsylvania craftsmanship was the long rifle, sometimes known as the Kentucky, because that is where it was used. The long rifle is a work of great art, a solid adaptation of known European features to the American frontier. We now know a good deal about the makers and the processes of manufacture, but the historical problems that remain, both about the craft itself and the use of the rifle on the frontier, are not settled. Chief of these is the development of the rifle. We do know that there was a period of incubation from the time of the development of the patch to the American Revolution. The golden age of the rifle was between 1780 and 1830, the period of handcrafted pieces, before the manufacture of Winchesters or Springfields. All phases of gunmaking were done by the same crafts-

of coverlets began. But we can hardly distinguish coverlets of linen and wool made by Hausmann in Lobachsville, Oley, from those made by Yankee weavers in the Connecticut valley. What Hausman did do was use his imagination and weave, on his four-harness loom, a tablecloth of bleached and unbleached linen, peasant damask. However, these forms were not new. Moreover, weavers itinerated and packed their looms on wagons, moving from farm to farm.

The patchwork quilt is soundly American, associated with the social phenomenon of the quilting bee. By 1840 printed cottons were plentiful and the colors were firm. But the quilt is somewhat older, having appeared about a century before, when all textiles had to be imported and when every scrap was valuable. This had produced the crazy-patch quilt with no basic design, joining all pieces.

Quilting bees, it must be confessed, may have been

Victorian-style sampler made by Mary H. Yoder of Oley in Sarah L. Boone's "select school" kept in that valley by the niece of Daniel Boone. Here young Dutch girls learned the social arts during the hot summers. *Courtesy Mrs. Wilmer Greulich*

Turned and painted "Lehn ware," carved decoys, and carved stencils in the Pennylvania Farm Museum, Landis Valley.

Stencil to mark quilts before quilting the designs.

Painted tin made in Pennsylvania is difficult to distinguish from that made elsewhere. This collection is probably native here. *Courtesy Mr. and Mrs. Walter Moser*

men and their skills were legendary: they were excellent carvers, engravers, blacksmiths, and woodworkers. The Pennsylvania rifle remains the finest achievement of our crafts.

Other crafts present similar problems. Tombstones are nearly unknown, so far as their manufacture goes. The best study we have is an exquisitely done appreciation by Eleanor Barba. Actually we know little about the stone-cutter's guild, for this seems to be the only craft where guild activity was extant. At first traditional folk designs were used; later more imaginative themes were adapted, nonrepresentational and representational.

With the so-called toleware, or painted tin, we also have a difficult field. Pennsylvania pieces are hard to distinguish from New England pieces. Also, considerable commercialized stenciling was employed, as on the plank chairs of the middle of the nineteenth century. Here perhaps we have moved out of the area of folk art as such, because these pieces were no longer hand crafted in the sense that they were now commercial products. These

Sunburst and flowers on the tombstone of Ellen, daughter of Johannes Mensch. Huffs Church burial ground.

Tombstones in the Pennsylvania mood from various cemeteries. *Photographs by Guy Reinert*

Sampler.

Coverlet made for Cornelia Griesemer by Hausmann of
Lobachsville, Pennsylvania, 1835

Coverlets

Coverlet on bed in Hope Lodge, Whitemarsh. *Courtesy
the Pennsylvania Historical and Museum Commission*

Lewis Miller's drawing of the old Brew House in the year 1801 shows the popularity of this beverage. Note the use of German and English languages. *Courtesy the Historical Society of York County*

Doll's bench. *Courtesy Mrs. Walter C. Moser*

Painted chest in European mood. *Courtesy Mr. Oliver Lewis Christmas*

The melting of traditions

Tombstone of Maria Elisabeth Neumann with interesting
floral decorations done around 1827. *Photograph courtesy
Mr. Edward W. Schlechter*

chairs and painted pieces are indistinguishable from other American forms, and we have moved from folk arts that were distinctively Germanic in mood to ones that are the common property of all Americans. Toleware and painted chairs were as American as baseball.

An interesting Old World custom did survive, and that was the making of a *putz* at Christmas. Wooden, clay, or tin figures were so arranged that they depicted the nativity of Our Lord. Several narrative groupings were followed, the Holy Family, the Nativity, the Annunciation, the shepherds in the hills, the three kings with camels, and the flight to Egypt. Related to the old medieval mystery plays, this tradition was retained by eighteenth-century German peasants and by the Pennsylvania Dutch. Associated with this was the old tradition of "illumination," celebrating the birthday of a prince with candles in the windows.

Putz with angels announcing the good tidings to the shepherds.

The last phase of Pennsylvania folk art—and still the most controversial—was painting the six-lobed star (*Sechsstern*) on barns. While European folk art is known to have used this design, it is only when barns began to be painted at all that these designs could appear.

The best information we have points to the year 1885, when O. K. Huber and Frank Rohrbach of Niantic began to paint designs on the barns of the upper Perkiomen Valley, from which this custom seems to have spread. (There are a few design-painted barns in the Lancaster region.) The first design these gentlemen used was a circle enclosing a six-lobed star, which was made by using the radius to form interesting arcs, an easy geometric figure. Widespread in European folk art, both carved and painted, this design has been traced by a European architect to the South Tyrol, where it was associated with the Christian monogram, I H S. In Europe this sign was always good luck and in Germany it appeared on door lintels and other external decorative features on the entrance to house and home. Since there were few separated barn structures in Europe, they could not appear on these. A manuscript from Erlangen, Germany, dated 1465, calls this a *Glücksymbol* (good-luck sign), and a later manuscript speaks of a *Glückstern auf das Jahr 1698,* a lucky star for the year 1698.

In Pennsylvania itinerating barn painters elaborated the *Sechsstern* and designs became ornate.

Now this design is popularly, and wrongly, called the *Hex* sign. This suggests that the design is put on barns to scare witches away. *Hex* means witch.

Now there is just no proof that stands the test of the laws of historical evidence to establish that the Pennsylvania Dutch barn sign was put there to scare witches away. This *Hex* theory seems to have been started by a New Englander and it has been adopted by many who should have known better. It is simply the wrong area of symbolic reference, a theory spun out of gossamer and advanced by those who profit from such things.

Lately evidence has come forward that helps to dispel some doubt. The key seems to be small charms, sometimes found in Pennsylvania barns, written on paper and folded, usually triangularly, and then nailed to barn rafters. The German text, although faulty, of one of them reads as follows:

Trollekopf, ich verbiete die mein haus und mein Hof, ich verbiete die mein Pferde- und Kiehstalle, ich verbiete dir meine Bettstelle, bis du alle Berge steigest . . . und über

Hier ruhen
die Gebeine von

Johañ Jacob Klein.

Er war gebohren den 25 December 1789.
und ist gestorben den 17 Märj 1826.
Er hat sein Alter in dieser Welt gebracht
auf 36 Jahre 2 Monate und 22 Tage.

If the *Sechstern* or six-lobed design found on the Pennsylvania barn is really a sign to ward off the witches, why put it on a tombstone? In Europe this design is often associated with plows, chairs, door lintels, and many other objects that are not talismanic in mood. No reputable European folklorist asserts that this design is talismanic. *Photograph by Reinert*

alle Wasser steigest. Dan kann der liebe Friede in mein Haus. In Namen Gottes, Des Sohns, und Gott der Heiligen Geistes. Amen.

Translation:

Troll-head! I forbid you my house and yard; I forbid you my horse stall and cow-barn; I forbid you my bedstead until you have climbed all mountains, and gone across all oceans. Then noble peace shall come to my house. In the name of God, the Son, and God the Holy Ghost. Amen.

An English-language charm has been found, dating from around 1890, which is here reproduced:

Now these charms are addressed to the trolls. Nowhere

had many names: Nusspuk, Kobald, Klaubautermann, Troll. Almost every region had its name.

Here in Pennsylvania we call him *'s Bucklich Maennli,* the little hunchback elf who has had many fine ballads composed in his honor. He was a trickster who caused the butter not to churn, who ripped up the newly planted onions, who scolded during milking, who made soup boil over, and who did a thousand-and-one household tricks. In England and New England he was also known: Longfellow has Pan-Puk-keewis teach the Indians how to gamble.

Perhaps those of us who have forgotten Germanic folklore may remember this fellow by his English name, Puck or Robin Goodfellow. Shakespeare's genius has

Trotter Head. I forbid thee my house and Premises. I forbid thee my horse and cow Stable. I forbid thee my Bed Stead, that thou mayest not Breathe upon me. Breathe Into Some other house. until thou hast Ascended Every hill. until thou hast Counted Every fence Post. and until thou hast Crossed Every Water. and thus Dear Day may Come Again Into my house. In the Name of God the Father, the Son: and the Blessed Holy Ghost Amen.

is the word *hex* used. And with trolls we are in a different world from that of witches.

There was an old Germanic belief that houses, barns, and stalls were inhabited by *Hausgeister,* house spirits, on whom the blame could be put when things went wrong. The old German troll, known in Scotland as *trow* and in Ireland as leprechaun, was the quick-change artist who was also known as Puca, Pook, Brownie, and so on. Half-animal in form, this dwarfish inhabitant of caves and hills sometimes dared to enter castles, guarded treasure, hunted in forests, punished grave-robbers, saved the poor farmer's cattle, and tidied up around the kitchen at night, sometimes even doing chores in the yard. He

immortalized him in *A Midsummer Night's Dream,* where he serves Oberon, king of fairies. And Shakespeare's Puck performs the same tricks as *'s Bucklich Maennli* in Pennsylvania. And "sweet Puck" must have his bowl of curds and cream, even if the kittens do lap it up, else the pottage will burn, the cheese curdle, and the ale lose its head. And on Pennsylvania farms, many a bowl of milk has been set out for *'s Bucklich Maennli.*

Puck was no witch. He is as far removed from witchcraft as the mood of *A Midsummer Night's Dream* is from the witches' scenes in *Macbeth.* Snow White fears the old witch but loves her dear dwarfs! Here we have two realms of folklore, one of black witchcraft, the other

The triumph of the Pennsylvania Dutch cabinetmaker's art: the Hottenstein *schrank*. Note the grasshopper carved in the center panel. *Courtesy the Henry Francis duPont Winterthur Museum*

the world of good fairies and the sweet little mischief-maker, Robin Goodfellow.

Here, I suggest, lies the meaning of the barn signs. These designs have no captions, of course, and thus we cannot say for sure that this is what they mean, but surely this view is not illogical and it is grounded in a common Indo-Germanic bit of folklore that is almost universally known.

Our Pennsylvania *'s Bucklich Maennli* may be somewhat cruder than Shakespeare's finely drawn character who, in spite of mirth, mischief, and melody, is still a worthy compeer of Peaseblossom, Cobweb, and Mustard Seed, who are also servants of the fairy king, Oberon.

This Puck theme, now forgotten, illustrates the fate of all aspects of Pennsylvania folk art. It emerged from a thought-world now forgotten. Both symbolic designs and barn signs were expressions of a world now lost to the contemporary scene. Hence folk art involves a folk mind; indeed, folk art comes from a commonly held fund of images and beliefs which are then graphically expressed.

This is how Pennsylvania folk art came to be. It arose when the Pennsylvania Dutch people still shared a common mental world. When that world passed, folk art became memory.

Whether that world was primitive or not, whether it was peasant, we should not venture. It certainly was not our modern bourgeois world of mass culture. But while it lived here, it did give meaning to America's finest folk art.

7

Folk Culture

As the Americanization process proceeded and Pennsylvania Dutch culture shriveled into its Germanic shell, as cultural contact with Germany was lost, and as knowledge of the German language and the ability to read and write it waned, a folk culture developed in the Pennsylvania heartland that in some measure still survives—an island in Anglo-Saxon America. This is the world of the child, proverb, superstition, folk medicine, and the like.

Those fortunate enough to have been born in this heartland, and who still know the dialect, can share this world. For it survives. It combines a rural milieu with a fundamentally Germanic view which comes from Alsace and the Rhineland, which breathes out the same romantic mood as *Des Knaben Wunderhorn.* Some of these pieces are among the oldest bits of German poetry and were in the main passed on by word of mouth from generation to generation, sometimes forgotten, sometimes altered.

First there was children's lore, beginning with counting-out rhymes. (Here I translate dialect materials freely, giving meter and rhyme precedence over sense.)

> One, two, three!
> You are free!

> One, two, three,
> Hickey, hockey, hee!

> Bacon and salt!
> Rooster says "Halt!"

> One head,
> Two head,
> Three head;
> Pig Head!

> I and Thou,
> Miller's cow—
> That art Thou!

> Butter like lard,
> Sugar like salt,
> Pepper goes up,
> He who catches
> Throws *out!*

> *Eins, zwey, drey,*
> Mommy caught a fly!
> The fly died,
> Mommy cried:
> *Eins, zwey, drey!*

> Hex foot, hex foot;
> Toad foot, toad foot!
> Long snout, long snout!
> Nothing out, nothing out!

> Dibble, dobble, thimble head!
> Set the farmer on his head;
> Who must out, I or Thou—

Or miller's old brown cow . . .
And that art Thou.

Play was largely imitation, repetition of acts that adults
or older children performed. After watching the militia
drill on Battalion Day in the towns, the children played
soldier:

> Left, right! Left, right!
> Keep your britches buttoned tight;
> Left, right, left right!
> Shine the buttons every night!

> One, two, three, four!
> March up to the kitchen door!
> Five, six, seven, eight!
> Back up to the garden gate!

> Attention men! Present your arms!
>   Today we march away!
> The war has come to Womelsdorf,
>   And home we cannot stay.

> So sharpen sabers, clean the guns!
>   Militia by the score!
> The en'my comes, soon he may be
>   By mamma's kitchen door.

The children also played church: Thus did they announce the hymn:

> The light is poor, my eyes are weak,
> To find this hymn will take all week.

Again:

> Hold up, hold up, good people dear!
> We shall not sing this hymn this year!

Then they sang a mock hymn:

> Ta, rah, de boom, de eh!
> Ta, rah, de boom, de eh!
> Tomorrow fishing we shall go,
> Next day again we go,
> And catch an entire bucket full.

Then one of the children would announce the Scripture:
"The Gospel according to Sauerkraut, the text is bean
soup," and he would start to preach a mock sermon:

> Here stand I on pulpit,
> Preaching like a blackbird,
> A rooster and hen,
> The sermon begins;
> A cow and calf,
> The sermon is half;

> A cat and mouse,
> The church leaves out,
> And we go home,
> And eat ham bone.

When a child hurt himself one would say, imitating the
powwow doctor:

> Owly, owly, keeley, kay!
> Tomorrow morn it's all away.

To ward off swarming bees and wasps one must say:

> Hummler, brummler,
> Do not sting
> Until devils
> Benediction bring.

Children laugh at the grownups when they pair off. However, the mysteries of adult life do not go by unnoticed:

> 'Tween Easter and Whitsun
> The weather is fair,
> The birds they are singing,
> And young people pair.

But choices are not always appreciated:

> My sweetheart is lovely,
> But rich she is not!
> What care I for money
> Sleeps not in my cot.

> The world is so big,
> The heavens are blue;
> What one doesn't want
> The other makes do.

And when the wedding is planned, one says:

> Hansel and Gretel,
> Two lusty wights!
> Hansel is crazy,
> Gretel not right.

And then when the kitten died, or the pet duckling, a
small hole was dug in the meadow and a funeral proces-
sion held, ending with these words:

> In the name of the Father,
> And of the Son,
> And in the hole she goes.

> Ashes to ashes,
> Dust to dust,
> If Reverend wont have him
> Satan must.

This spirit of mockery was widespread among children. Thus

> Hamburg girls wear bright red coats,
> Bloom like roses, stink like goats.

> Kutztown is a rotten town,
> Bone-dry bread that's coarse and brown,
> Hickory shells and blackberry juice—
> Kutztown lets the devils loose.

Scorn moves out to the ballad form:

> "Now Bill, I want to ask you something:
> Who are those girls down at the spring?"
>   Dibble, ribble; dibble, ribble; dibble, ribble de dee!

> "One is as dumb as uncle's mule,
> But goes with bright boys at the school."
>   Dibble, ribble; dibble, ribble; dibble, ribble de dee.

> "The other's nose is fencerail long
> And twangles when she sings a song!"
>   Dibble, ribble; dibble, ribble; dibble, ribble de dee.

> "The other dresses up for holidays,
> Still keeps her country look and ways."
>   Dibble, ribble; dibble, ribble; dibble, ribble de dee.

> Eenie, meenie, ink-well knot,
> Go to school to learn what's what!
> When home you come and nothing know
> We'll whack your backside down below!

When a child has eaten too much one says:

> One hundred thousand apple cakes
> Make an entire wagon full;
> But if we eat too many now
> We'll get as fat as daddy's sow.

> No mason ever will get rich
> For he drinks what he does earn.

> Rosie Ritter is my name,
> A maiden brave am I;
> Red stockings do I wear,
> And sew and knit can I;
> I make the wheels to go, to go,
> There's more that I do dare.

When children run in and out of the house, mother says:

> Men and dogs stay out;
> Women and cats stay in;
> Men work; dogs bark;
> Women broom; cats meow.

Impious persons were ridiculed:

> He who prayerless starts to eat
> And prayerless finishes his meat
> Is like my ox and stupid mule
> And does not live by God's good rule.

Or again:

> The time shall very soon be here
> When pious persons shed a tear,
> When bears and wolves the world do rule
> And to dark death send every fool.

The mood may be somewhat lighter:

> Jim along Josey,
> Bullfrog's in the spring,
> The water is much too cold
> For him to take a swim.

Or sometimes it is total rejection:

> Sauerkraut I do not like,
> Turnips are too sweet;
> Farmers' girls they please me not,
> I see their great big feet.

> Yankee doodle oatmeal sack,
> Give a chew of raw tabac;
> Yankee doodle dandy,
> Give a bottle of brandy.

Grandfather's lap was where folklore was passed on. Here "patty cake" was taught:

> Botschy, botschy, doughy ball,
> Bakers give this funny call:
> If you would tasty cookies bake
> These seven things you have to take:
> Sugar, butter, salt, and lard,
> Eggs, flour, saffron—beaten hard!

Riding the knee-horse:

> Ridey, ridey horsey,
> Every hour a miley;
> Every mile a place to drink,
> *Lift* the glasses! Let them clink!
>   (With "lift" the child is raised.)

> Dross, dross, drilly,
> Farmer lost his filly;
> The filly runs away,
> Farmer *falls* on clay.
>   (With "falls" the child is dropped some.)

Or riding hobby horse:

> Hoppi, hoppi, hoppi,
> Pony goes galoppi;
> Over stock, over stone,
> Never crack the left shin bone;
> Always at galoppi,
> Hoppi, hoppi, hoppi.

Counting the fingers:

> Little finger,
> Stupid finger,
> Long finger,
> Louse cracker,
> Oats smacker.

Now, beginning with the thumb:

> This is the thumb,
> This shakes plums,
> This picks them up,
> This drags them home;
> And this little fellow eats them all.

Counting the days of the week:

> Monday is Sunday's brother,
> Tuesday is quite yet another;
> Wednesday go to church to pray,
> Thursday is half holiday;
> Friday 'tis too late to spin,
> Saturday half-holiday again.

When the child pounds on the floor with a mallet, mother says:

> Locksmith, locksmith hammer on,
> Iron must be pounded down;
> Hammer, hammer, free from wrong,
> Makes you fat and big and strong.

Watching the ducks on the pond, the child might say:

> All my ducklings
> Swim by pair;
> Heads in the water,
> Tails in the air.

When the child is ready for bed, a prayer is said, the old traditional prayer of the fourteen angels:

> Evenings when I go to sleep
> Fourteen angels vigil keep;
> Two to rest my weary head,
> Two to keep my feet abed;
> Two to left, two to right;
> Two to keep me covered tight;
> Two to wake me, two to lead
> My soul to God with each good deed.

And when the child is tucked in mother said:

> Good evening, good night,
> By roses held tight,
> By peg and pin
> And covers held in;
> At morning, God willing,
> You'll be up again.

And finally the day is closed with an old familiar lullaby:

> Sleep, baby, sleep,
> Daddy tends the sheep,
> Mother tends the little lambs
> And brings a nice full titty home,
> Sleep, baby, sleep.

As children grow older, their rational powers increase. One of the areas of folk culture was the riddle, some of which are among the oldest bits of folk literature. Here are a few:

> Whoever makes it, tells it not;
> Whoever takes it, knows it not;
> Whoever knows it, wants it not.   Counterfeit money.

> In our country was a man:
> Riddle was his name.
> Of saddlerback was he made;
> Three times have I said his name.   "Was."

> White as snow,
> Green as grass,
> Red as blood,
> Black as a hat.   A red cherry.

> In Weisenberg is a pond
> Where grows a yellow flower;
> He who would have the yellow flower
> Must break all Weisenberg.   An egg.

> Iron horses, flaxen tail,
> The faster that the horse does run,
> The shorter does his tail become.   Needle and thread.

> High as a house,
> Low as a mouse;
> Rough as a rail,
> Smooth as a pail;
> Bitter as gall—
> Sweet to us all.   Chestnut.

> A mill with seven corners,
> In each are seven bags;
> On each bag sit seven cats,

Each cat has seven kittens;
Miller and wife come in:
How many feet now therein?   Four. Cats have paws.

A maiden went over the Rhine
To fetch her mistress some wine;
Neither glass nor keg had she.
Wherein did she carry it?   In the grapes.

A farmer sees it every day,
A king seldom, God never.   His equal.

Why do farmers build pig sties between house and barn?   For pigs.

What changes name on shortest notice?   A woman in marriage.

What kind of stones are found in water?   Wet ones.

What grows on its tail?   A turnip.

When is a fox a fox?   When he is alone.

Why does the rooster close his eyes when he crows?   He knows it by heart.

Where did Adam strike the first nail?   On its head.

Which candles burn longer, those of tallow or those of wax?   They burn shorter, not longer.

What is finished yet made every day?   A bed.

Where did you sit when you went to school?   When I went I walked.

On what side do dogs have most hair?   The outside.

Have you ever been taken out to hunt *Elwetritches?* Have you ever been put out, on a cold winter night, in the dark of the moon, to catch this elusive relative of the American snipe? Waiting where paths cross in deep woods, alone with wailing wind, the "drivers" having left

to flush the quarry, you wait, and wait, and wait, and wait.

Beliefs could change frames of reference easily. Deep in the consciousness of Pennsylvania Dutch people were remnants of old Germanic views concerning the ghostly rider. This story has been often repeated and it has been etched into these people's consciousness by Washington Irving's story of the headless horseman, known in Ger-

One modern potter's conception of the *Elwetritsch.*

man as *Der Schimmelreiter.* This biblical idea was that of *der wilde Jäger,* a religious and apocalyptic symbol related to Wodan, ghostly leader of a ghostly army. In classical mythology this was Mercury, one of the oldest of human archetypes. References to the headless rider can still be heard among rural Pennsylvania Dutch people. He is not always headless.

Another image, somewhat confused with these figures, is the biblical image of Elias with his fiery wagon, the moon-man who struggles against the forces of good. This is likewise an apocalyptic figure.

Yet another surviving belief takes the form of small iron figures placed in barns to drive diseases from animals. These cast-iron figures were used in southern Germany and they were seen in barns near Kutztown around the turn of the twentieth century. In Bavaria and other Old-World regions, they were placed in stalls because St. Leonard was the patron of veterinary medicine and cared

"And I saw heaven opened, and behold a white horse;
and he that sat upon him was called Faithful and True,
and in righteousness does he judge and make war. . . .
And out of his mouth goeth a sharp sword, that with it
he shall smite the nations; and he shall rule them with a
rod of iron." Revelation 19: 11-16. This is an apocalyptic
image on a plate made by David Spinner. *Courtesy the
Metropolitan Museum of Art. Gift of Mrs. Robert W.
deForrest*

Cast-iron figures like these stood in barns in the Kutz-town area at the beginning of the twentieth century. Diseases were to enter these animals instead of flesh-and-blood ones. *Courtesy Philip F. Cowan*

for animals; these were known as St. Leonard's figures. In human affairs they often became phallic symbols, but as such they have not been found in Pennsylvania. Here they were used to ward off animal diseases, like nailing horseshoes to barns.

Fertility symbols also are known. Lead and iron toads were set up on nightstands to assure fertility. Cows and rabbits were likewise fertility symbols. Impotence on the other hand was traced to all sorts of sicknesses like headaches, "possession," ligatures. Some animals like bats were hated because, it was said, they fly into one's hair and piss in one's eyes.

Now let us turn to the *hex*. *Hex* means "witch." Like all European and American peoples of the time, no more, and no less, Pennsylvania Dutch people believed in witches. However, compared with what took place in Puritan New England, I must suggest that the Pennsylvania Dutch were not consumed by heady superstition. Witchcraft was a composite belief and we should carefully separate this belief into its component elements.

The persecution of witches (*Hexen*) was a medieval process of such prevalance that it may be called a mania. "Witchhunt" is still a nasty word.

To insure pregnancy a childless wife furtively placed this figure on the night stand in the bedroom, a charm which, it was believed, would make for fertility. The toad had early associations with midwifery and in Switzerland a saucer of milk was sometimes put out for it. Some even believed that toads sucked milk from cows. This one was made by Jim Hill of Fleetwood. *Courtesy Mr. William Shade*

This idea of the witch (*Hex*) was completely fashioned by 1490. It included the following elements: devil-pact, blood-sucking, heresy, cause of sexual impotence, flying, ability to change human beings into animals. Few of these elements dominated in the tolerant, easy-going land of Pennsylvania.

There were *Hex* trials in Europe as late as 1715, when the august theological faculty of Tübingen university banned one. In 1728 a witch was tried in Berlin. No serious trial of a witch ever took place in Pennsylvania; the one that was recorded ended in acquittal; however, if the common reasoning were therefore to be followed, then *all* New England Puritans, *all* Tübingen theologians down to the present day, and *all* Berliners would be believers in the ugly creature with crooked nose, deep-set eyes, and red hair, hunched, haggard, and with peaked hat, who rides her broom across October skies. It is indeed a cruel hoax to claim that the barn sign, a good luck symbol associated, I believe, with "sweet Puck," is to ward off witches.

Yet, if it be cruel hoax to associate barn signs with witchcraft, it is downright stupid to claim that folk medicine—*powwowing,* as it is called—is also witchcraft. Here I claim that folk medicine conjures up a vision of dancing medicine men in ugly masks, incanting spells against men, demons, and sorcerers, who heal by manipulating spirits.

Powwow is an Indian word. It meant council, conference as a noun, and to confer and to counsel as a verb. Now it is applied to faith-healing and to folk medicine among the Pennsylvania Dutch. This is, I believe, a fundamental misapplication of meaning.

The Pennsylvania Dutch word for the act of faith-healing is *braucherey.* This is a corruption of the Hebrew word *baruch,* which means "to bless." And this is precisely what the so-called "*powwow* doctor" does; he blesses wounds, sores, warts, illnesses. When a vaccination festers, mother blesses it with a short charm-formula. *Powwow* books, which never were known in the older days by that title, were collections of short prayers or benedictions for use in specific health situations.

This is, of course, magic or faith-healing. It goes back to ancient Indo-Germanic sources and was a typical experience among most people. In India this was the only kind of medicine for many years. It carried an occult mood, which was revived by the Renaissance humanism of the philosophers. Always somewhat esoteric, it attached itself to great names, to thinkers of reputation, like Albertus Magnus (Albert the Great, 1193–1280) who was falsely credited with writing *Bewährte und approbirte sympathetische und natürlicher Egyptische Geheimnisse für Menschen und Vieh,* a work printed in Allentown during the nineteenth century. Other similar works arose, like *Der Verborgene Artzt,* New Berlin, 1830.

What the folk doctor does is to use an old verbal charm or incanted formula to bless wound or illness. Generally poetical, these are among the oldest bits of High German verse, going back to the thirteenth century, thus attesting to their antiquity. Here is one designed to stop bleeding:

Auf Christi Grab wachsen Drei Rosen,	Three roses grow on Christ's grave:
Die erste is gütig,	The first is gracious,

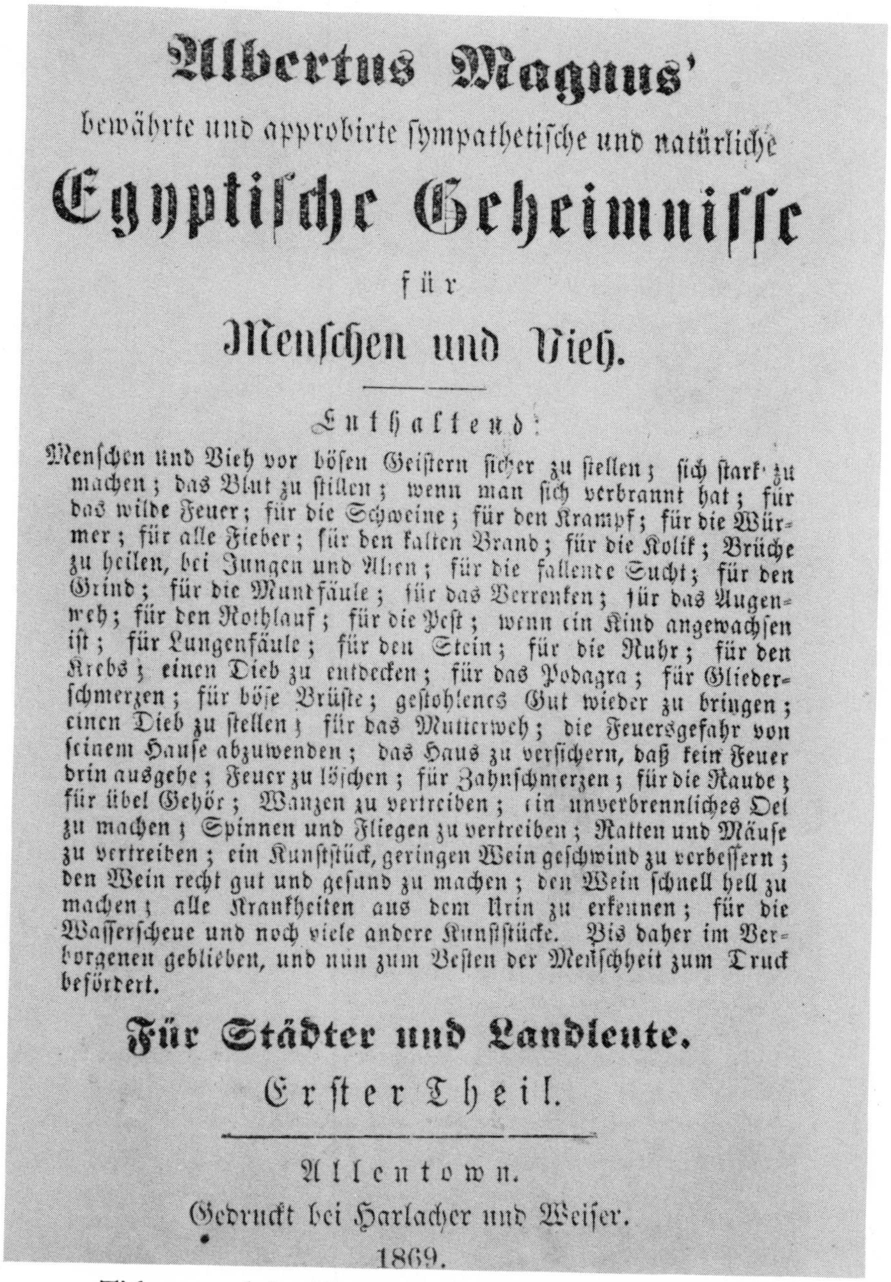

Albertus Magnus'

bewährte und approbirte sympathetische und natürliche

Egyptische Geheimnisse

für

Menschen und Vieh.

———

Enthaltend:

Menschen und Vieh vor bösen Geistern sicher zu stellen; sich stark zu machen; das Blut zu stillen; wenn man sich verbrannt hat; für das wilde Feuer; für die Schweine; für den Krampf; für die Würmer; für alle Fieber; für den kalten Brand; für die Kolik; Brüche zu heilen, bei Jungen und Alten; für die fallende Sucht; für den Grind; für die Mundfäule; für das Verrenken; für das Augenweh; für den Rothlauf; für die Pest; wenn ein Kind angewachsen ist; für Lungenfäule; für den Stein; für die Ruhr; für den Krebs; einen Dieb zu entdecken; für das Podagra; für Gliederschmerzen; für böse Brüste; gestohlenes Gut wieder zu bringen; einen Dieb zu stellen; für das Mutterweh; die Feuersgefahr von seinem Hause abzuwenden; das Haus zu versichern, daß kein Feuer drin ausgehe; Feuer zu löschen; für Zahnschmerzen; für die Raude; für übel Gehör; Wanzen zu vertreiben; ein unverbrennliches Oel zu machen; Spinnen und Fliegen zu vertreiben; Ratten und Mäuse zu vertreiben; ein Kunststück, geringen Wein geschwind zu verbessern; den Wein recht gut und gesund zu machen; den Wein schnell hell zu machen; alle Krankheiten aus dem Urin zu erkennen; für die Wasserscheue und noch viele andere Kunststücke. Bis daher im Verborgenen geblieben, und nun zum Besten der Menschheit zum Druck befördert.

Für Städter und Landleute.

Erster Theil.

———

Allentown.

Gedruckt bei Harlacher und Weiser.

1869.

Title page of the Allentown edition of Albertus Magnus's *Egyptian Secrets,* a book of folk medicine. It has several parts, each with a differing title page.

Beware! Beware of this *Aussprache* (prophecy) of God through His servant Gottlieb Daniel Hoffmann. For this God asks whether He is not a God who is nigh at hand rather than a God who is far off, who can ferret out those who secretly hide. If He is the one who fills heaven and earth and who moves mountains, then we should prophesy in His name. Just how this charm was used is not clear.

Die Ander ist nach herrschen viel	The second would rule,
Blut steh still, und wunde heil.	Blood stand still, wound heal!

This was magic, *Zauber,* which goes back to alchemy and to the desire to control natural processes; but it is white magic, done in the Lord's name, and not black magic; the Faust legend was almost unknown in Pennsylvania.

Powwowing—again that ungainly Indian word, here misapplied—is then nothing else than these old medical theories which seek to exorcise spirits by means of bless-

Der
lange verborgene
Schaz
und
Haus-Freund,
oder
getreuer und christlicher
Unterricht für Jedermann.

Enthaltend

Wunderbare und erprobte Mittel und Künste, für
die Gebrechen der Menschen und am Vieh.

Aus den arabischen Schriften des weisen Alchymisten
Omar Arey, Emir Chemir Tschasmir,
ins Deutsche übersetzt und mit noch vielen
andern Künsten vermehrt.

Zweite vermehrte und verbesserte amerikan. Auflage.

Herausgegeben von J. H......s.

Gedruckt in Pennsylvanien, A. D. 1847.

Title page of the *Long Lost Friend,* a so-called powwow
book, said to have been published in Reading. Although
it proclaims itself a "Christian book," it also claims to
have been taken from the alchemical writings of wise
Arabs and translated into German from the Arabic.

ing wounds and sicknesses with praayers. Old and well-known exorcism of spirits, which was not ecclesiastically approved, was part of the folk attitude towards religion. Before medicine had become materialist, using drugs to cure, this view that spirit controlled bodily processes was well known. Paracelsus (1493–1541) had tried to establish medicine by freeing it from alchemy and this significant but still-neglected thinker of the northern Renaissance believed that we cannot know disease unless we also know how nature reveals herself.

12

wenn du es bei dir hast und wirst gebunden, so springen alle Stricke und Schlösser von dir, und wirst auch nicht geschlossen.

Oder:

Nimm Radlichor, iß sie nüchtern, so kann man dich nicht mehr hauen; so du sie in dem Mund trägst, so überwindest du alle deine Feinde.

Oder:

Der seine eigene Sales essen kann, der ist unüberwindlich.

Sich bei den Leuten angenehm zu machen.

Trage eines Wiedhopfen Aug bei dir, wenn du es vornen auf der Brust trägst, so werden dir deine Feinde hold, und so du es in dem Beutel trägst, so gewinnst du an allem, was du kaufest.

Einen zu stellen, daß er nicht weichen kann.

Nimm eine Nadel, mit welcher ein Todter eingenäht wurde, steck sie in seine Fußstapfen, so kann er nicht weggehen.

Glück im Spiel und sich beliebt bei den Menschen zu machen.

Nimm deinen rechten Daumen in deine Hand und steck sie in den rechten Sack, wenn man einen armen Sünder hinrichtet, so hast du Glück im Spiel und bist beliebt bei den Menschen.

Eine Jungfer zu probiren, ob sie keusch ist.

Rettigsaft in die Hand gethan, so grabelt sie nicht.

Daß dich eine lieben muß.

Nimm Federn von einem Hahnenschwanz, drücke sie ihr dreimal in die Hand. Probatum.

Oder:

Nimm eine Turteltauben-Zunge in den Mund, rede mit ihr lieblich, küsse sie hernach auf den Mund, so hat sie dich so lieb, daß sie dich nicht mehr lassen kann.

Oder wenn dir eine nichts versagen soll.

So nimm die Turteltauben-Zunge in den Mund und küsse sie damit, so kann sie dir nichts versagen.

Page of recipes from Albertus Magnus's *Egyptian Secrets*. The second one from the bottom tells how to make someone love you: Take the tongue of a turtledove in your mouth, speak lovingly to the beloved, then kiss her on the mouth, and she will love you so that she will nevermore leave you. Of course, one must first catch the turtledove!

§ 4 §

Wenn einem Frauenzimmer die Mutter aufsteigt, und gut für den Husten.

Nimm für 2 kr. Pomeranzenschaalen, für 2 kr. Aloe, für 2 kr. Mühren, dieses in eine Bouteille gethan, Morgens und Abends davon getrunken.

Warzen zu vertreiben.

Nimm Nußblüthe, reibe die Warzen damit, sie heilen.

Eine Citation, eine Hexe herkommen zu lassen.

Nimm einen ungelöschten Hafen, Garn von einem Mägdlein gesponnen, welches noch nicht sieben Jahre alt ist, das Wasser von dem Thier in den Hafen gethan, darnach nimm ein Ei von einer schwarzen Henne, und nimm von dem Garn und fahre dreimal um das Ei herum, und sprich in drei Teufelsnamen, hernach thue das Ei in den Hafen in das Wasser, den Hafen gut zugeklebt, daß kein Dampf herauskommt, der Kopf am Deckel muß zu unterst sein; wenn man den Hafen zu dem Feuer stellt, spricht man: Lucifer, Teufel stell mir den Zauberer oder die Zauberin in's drei Teufels Namen.

Wenn einem etwas gestohlen wird.

Wenn einem etwas gestohlen wird, so wird dieses auch gemacht, wie es oben steht, man nimmt Wasser, schöpft es in den Bach hinunter, und schneidet drei Spänlein von der Schwelle, wo der Dieb darüber gelaufen ist, das Wasser muß auch in's drei Teufels Namen geschöpft werden.

Daß keine Hexe aus der Kirche komme.

Kauf ein paar neue Schuhe, schmiere sie an einem Sonnabend an den Ortsohlen mit Schmeer, sodann ziehe sie an und gehe damit in die Kirche, so kann keine hinaus, du gehst denn voran.

Von Hexen und Zauberei.

Hänge eine Meerzwiebel über die erste Thüre des Hauses, so wird kein Mensch darinnen verderben.

Hexen zu schlagen.

Nimm das Kutter, so im Hause drei Tage zusammengefeget wird, laß es drei Tage liegen, und am dritten Tag leg ein

This page from Albertus Magnus's *Egyptian Secrets* brings us as close to devil-pact as we get in Pennsylvania, where the Faust legend was not well known. Here is how we get rid of a witch (*Hex*). Take an unwashed jar; take thread spun by a maiden not yet seven years of age; put water from an animal into the jar. Then take an egg from a black hen, wrap the thread around the egg three times, and speak forth the three devil-names. Then put the egg in the water, close the jar, turn it upside down so no moisture escapes, and set it near the fire, saying, "Lucifer, get rid of the witch in the name of the three devils."

Thus folk medicine, of which the Pennsylvania Dutch powwowing was a part, was a spiritual manifestation. It sought to control by spirit. However, the folk doctor did not eschew drugs. Indeed, herbs and medicinal substances were used, some with sound empirical reason, for example, belladonna (atropine). Still, most folk medicine joins spiritual world views with some empiricism. It was not modern science.

Folk medicine implies many ideas, some of which are now obsolete. It also suggests an interesting theory of knowing by means of the "signature." Everything has its core, or heart, by which it may be known. Through this signature it may be controlled, if one has the hammer to strike its bell, as Jacob Boehme wrote. Through this, or through knowledge of this, it may be manipulated. Just as an individual person is represented by his signature, his handwritten name, so every object has a key or token by which it may be grasped, a symptom by which it may be managed, controlled. Folk medicine is the manipulation of spirit by means of the signature: hemorrhages are cured by blood stones, blood being the signature, the common key. Yellow flowers cure jaundice.

This brings us to the omniscient folk physician, the so-called powwow doctor, who in deep secrecy has been given power to know all signatures and is custodian of the secretive manipulatory wisdom. The ancient Greeks gave this knowledge to priests, the power that Hippocrates gave to infant medicine and which physicians now claim. These magical powers were not empirical, based on proven experimental facts; still, we should approach Pennsylvania folk medicine, not from the side of the occult, but from the point of view of its philosophical implications, residual survivals of ancient points of view.

So powwowing—what a barbarous name, grossly used—is simply exorcising illnesses by means of control of signatures.

Associated with folk medicine was belief in the power of stars and heavenly bodies over human destinies. This is also old, coming from Babylon, Assyria, and Hellenistic cultural areas. It embraced the notion that a person's fate was reflected in the configuration of planets and stars. In full retrospect this view did not loom large among the Pennsylvania Dutch, even though the almanacs carried these views. What did continue was the custom of planting various crops by following the zodiac.

Bound to astrology was the view that comets were portents of death, revealing coming punishment. After Isaac Newton's discoveries, such beliefs began to moderate and fade out. Paracelsus's old view that new stars, like comets, were part of a virginal creation, God working anew, and that they brought their own revelations was reflected in Pastor Daniel Schuhmacher's drawing of the comet that passed across the Pennsylvania heavens just before the American Revolution.

Disunity of calendar reckonings, controversy about old and new styles, varied beginnings of the new year made New Year customs change. After 1691 continental Europe, Catholic and Protestant alike, followed the decision of Pope Innocent XII setting January first as New Year's Day. This replaced the first of March. In Pennsylvania New Year's eve was a time of spirits, when all subhuman forces were on the move and could be frightened by bells and alarms, and by shooting guns. Few masks were known to have been worn and the mummer's tradition is not Pennsylvania Dutch as such. However, greetings were exchanged. To counteract the pagan New Years' customs, men like Pastor Schuhmacher sent greetings to their friends in traditional language.

The most important day on the Pennsylvania Dutch calendar was the second day of February, our national holiday, *Grundsowdaag* (Groundhog day). This was known in Europe as *Lichtmesstag*. This comes from the old Roman festival of lights, which under Christian influences was transformed into the day of the purification of Mary. In Europe many customs were associated with this day, including blessing candles. In the Pennsylvania Dutch folk mind, one belief seems to dominate: on this date the sun was seen to make its first leap toward the spring equinox, therefore it became a day of decision, especially for determining weather:

Lichtmess im Klee	Candlemass in clover,
Ostern im Schnee.	Easter in snow.

This proverb has now grown up. Now a lowly animal, the woodchuck or groundhog, makes the grand decision whether there shall be six more weeks of winter. Some people say that it is better to see a wolf on Candlemas than the sun. On this day of the year the future weather turns.

In Catholic lands December sixth was Saint Nicholas Day, named in honor of an Asia Minor bishop who died *ca.* A.D. 300 and who was honored for his wide-ranging good works. Veneration of him appeared in the Rhineland, which became the center of a cult of Saint Nicholas. However, after the Reformation had done away with the year of saints' days, Protestants pushed this to

Pastor Daniel Schuhmacher's New Year's Greeting to
"Liessabetha Grimmin" in Weissenburg, Lehigh County,
1772. Note the sample alphabet at the bottom.

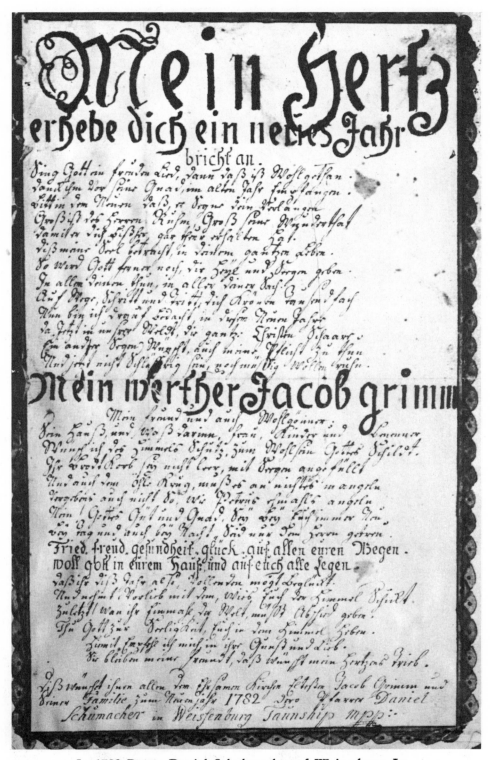

In 1782 Pastor Daniel Schuhmacher of Weisenberg, Lehigh County, sent this New Year's Greeting to his elder, Jacob Grimm.

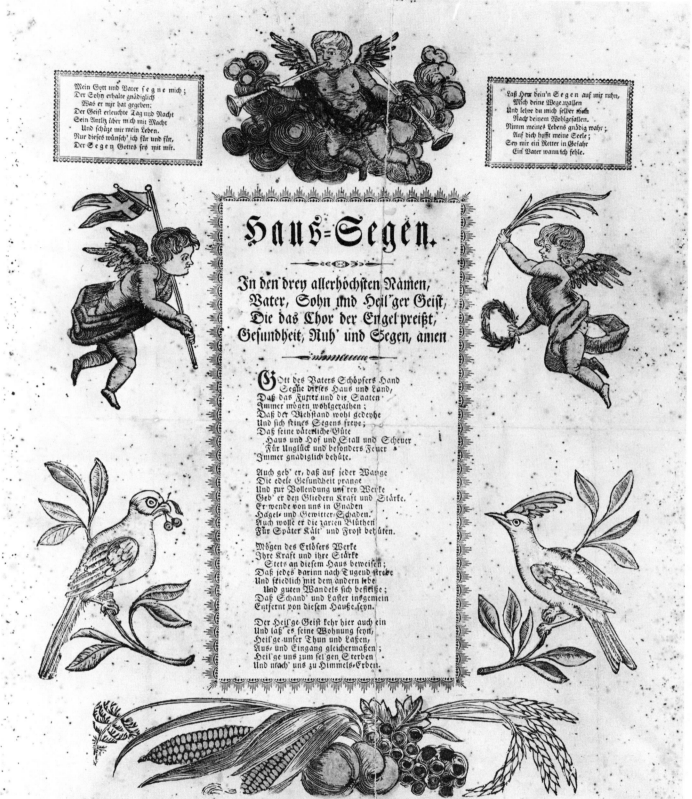

Like printed "fat angel" style birth certificates, these house blessings also were printed in outline and then colored by hand. The High German poem, done by some local folk poet, was in traditional pattern and may even be old.

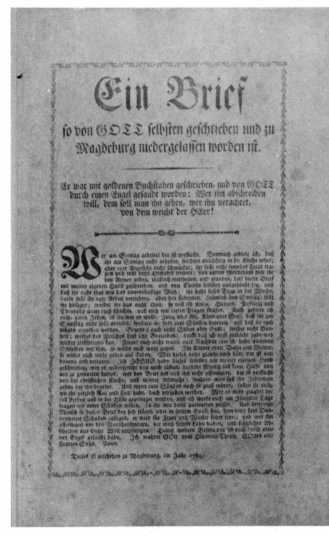

The Letter from Heaven (*Himmelsbrief*), which God sent down in the year 1783 and which was often reprinted in Pennsylvania. Sometimes it was translated and given out by tradesmen as souvenirs and gifts.

Christmas eve, when they expected the coming of *Beltznickel*, a figure now merged with Father Christmas, Santa Claus, and so on. The two traditions join. In the older view, however, *Beltznickel* may come any time during Advent, ringing sleigh bells, bringing small gifts for children—nuts, candies, fruits. He throws the gifts on the floor, demanding a "piece" performed by the children. They have prepared for this for months, and they say a poem or sing a song. He remains stern, with grim, forbidding countenance—a far cry from the jolly fat man with the merry "Ho, Ho, Ho!" When *Beltznickel's* whip rattled the windows, the children were

frightened and he was a creature to be feared. Sunday School festivals in the Pennsylvania Dutch countryside continue this tradition of saying a "piece" for him, even though he may not show up.

Weddings among the Pennsylvania Dutch were never so raucous as among other peoples. The one lusty aspect was the "bull band" on the evening of the wedding after the wedded pair had gone to their room. Then tubs, pots, pans, kegs, and bells were noised, thumped, pounded, rung, and whacked with zest, and the newlyweds were aroused to pay out a small gift.

Often condemned by the church, the *Himmelsbrief* (letter from heaven) was widely circulated in Penn-

"The Graveside Singer" was a collection of German poetry dealing with death and the consolation of the bereaved. It was compiled by Pastor Hermann of Kutztown and went through several local editions before being stereotyped in this Philadelphia edition. This was one of the most popular of Pennsylvania Dutch works.

sylvania, both in English and German. It was thought to protect a person from evil, a talisman. This was the text of a letter that is actually very old—one author suggests a fourth-century origin—which came down, it was said, at certain places in Germany from the heavens. It was passed along, sometimes as a chain letter for a fee, sometimes given away as a present. The Northampton county barber, George Beil, passed out an English version to his customers as late as 1916. It was basically a warning against impiety and ir-religion.

Several folk books also were in common use. The oldest of these was *Das Hertz des Menschen,* reprinted as early as 1822 in Reading, an old prayerbook which some say has affinity with the desert prophets of southern France. Another popular book of folk prayers was *'S Habermännlein,* known also as the golden Haber-mann, probably assembled by the theologian Johann Habermann (1516–1590). Also, the Reverend Alfred Hermann, Kutztown pastor, compiled the most popular work of devotion used among the Pennsylvania Dutch, *Der Sänger am Grabe,* which was used both for funerals and for consoling the bereaved. It went through many editions in Kutztown, as well as a larger stereotype edition by Kohler of Philadelphia. Not original, the work collects over two hundred German pieces. Sources are not given; some poems may be of American origin.

In 1880 Ludwig August Wollenweber published *Die Berg Maria* (Mountain Mary), which gathered much of the Pennsylvania Dutch folk consciousness into an historical tale. He had been born at Ixheim in the Palatinate, near Zweibrücken, and was a printer by trade, who became involved in liberal movements during the 1830s, fleeing to America. He had established the *Philadelphische Demokrat* and edited it for several years, later moving to Womelsdorf, where he wrote dialect pieces for Pennsylvania newspapers under the *nom de plume* of "Der alte vom Berge."

Die Berg Maria is a sentimental novel about Theodor Benz and Maria Jung, and their migration to Penn-sylvania. Here, with sugar-sweet sentiment, Wollen-weber relates the stories of the migration, the heroic measures of the indentured immigrants who survived bitter years, the brave patriots who fought and (like Theodor) died for their new land, Mary's selfless service to the sick and ailing settlers of the Oley Hills—all matters of legend and story. Now Mary and Theodor became living characters in the folk mind.

Pennsylvania Dutch culture, therefore, has matured. It is beginning to form its own myths.

One more book must be mentioned: M. L. Weems's *Das Leben des Georg Waschington,* Baltimore, 1817, and Lebanon, 1820, which saw translation into German in several editions. The new land had impressed itself upon an Old-World culture.

8
Dialect Literature

hile the Pennsylvania Dutch were reading Luther's version of the Bible, and High German newspapers, singing hymns by Paul Gerhard and Joachim Neander, and writing, printing, and reading their own materials in High German, they were speaking a *patois* on farm and at home, the dialect called Pennsylvania Dutch that has attracted so much attention and is still heard today, not only in Pennsylvania but through the midwest and parts of Canada. Like many regions in old Germany, there was in Pennsylvania a difference between how German was written and how it was spoken. Dialect is really a way of speaking: *Berg* becomes *berick* and *Markt* becomes *marick.* The changes are regular.

As early as 1742, when Count Zinzendorf, who was a highly literate man, was visiting America, he noted the distinctive dialect and honored it by trying to speak it. German travelers in the Confederation (1783) were not so kind; they suggested that it was "fustian salmagundy of English and German," a mixture that purists should shun.

Actually, the base on which Pennsylvania Dutch dialect was built was a regular departure from standard German. It follows certain rules for its consonantal shift from the older tongue. Thus High German *Thür* becomes the Dutch *Dier* (door). High German *Schnabel* becomes *Schnawel* (beak). *Th*s become *D*s, *B*s become *W*s. This shift has been well documented and the Pennsylvania Dutch dialect emerged on this base, an orderly change from standard High German.

The vocabulary originally was Germanic and antique. Many older words here survive as relics: *Gaul* (horse) is a word for the linguistic museum. The ungainly *Aussteyerkischt* (dower chest) is more expressive than the German *Truhe.* This antique inherited vocabulary has been augmented by much borrowing from English. The appearance of the magnificent *Pfälsisches Wörterbuch,* the great dialect dictionary now in process of publication, will certify the soundness of the Pennsylvania dialect.

However, when migration ceased, or slowed, dependence upon High German began to wane and as a result new words were borrowed from English. Also, new things were invented for which no words existed—an exceptionally large part of the language—hence vocabulary had to be created: *riegelweg* (railway), *machene* (automobile), *radio, powwow.* New expressions and environmental pressures made for creativity in augmenting the vocabulary. Sometimes words were taken artificially and used in only one situation, such as the cuss-word still employed when one hits a rock while ploughing: *Bullemefransais,* which corrupts *parlez-vous français.*

Yet, for all its vigor and pathos—and it can still move strong men to tears—dialect literature was an after thought, which came after a vigorous period of High German literature was over. For nearly two centuries High German was the literary language of the Pennsylvania Dutch; by 1830 forty-seven places had presses that

Language problems existed from the start. When a Pennsylvania Dutchman made his last will and testament he had to get an exemplification of it in English so that it could be probated. Here is such an exemplification for the will of Matthias Baumann, leader of the Newborn sect in Oley, dated February 27, 1727.

were printing materials in this language—thirty-one in Pennsylvania, three in Maryland, four in Ohio, five in Virginia, and scattered ones elsewhere. The Lutheran Bible had three American editions before 1782, when the first English one appeared in Philadelphia, and in 1813 a German Bible was printed in Somerset, west of the mountains.

When the German school passed out of existence and the German language was no longer taught, and when the impact of the romantic stress on folk language came

Whereas Mathias Bauman of Oley in y° County of Philad°: in y° Province of Pennsylvania, Did by his last will and Testament leave his land and Plantation Scituate in Oley aforesaid: y° one half to Cathrine his wife for and during her Natural life Now this agreement Witnesseth That Peter Andrew and Cathrine his wife for and in Consideration of fforty pounds Currant — mony of Pennsylvania To them in hand paid by Samuel High Have Bargained and Sold and by these presents do bargain and Sell unto y° Said Sam.ll High his heirs and assigns, All their right Title Interest property Claime and demand In and to y° above Said Plantation and Tract of Land and all and every part thereof (by Virtue of y° Said last will and Testament or otherways) To have and to hold the Said Moiety or one half of y° Said Land plantation and premises unto y° Said Samuel High his heirs & Assigns forever: Without any further Trouble let Suit hindorance disturbance or Molestation of him y° Said Peter Andrew or Cathrine his wife or from their heirs Execd.rs or Administrators or any other person whatsoever, by their Consent means or procurement. And that I the Said Peter Andrew and Cathrine my Wife Shall & will warrant and forever defend by these presents, y° Said Land plantation and Premises: Now being in the actual and peaceable possession and Seizin, of the Said Sam.ll High his Heirs Execd.rs admd.rs and assigns: Witness my hand and Seal dated y° Twenty Ninth day of May anno Domini one thousand Seven hundred & Thirty

Sealed & delivered in
y° Presence of us

The language problem continued in legal matters. Thus when Matthias Baumann of Oley died and his land was parceled out among his heirs according to his will, they had to get an English-language exemplification to use in the courts. This was dated May 29, 1730. The signature was in German script.

Es waren Zehn.

Von W. Donner.

Es waren Zehn !—Das war ein Kampf !
Da galt es sich zu wehren.
Da floß der Schweiß von früh bis spät,
Die alle zu ernähren !

Es waren Zehn—Nun sind sie groß,
Vier Mädchen und sechs Jungen.
Des Vaters schwiel'ge Arbeitsfaust,
Sie hat die Noth bezwungen.

Es waren Zehn !—Das sieht man gleich !
Schau', wie die Knochen beben !
Nun ruh' dich aus, du müder Greis,
Jetzt sollst du sorglos leben !

Es waren Zehn !—Der Aelt'ste sprach:
„Willst nicht zum Michel gehen ?
Sieh' da, wo jetzt dein Armstuhl steht,
Muß uns're Wiege stehen !"

Es waren Zehn—!—Der Vater ging.
Doch Michel meinte weise,
'wär besser, denn es werd' schon kalt,
Wenn er zum Peter reise.

Es waren Zehn !—Der Peter brummt:
„Zu eng sind uns're Stübchen,
Der Vater hustet häufig sehr,
Und weckt dann unser Bübchen."

Es waren Zehn ! — — wohin denn nun ?
Be'm Paul wollt' er's probiren.
Doch der: „Mein Webstuhl knarrt so sehr,
Das wird dich wohl geniren."

Es waren Zehn !—Der Alte denkt:
„Dem Max komm' ich gelegen !"
Doch der: „Ach, meine Frau ist schwach,
Die kann dich nicht verpflegen !"

Es waren Zehn !—Zum Jüngsten ging
Der Greis mit seinem Päckchen.
„Die Schwiegermutter zog jüngst ein,
Besetzt ist jedes Eckchen!"

Es waren Zehn !—Der Vater weint
Im Stillen heiße Thränen. — —
Es bleiben doch die Töchter noch
Ihm übrig von den Zehnen.

Es waren Zehn !—Der Aermste ging
Zur Ersten, Zweiten, Dritten.—
Die Jüngste hab' am meisten Platz,
Dort sei er gut gelitten !—

Es waren Zehn !—Der Greis wankt müd'
Zur jüngsten Tochter Lore,
Sie war des Todtengräbers Weib
Und wohnt' im Friedhofsthore !

Es waren Zehn !—Der Vater fand
Hier endlich auch ein Stübchen,
Doch schon am dritten Tage sprach
Zu ihm das Enkelbübchen:

Es wären Zehn !—sagt Mütterchen,
Sie wollt' dich auch nicht haben;
Am besten sei's, wenn Vater dir
Recht bald ein Grab könnt graben !"

Es waren Zehn !—Dem Alten deucht,
Ein Schwert hab' ihn durchstochen !
Er sinkt zurück in seinen Stuhl,—
Das Herz war ihm gebrochen !

Example of High German poem appearing in the almanacs of eastern Pennsylvania. Works from Europe and America, in High German as well as dialect, appeared.

Das Lied von Gottes Herrlichkeit.

Es klingt so weit, durch alle Zeit
Das Lied von Gottes Herrlichkeit;
Wie Harfenklang, wie Sphärensang
Zieht's durch die Welt mit Feiergang.

Bald rauscht es sacht, bald stürmt's mit Macht,
Bald wogt's in ruhig schöner Pracht;
Zur Nacht zumal bei Sternenstrahl
Geht's wunderbar durch Wald und Thal.

Und blüht der Hain im Frühlingsschein,
Dann stimmet alle Welt mit ein—
Der Blumenflor, der Vögelchor:
Ein Jedes singt, ob's stumm zuvor.

Es schallet fort von Ort zu Ort,
Als wär's ein Auferstehungswort,
Und wo es wallt, und wo es schallt,
Wacht auf des Lebens Allgewalt.

O, singt es laut und Gott vertraut,
Wenn Gram auf eurem Auge thaut;
Es führt euch weit zur Ewigkeit,
Das Lied von Gottes Herrlichkeit.

Example of the High German religious verse that was printed in the Pennsylvania almanacs as late as 1900. This shows a continuation of that language.

Datestone on a house along the Swamp Pike, in New Hanover Township, Montgomery County. Even at this late date the German language was used. *Photograph courtesy Mr. Edward W. Schlechter*

from Germany, writing dialect became possible. However, we can do better than that! On September 11, 1850, Joseph Jung wrote in the *Doylestown Morgenstern*:

> We . . . hit upon the idea, since we had been born in America, of writing jokes or bits of foolery in Pennsylvania German dialect, and this over ten years ago. The articles were well received and soon similar articles began to come, too, from other sources. Would-be wise men and journalists not exactly right in their heads immediately turned up their noses and tried to make this innocent dialect an object of contempt. . . . Pennsylvania German is beginning to be popular and we take the credit for introducing it.

This newspaper material, anecdotal and humorous, has never been collected and has been little studied, even

The familiar blue paper covers of the publications of the Pennsylvania German Society.

though it forms the earliest phase of Pennsylvania Dutch dialect literature. The able editors of these newspapers, then, like Albrecht Kneule of the *Bauern-Freund und Pennsburg Demokrat,* Conrad Gehring of the *Kutztown Journal,* and Moritz Loeb of the *Doylestown Morgenstern,* were advocates of this movement.

Soon the almanacs, too, which were also popular products of the provincial presses, began to print dialect pieces, anecdotal and humorous. Spelling moved from European to English-style, as did the dialects spoken. These materials have not been studied, either; while scholars have been busy reprinting second-hand newspaper pieces, they have neglected these primary sources in newspaper and almanac.

Spelling has, of course, been the problem, perhaps one that reveals the ultimate irrational character of dialect for literary purposes. In his fine anthology of Pennsylvania Dutch poetry, Professor Reichard let each writer spell for himself. This wise decision was more than expediency, for it gave useful insight into the writer's view of dialect. It also serves to separate those who wrote with a German ear from those who were writing from English phonetic experience.

Surveying the field of dialect literature, we note that the beginning of the twentieth century marks a point of transition. Before that time most writers had grown up in an environment wherein High German was still alive. They conceived of dialect sounds in German phonetics. This separates them from those who wrote in the twentieth century from the English phonetic scheme. Some make Pennsylvania Dutch dialect look like the Hottentot.

It is ironic that dialect literature first appeared in modest form in puppet plays performed by a Philadelphia Scotsman, Hugh Lindsay, an itinerating Philadelphia humorist who offered some dramas every evening but Sunday at the Philadelphia theater operated by J. H. Myers, an old German comedian. Lindsay was also magician, puppeteer, and ventriloquist; his characters were the stereotyped "Dumb Dutch" who spoke vernacular, mouthing coarse, vulgar jokes. Lindsay had no followers in Pennsylvania German literature. About the same time, Lewis Miller, the carpenter-folk artist of York was writing songs in dialect, ditties, and other small bits.

The full range of dialect poetry becomes clear when we peruse Professor Reichard's anthology, *Pennsylvania German Verse* (Norristown, 1940), which gathers ninety-six poets, and several more anonymous ones, in a rich treasury of verse that bares the soul of the Penn-

Die Lederhose.—„Alle verzehn Dag neie Hose' vor Eich; Schlingel, das geht m'r iwers Bohnelied"—rief mein pfälzer Freund, als seine drei Sprößlinge wieder 'mal nach Hause kamen, die Taschentücher um die Knie gebunden und sonstige Defecte an unaussprechlicherer Stelle ihrer Beinbekleidung, so gut es eben ging, mit der Hand verdeckend. „Lederhose gehöre Eich, Ihr dunnerwetters Kerl, un' das mit doppelte Sticker uf die Knie un' sunst wohin, un' gleich geht Ihr mir mit zum Säcklermäster, der soll sie Eich ahnmesse uf der Stell' — Eich will ich schun krieche." Gesagt—gethan. Die Lederhosen werden angefertigt und der Vater freut sich seiner köstlichen Idee, und noch mehr der bald in scheinbarer Unverwüstlichkeit vor ihm liegenden Hosen. Gleich werden sie den Jungens angethan. Diese schreien zwar trostlos: „Vater, so könne m'r net gehe, m'r sehe so aus wie die Schornstänfeger—," aber der Vater, mit Wohlgefallen sie betrachtend, erwidert ruhig und befriedigt: „Thut nix, davor habt Ihr jetzt e' haltbar' Hos'; die verreißt Ihr mir nit, do bin ich Eich gut davor."—Einige Tage nur waren verstrichen, da springen die Jungen frohlockend in die Stube vor den Vater hin: „Etsch, Etsch, guck' amol do!" und o Schrecken! in röthlich strahlender Rundung lachen dem verblüfften Vater die naiven Kehrseiten seiner Jungen höhnisch aus den vernichteten Lederhosen entgegen. „Gell, do guckst D'!" — „Ihr Gewitter-

Oeser wie habt Ihr das blos ahngestellt?"— „Ei, Aener hot sich immer uf de Schleifstän' gesetzt, und mir Annern zwä hawe' gedreht."

An obviously European story told in dialect with accompanying cartoon, as presented in the *Adler* almanac for 1888. Lederhosen were not worn in Pennsylvania. Also, the language is somewhat strange to our ears.

sylvania German people. When we add this dialect verse to the High German poetry of the earlier periods, we gain a full exposition of the Pennsylvania German spirit.

Henry Harbaugh (1817–1867) remains the classical writer of Pennsylvania dialect verse. Born near Waynsborough on a farm that was firmly etched in his poetical imagination, he was directed to writing dialect by Philip Schaff, church historian at Mercersburg. Harbaugh's slim volume, *Harfe,* portions of which may still be heard recited from memory in eastern Pennsylvania, appeared during the 1850s and 1860s in the magazine that he was editing, *The Guardian.* This volume gives fifteen precious poems, along with four translations by Harbaugh himself, a memorial by Clement Z. Weiser in dialect and an interesting *Wortverzeichniss* (word list) in High German, toward which the language of these poems was directed.

Henry Harbaugh was far more than a naïf folk poet writing occasional ditties for his own amusement. He was seeking to start a literary tradition—which he did— Pennsylvania Dutch dialect literature. Acquainted with Hebel's *Allemannische Gedichte,* he was conscious of attempting to build a *Volkssprache* (folk language), and he combined with this a nostalgia for the good old days of his youth, for pleasant days now past, which he could not project in his sermons. Harbaugh was a *Volksmann* (man of the people) as well as popular humanist, perceptively appreciating the older times that were being overwhelmed by the technological culture then coming.

Heit is 's 'xactly zwanzig Johr   Today it is just twenty years

Das ich bin owwe naus: Since I began to roam,
Nau bin ich widder lewig   Now, safely back, I stand
    z'rick   once more
Und steh am Schulhaus an d'r   Before the quaint old school-
    Krick   house door
Juscht nechscht an's Dady's   Close by my father's house.
    haus.

Harbaugh also describes the non-Germanic idea of the "gentleman," the sporty youth with fancy buggies and fast pacers; he longs for the fireplace and sleeping room of his youth. Sentiment, nature-love, and folklore come to expression in his deeply intuited verse.

As he wished, Harbaugh was the beginning of a fruitful and honorable tradition. There were many others who followed. There was Edward Hermany, born in Lehigh County, who wrote between 1860 and 1872, using a unique style of spelling to express his many moods. It was editors like L. A. Wollenweber, newer immigrants, who became advocates of folk literature in dialect; here was a man who fell in love with the culture of the Colonial Germans; he wrote several novelettes in High German on Pennsylvania themes and he compiled *Gemälde aus den Pennsylvanischen Volksleben* (Philadelphia and Leipzig, 1869), which was the first effort to bring the Pennsylvania Dutch folk mind into perspective. Wollenweber also wrote dramatic works, which appeared as sketches in newspapers.

Among native-born writers, Henry L. Fisher of York and Rachel Bahn were both related to Henry Harbaugh. Fisher, a York attorney, associated the old Market House in York with the Kreutz Creek valley scene, giving us imaginative comprehension of the Pennsylvania mood. Eli Keller, born in Northampton County, portrayed in prose and verse a rural nostalgia and pride for his land, tongue, and people. One of the best-known bits of Keller's verse is

Ich schwetz in der deutsche   I speak the German tongue,
    Sproch,
Lieb sie ah und halt sie hoch: Love it too and hold it high,
Sie is ah ken Huren Kind,   And it is no whore's child
Das mer in de Hecke fint—   That we find in the hedges;
Sie kommt her vom schöne   It comes to us from the lovely
    Rhein   Rhine,
Wu sie Trauwe hen—und   There they have grapes—and
    Wei.   wine.

The spelling here is for German readers. Also, during the Civil War, Edward H. Rauch (b. 1820) wrote a pamphlet of verse, *De Campain Briefe fun Pit Schweffelbrenner,* which was published in Lancaster, thus beginning a fine career as a dialect writer. In 1873 he started

On this tombstone the inscription is still in German but the given name and family name have been englished. Here we stand on the boundary of the two languages.

the *Pennsylvania Dutchman,* a magazine in both English and German, which saw only three issues. Several years later he published a *Pennsylvania Dutch Handbook,* which was dictionary, literary work, and anthology. His work was notable for his translations. Here is Rauch's rendering of the ghost's speech in *Hamlet,* I,v:

GHOST: *Ich bin deim dawdy si schpook:*
        G'sentenced der a tzeitlong rumm lawfe nauchts,

Clock face of Joseph Weiss, also of Allentown, to which folk designs have been added. *Courtesy Mrs. Walter C. Moser*

Clock face of Joseph Geiger, 1787, of Allentown (then Northampton) in an obviously European mood. *Courtesy Mr. Tom Schmoyer*

European influences

The folk arts of Pennsylvania have returned to Europe again. Our provincial arts are now exhibited at a famous watering-place for the eighteenth-century aristocracy. Here are the Pennsylvania Dutch rooms in the American Museum in Great Britain.

Americanized designs

Toleware from Pennsylvania. It is difficult to separate what was made in Pennsylvania from other pieces. *Courtesy Mrs. Walter C. Moser*

Reverse painting on glass was known as early as the Italian Renaissance, if not earlier. Here is a mixture of American and European pieces. *Courtesy Mrs. Walter C. Moser*

Un im dawg fescht stecke im fire,
Bis de schlechty sucha os ich gadu hob in meina
Nadoor's dawga,
Ous gabrenn'd in ous g'lozeerd sin . . .

In 1884 Rauch also saw performed on an Allentown stage his *Rip van Winkel*, a romantic drama in two acts, an adaptation of Washington Irving's story in which the scene has been changed from the Catskills to the Poconos and in which George III is replaced by George Washington. Rauch was no purist, as can be seen from his spelling, and he borrowed English words with liberality. He also made other translations.

A. R. Horne, born of Mennonite background in Bucks County, became principal of the Normal School in Kutztown where, in spite of the attitude of the Pennsylvania Department of Public Instruction, he became a staunch advocate of Pennsylvania Dutch culture. He compiled a handbook, *The Pennsylvania Manual for Pronouncing, Speaking, and Writing English*, which had several printings, each an expansion: 1886, 1896, 1905, 1910. Its second part was a grammar and dialect dictionary. Horne's dialect verse was nostalgic and sentimental.

Lebanon-born Lee Light Grumbine, younger brother of Ezra Grumbine, was a college-bred teacher at Cornell who has given us some excellent poems, especially *Der Alt Dengelstock* and the introspective longer piece, *Sonntag Morgeds an de Ziegel Kerch.* His rendering of Longfellow's *Psalm of Life* in the dialect was notable.

Thomas C. Zimmermann, newspaper editor born in Lebanon County in 1858, was noteworthy in that he

Under various titles the Pennsylvania German Magazine came out and forms a rich treasury of materials dealing with the Pennsylvania Dutch. Here are two different covers.

translated some High German works into the dialect, works by Claudius, Chamisee, Eichendorf, Goethe, Uhland, and especially Schiller. His most successful transla-

The almanac of the old Reading *Adler* was really a joke book, full of the lusty humor of the people.

tion was *Die Nacht for de Chrischdaag* by Clement C. Moore:

'S waar die Nacht for de Chrischdaag und dorch es ganz Haus
Verregt sich ke' Thierli, net emol en Maus:
Die Strümpf warre schnock im Schornschte gehunke,
In der Hoffnung der "Nick" dheet graad runner dschumpe: . . .

Translations from English literature also were popular. In 1880 Alfred C. Moss and Edward J. Newhard performed a version of *Pinafore* in dialect in Allentown

and it became an instant hit, playing to large audiences. The spelling still was inconsistent, a mixture of German and English, but it did not have the warmth of native dialect verse.

In 1891 Charles Calvin Ziegler (1854–1930) published a slender volume of dialect verse, *Draus und Daheem, Gedichte in Pennsylvänisch Deitsch,* which, although it was brought out in Germany, received favorable notices here in America, including historian John

Here we see the boundary of Pennsylvania Dutch culture in this tombstone in St. Gabriel's Church, Douglasville. The skull and crossbones are not typical of the Pennsylvania Dutch, nor is the English-language verse:

> Remov'd from Noise and Care
> This silent Place I Chose
> Where Death should end my Year
> To Take a Sweet Repose
> Here in a peacefull Place
> My Ashes must Remain
> My Saviour shall mee Keep
> And raise mee up A Gain.

Photograph by W. W. Dietrich

Fiske's opinion that it was a "charming book." Some persons consider Ziegler to be Pennsylvania's finest dialect writer and in view of the scope of his moods and the versatility of his images, he is hard to beat. Educated at Harvard, his verse moves from belly-shaking laughter to a mystical vision of the unity of life, from satire to lovely and feeling translations. He was urged to continue his interests by Professor Barrett Wendel, who encouraged him to use his people's language with tenderness. On his graduation from Harvard he wrote:

Heit graduir ich, und mit Ehr: Today I graduate with honors

"BRENASEL" STHORIES.

IN PENSILVANY DEITSCH.

BY PROF. JIM BRENASEL.

(FER EN LONGHY TZEIT DER SPECIAL PENSILVANY
DEITSCH CONTRIBUTOR TSU DA "READING
SUNDAY MORNING REVIEW.)

———————

EPHRATA, PA.:
J. W. VON NIEDA, AUTHOR UN PUBLISHER.
1878.

An early attempt at Pennsylvania Dutch narrative prose.
Photograph courtesy Mr. Edward W. Schlechter

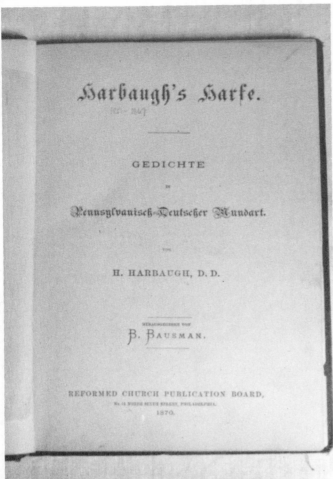

Title page of Henry Harbaugh's *Harfe,* probably the best of the collections of dialect poetry.

Night"; Bryant's "Thanatopsis"; O. W. Holmes's, "The September Gale"; Emerson's "It was one of those charmed days." Here the influence of his Harvard teachers is evident. He also wrote in High German and English, being an accomplished verse-smith in three languages. If Henry Harbaugh's *Harfe* was the nostalgic start of Pennsylvania dialect verse, then Ziegler's *Draus und Daheem,* while still nostalgic, is a portent of things to come.

Pennsylvania dialect verse of the nineteenth century was therefore part of a first period of literary achievement, which should be viewed from the point of view of its context. It was in truth only a frail shoot, stimulated by German romanticism, and it retained the features of that attitude: nostalgia, folksy humor, sentimentality. And when it translated, it did so from American poetry, showing wherein its roots lay.

Toward the end of the nineteenth century, Daniel Miller began to publish *The Reformed Church Record,* which contained a column of dialect prose and verse and included verses by P. T. Eisenbrown, George Mays, J. F. B. Rhoads, John Vogt, Isaac S. Stahr, and J. S. Mengel, most of whom were either clergymen or physicians.

The derivative and imitative character of dialect verse is seen from the fact that few influences from German writers appeared, while in its *corpus* there is much translation from English and American writers. The Pennsylvania Dutch had forgotten Germanic ways.

One favorite for translation was Longfellow's "The Village Blacksmith," a poem that children learned in English schools. Here is H. L. Fisher's rendering of the first two lines:

> *Dort unna 'm alte Keschtebaum*
> *Dort war der alt Schmidtschop . . .*

And Auld Lang Syne is thus begun:

> *Sol alt bekanntschaft nimmermehr*
> *Bei uns erinnert sein? . . .*

He also put into dialect the celebrated recruiting ballad of the Civil War:

> *Wir kumme, Fater Abraham,*
> *Drei hunnert tausend meh' . . .*

And George Mays began Longfellow's "Song of Life"

> *Sag me net mit betruebten Mut*
> *'N lehre Traum is 's Leben gar . . .*

Mer marche 'rum darch grosse Crowds,	We march about through great crowds,
Das is 'n Wese—Music, shouts,	This is some business— music, shouts
Als wann der Bresident do waer.	As if the President were here.

Ich nem mei Schere im grosse Show—	I take my part in the great show,
Grik mer Diploma—"magna cum"—	Get my diploma, *magna cum;*
Es scheint ich bin doch net so dumm	It seems I am not so stupid
Wie dheel von denne Yankees do . . .	As some Yankees around here.

Ziegler excelled at translations: Longfellow's "Snowflakes," "The Reaper and the Plow," "Hymn to the

What is significant is that it is American and not German poets who are the forces stirring the muse in the Pennsylvania dialect.

Meanwhile, the almanacs that were appearing in nearly every town from the provincial printshops continued the newspaper tradition of bringing out anecdotal and humorous pieces in dialects of all kinds. Many of

kerzlich en Kalb krickt hot un ansemol en wenig kickt, wie die Sällie anfangt:

"Juscht en Dahler un Dreiviertel die Woch und von Morgets bis Owets schaffe wie en Nigger—ich duh's meinersechs nimme lang! Nau steh mir still, dreckig Thier, oder ich kick dich dass du brillst. Juscht en Dahler und Dreiviertel for so dreckige Küh zu melke, un alle Woch an Wäsch, die zwee Ziwer voll macht, ich duh's gewiss net meh lang. Nau kick noch emol, denoh kick ich dichi—

The graveyard on the farm where Henry Harbaugh grew up. Of this he wrote:

Dort gab ich ihr mei Färewell	'Twas there I gave her my good-bye
Ich weinte als ich's gab,	There, did her blessing crave,
'S war's letschte Mol in däre Welt	And, oh, with what a mother's heart
Das ich ihr's gewe hab!	She that sought blessing gave;
Befor ich widder kumme bin	It was the last,—ere I returned
War sie in ihrem Grab.	She rested in her grave.

them are clearly of local origin. Here is one from the *Adler Calender* for 1904, just at the turn of the century:

WAS DIE SÄLLIE ZU SICH SELWER GESCHWÄTZT HOT.

Mister Drucker: Ich hab do letzt im Fudergang der Mahd zugehorcht, wie sie beim Melke for sich selbert geschwätzt hot. Ofkohrs hot sie net gewisst, dass ich im Fudergang bin, sonst hätt sie's net geduh. Nau, for euch zu weise was dehl Mäd for Gedanke hen, will ich euch der Sällie ihr Selbstgespräch do shicke.

Sie hot sich unnig die wollstrehmig Kuh gehockt, die erst

Ich muss kickige Küh melke un die Mary leit mit ihrem John im Bett, ich muss sie for Breckfest rufe un denoh muss mer schier als noch en Stund warte, eb sie reddy sin— for was kann ich net ah heiern; ich wess die Zeit, dass die Mary Küh gemokle hot, so gut wie ich, und nau leit sie im Bett bis die Erwed geschafft is—Kickhst du Räskel schun wieder!—(Desmol tschumpt die Säly uf und kickt die wollstremig Kuh in die Rippe, und hockt sich dernoh unnig die scheckig kuh.)

Des is aus un vorbei!—Die erst Chänce, dass ich krick, heier ich—darnoh melk ich mei eegene Küh oder gar kenne. Juscht loss mich der Fred nochemol von der Singschul hehm sehne, ich gebs ihn zu versteh'n dass ich en scheb Fedder-

Sunbonnets and Shoofly Pies

Im Ernfeld.

Von H. L Fischer, Esq., York, Pa.

Im Ernfeld wars net so wie nau,
  Mit Pätente Maschine;
Es war en große Cumpanie
Un juscht en rechte Dschubilie,
  En Dagloh zu verdiene,
Mer hot so viel dazu gelacht,
Es hot die Erwet leicht gemacht.

Die Prentißbuwe aus der Stadt
  Sin ah als kumme ernte;
Sie hen zwee Woche Freiheit ghat
Bun Handwerkserwet in der Stadt—
  So halwer ausgelernte;
Erscht ware sie als matt un bleech,
Doch uf zu alle Deiwelsstreech.

Sie ware Morgets artlich faul
  Un sin net früh ufgstanne;
Im Bett hen sie sich rum gedreht,
Bis sie als gheert hen, daß die Meed
  Schun rapple mit de Panne;
Un sell war ah die eenzig Jacht,
Wu selle Kerls hot wacker gemacht.

Dann wanns emol bal Mittag war,
  Hot's Mittagshorn geblose,
Des hot sie wieder umgerührt—
Was hen die Stadtkerls als gedschiert,

  Wie freiheitsfroh' Franzose;
So'n Appetit for Mittagesse!
Was hen die Stadtkerls doch als gesse!

Un wann sie s Horn geblose hen,
  Dann hot der Wasser gheilt;
Wie gschwind war Sichel, Reff un Sens
Un Reche ghanke uf der Fens,
  Un heemzu hen mer g'eilt;
Noth wann mer als sin kumme so,
Was war der Wasser doch so froh!

Noch Mittag war en Stund noch Ruh,
  Im Schatte dort so kühl.
Die Alte hen ihr Peife gschmokt,
Die Buwe hen die Meed geplogt,
  Ebmols schier gar zu viel;
Sie hen ebmols net kenne ruge,
Bei so unruhige, knitze Buwe.

Es ware als zwee extra Ims—
  's is wohr—es is keen Traam;
Es Zehuhr- un's Vieruhr-Stück,
Hen mer oft gesse an der Krick,
  Am alte Keschtebaam:
Un besser hot's uns gschmackt dort draus,
Als 's bescht am Disch im feinschte Haus.

Was hen die Meed uns als gebrocht
  In selle große Körb?
Ei, frische Weck un Brod un Fleesch,
Butter un Pickels, Milch un Käs,
  Un Eppelpei so merb.
Un 's war nix bessers in der Welt,
Als so en Esse draus im Feld.

Sell war en schöne Cumpanie,
  Lebhafte junge Leit.
Die Meed hen grecht un glacht un gsunge,
Die Buwe hen'ne noch gebunne—
  Ich wot 's weer noch so heut.
O, was 'n Cumpanie alleweil,
Zwee Mann, zwee Esel un zwee Gäul!

Wie lohnsam is 's im Ernfeld nau!
  Doch geht die Erwet schmärter.
's werd nix gemeht nau mit der Sens,
Als juscht en Gmaht so an der Fens,
  Die Rieper drin zu stärte.
Mer sin als all um's Stück rum gange,
Bis mer den alte Has hen gfange.

Von Weitem hot's als viel geguckt
  Als wie en Trupp Schneegäns,
Der Rieper macht en große Jacht;
  Doch was hot als die Musik gmacht?
Es Bloshorn un die Sens.
Un wann mer hen die Sens als gschliffe,
Noth hen die Vögel 's ärgscht gepiffe.

Dialect poem by H. L. Fisher, of York, as printed in the *Adler* almanac for 1888. Notice that the spelling of the dialect is attuned to those who read German.

bett un bal hunnert Dah'ler Cäsch Geld—ich will wette, sell macht's fertig, un wann er's vetseh will, dann werd er beigosch des neechscht mol gesäckt un em Annere selle Hints geschmisse. Ich melk ken sechs Küh meh un duh all die anner Erwed for en Dahler un Dreiviertel die Woch. Fangst du an zu trippele, du schekige Hex—wart juscht bis dich epper schunscht melkt—die Ditz werre dir noch annerschter gerisse werre. Ich heier eb drei Monat sum sin— werscht's sehne. Annere Leut ihr Bäbykleeder wäsche, sell bin ich ledig—ich wäsch mei eegene! Die Woch noch, sell is all—loss sie epper schunscht kriege, ich geh hehm un krick mei Sach reddy. Wann's der Fred net is, dann is 's *epper schunscht—der Joe hot mir do letzt die Hand net for niks gebe.*

(Sell hot des Selbstgspräch geendt, for die Stalldähr is ufgange un sie hot gemeent es deet epper kumme. Sie hot awer bis alleweil net ausgefunne, dass ich im Fudergang Alles mit angehört hab—aber wette will ich, dass die Sällie heiert—so geschwindt wie sie epper frogt devor.—Es is en Tschäns do fer epper, sell is plehn wie der Dag.)
Dummeldich.

Translation:

HOW SALLY TALKED TO HERSELF

Mister Printer: A while ago, from the feeding-passage in a barn I heard a maid talking to herself while she was milking. Of course, she did not know that I was in the feeding-passage or else she wouldn't have done it. Now, so you may know what kind of thoughts such girls have, I send along Sally's speech to herself.

As she sat beneath a fresh cow which just had calved and which kicked now and then, Sally began:

"Just a dollar and three quarters a week and work like a nigger from morning to night—I'll not do it very much longer! Now stand still, you dirty beast, or I'll kick you so you cry. Just a dollar and three quarters to milk such dirty cows, and a wash every week which makes two tubs full; I surely won't do it much longer. If you kick once more I'll kick you! I have to milk these kicking cows and Mary lies in bed with her John; I have to call them for breakfast and then we have to wait almost an hour before they are ready—why can't I marry. I remember the time when Mary

Sunday morning at the Ziegel Church. (*From a photograph by W. W. Dietrich.*) This is how Lee Light Grumbine described this experience:

Der Klingel-klang der Sonntag's Klocke—	The cling-clang of the Sunday bell,
Die Vögel im Thurm verstort un' verschrocke—	Disturbs and scares the birds in the tower,
Zum Gottesdienst die Leut zu locke,	And bids the people to worship,
Durchs Stille Thal schallt,	Resounding through the still valley.
Statts in der Faulheit dehe'm rum hocke,—	Instead of sitting around lazily at home,
Üwer Hüwel und wald.	Over hill and woods.

milked cows, just like me, and now she lies in the bed while the work is being done. You rascal, you kicked again! (With this Sally jumped up and kicked the fresh cow in the ribs, and then she sat down again beneath the mottled cow.)

"This is over and done with! The first chance that I get I'll marry, thereafter I'll milk my own cows or none at all. Just let Fred bring me home from singing school and I'll give him to understand that I have a pretty featherbed and almost a hundred dollars in cash, and I'll bet that'll clinch it, and if he doesn't want to understand then he will be jostled again and other hints thrown his way. I'll milk no six cows anymore and do other work for just a dollar and three quarters a week. Are you starting to walk off, you wretched witch! Just wait until someone else milks you! Then your teats will be torn differently! I'll marry before three months are out, you'll see! I'm tired of washing other people's baby things—I'll wash my own! This week yet, that's all! Just let them get someone else, I'll go home and get my things ready. If it's not Fred, then it'll be somebody else; Joe didn't give me the hand for nothing."

(This ended the speech to herself, for the barn door opened and she thought that someone came in. She never did find out that I stood in the feeding-passage all the time and listened—but I'll bet that Sally marries, as soon as someone asks her. Here is a chance for someone, which is as plain as day.)

Hurry-up.

Almanacs and newspapers are full of such pieces, a vast area of dialect literature that has not even been studied, not to mention being collected in anthologies. In these pieces, we say, the Pennsylvania German dialect came of age.

These old German almanacs contained a sparkling mixture of languages, moving from High German poetry written both abroad and in America, from High German anecdotes and many kinds of south German dialect pieces obviously of European origin, to the following kind of local story, obviously written in Reading, and still spelled for German readers. This appeared in the *Adler Calendar* for 1885.

EN TRÄMP STORY

Er hot arrick müd geguckt, der arm Kerl, wie er üwer die Lenkeschter Brick geloffe kumme is een Owed letscht Summer. Er war noch en junger Kerl, awer sei Kleeder ware lumpig un er war dreckig un verschwitzt un ausgewohre, un des hot ihn alt gucke mache un schwach. Er is langsam sei Weg fort geloffe un es letscht kummt er an die Penn Schtross. Wie er so weit kumme war, trafft er zwee fäncy gedresste junge Kerl an, so vun der Sort was mer "Dudes" heest. Die hen dan grad gemeent do wär nau en bully Tschäns for en wennig G'spass.

"Hello!" ruft der eend vun ihme, "wie gehts Laafe draus Wescht?"

"Ich weess es net," sagt der Trämp, "ich bin rei kumme im me Pälace Car."

"Was hoscht g'schaft dort draus?"

"Dudes uffgebroche for Riegelweg Ballast."

Des hot die Zwee bös gemacht, weil die Leut, was neekscht ware, so mächtig gelacht hen.

"Wann d' runner kummscht an die Cherry Alley, schlag ich die Schtoffens aus dir!" kreischt noh eens vun dene Dudes.

"Es is plenty Platz grad do," sagt der Trämp.

"All recht—Look out!"—Un sie sin an nanner. Die Dudes sin grad all beed uff der Trämp getschumpt, un dann is ebbes g'happent. Es hot gekleppert for en Sekund oder zwee. Dann hot der eend Dude sich z'samme gelese aus de Specht von me Bauerewage Rad was er nei verwickelt war, un der anner war an der Erwet for sei Zähn aus em Hals zo hole was ebber ihm nei geschlage hot g'hatte, un sei Nas war breet g'schlage un hot geblut wie en Sau.

Der armselig Trämp war bei dere Zeit schun langsam uff em Weg die Penn Schtross nuff. "Es duht mich allemol schlecht fühle mache wann so uffgefiederte kräftige junge Kerl en armer Deiwel wie mich leddere wölle," hot er gemeent. "Ich hab nix rechts gesse in drei Dag, schunscht hätt ich sie verleicht weh geduh!"

Translation:

A TRAMP STORY

He looked very tired, the poor fellow, as he came walking across the Lancaster bridge one evening last summer. He was still a young man, but his clothes were lumpy and he was dirty and sweaty and worn out, and this made him look old and weak. Slowly he went his way and finally came to Penn street. When he had come this far he met two fancily dressed young fellows of the kind that we call "dudes." They thought that here was a chance for some bully fun.

"Hello!" the one called out to him, "how's the walking out west?"

"I don't know," the man said, "I came in on a Palace Car."

"What did you work out there?"

"I broke up dudes to make railroad ballast."

This made the two angry, because the people who heard it laughed heartily.

"If you come down to Cherry Alley we'll knock the stuffings out of you," one of the dudes cried out.

"There's plenty of room right here," said the Tramp.

"All right—look out!"—and they went at it. Both dudes jumped on the tramp right away, and then something happened. It thundered for a second or two. Then the one dude picked himself out of the tracks of a farm-wagon wheel where he was wrapped up, and the other was at work picking his teeth out of his neck where someone had hit them, and his nose was knocked broad and he bled like a sow.

The poor tramp by this time was slowly going his way up Penn Street. "It makes me feel bad when such overfed young fellows want to beat up an old devil like me," he mused. "I haven't eaten right for three days, else I might have hurt them."

After Pennsylvania Dutch dialect writing had reached such elasticity and competence in a German-oriented environment, being spelled for readers of the German language, a second stage appeared wherein dialect was written for those who were taught to read English. This change was gradual, having been evident earlier; and it was to be opposed by several writers who were well-acquainted with German dialect literature. Still, as the twentieth century advanced, dialect writing became the toy of the chauvinist, a vehicle for the "professional" Pennsylvania Dutchman.

Dr. Ezra Grumbine, born in 1848, whose main works were written in English, was one of the earliest writers oriented toward the English language; but this was not true of the scholar and linguist, Charles C. More, who, while residing in Europe, made a formal study of European dialects and approached the problem with scholarly self-consciousness. Some of More's work was of first quality. Louise Weitzel was columnist for the *Lititz Express,* offering both prose and verse for many years, even as she lamented the dearth of dialect writers. Indeed, many local newspapers published columnists who employed dialect for many purposes, like Astor C. Wuchter, whose philosophical and anecdotal works were a medium for his fine sense of vocabulary. Thomas Hess Harter made the pen-name Boonastiel famous in the Bellefonte *Keystone Gazette;* with Harter satire was an expression of his strong ideas. Harvey M. Miller made "Solly Hulsbuck" famous in his volumes of *Pennsylvania Dutch Poems* (1906) and *Pennsylvania German Poems* (1906). Miller also wrote prose, which came out as *Pennsylvania German Stories* (1907) and *G'shboss und Arnscht* (Fun and Seriousness) (1939).

In 1927 an important event took place in Pennsylvania Dutch dialect literature: Clarence Iobst and Edward Clewell of Emmaus put on a skit, the start of a remarkable career as Pennsylvania German playwrights. On April 28, 1928, a play called *"En Quart Millich un en Halb Beint Rahm"* (A Quart of Milk and a Half Pint of Cream) had its first performance and before the public was satisfied the show played five times. Going on the road, it ran for at least sixty performances, making it the most successful dialect play. As in Elizabethan drama, all the roles were played by males. The plot appears from the symbolism of its title: the wife is a quart of milk while the husband is a half-pint of cream. In a situation of folksy gossip, but realistic, spry, and not bawdy, this play was performed before cosmopolitan audiences as many as fifteen hundred times.

The successor to Clarence Iobst was Paul Wieand—producer, actor, writer, craftsman, painter. His folklore players were widely known and he was the first to employ

radio as a medium for folk drama. He adapted an English play, *"Der Kreitzweg Schtor"* (*The Crossroads Store*), wherein he wrote many songs to well-known tunes. He also wrote many other works, one of which was played at the Allentown Civic Little Theater as well as in many counties of eastern Pennsylvania. He teamed with Harry H. Reichard to play the skit over an Allentown radio station, "Asebe and Sabine," a continuing drama that ran for many years.

Of course, the high point in any dramatic literature is translation of Shakespeare. Ralph Wiest Schlosser, college president, carried this sort of translation to its pinnacle, having put much of the bard into the dialect, some of which has been performed. Here is Portia's speech from the *Merchant of Venice:*

PORTIA: *Barmharzichkeit lost sich net zwinge;*
    es fallt wie der warm Rege fum Himmel uff
        die Aerd;
    es bringt en doppeleter Seege;
    es dut deem gut der gebt un dem der nemmt;
    im schtarrickschte is es mechtichscht;
    es is besser agsehne im e Kehnich as sei Kron,
    Me Kehnich sei Macht is uscht in weltliche Dinge,
    awwer doch erschtaernst die Leit un der sel
    farriche sie sich weeich Kehnich un nemme sich
        in Acht.
    Awwer Barmharzichkeit is greeser as me Kehnich
        sei Macht.
    Es finnt sich in die Kehnich ihre Haerzer;
    es gmant eem an die Nadur Gottes.
    Weltliche Macht weist sich's menscht wie Gottes
    wass Barmharzichkeit en Sals is zu Gerechtigkeit.
    Un nau Jut, wann du Gerechtigkeit noch bischt,
    denk mol dra dass kens fun uns seelich waerre
    kennt darrich Gerechtigkeit alee. Mir beete
    dass Gott sich erbarme soll iwwer uns,
    und im seeme Gebet das mir selwer gneedich
        sei mechte.
    Ich hab des nau gsat das du net so hart sei
        meechscht
    uff den Mann. Awwer wann du schtuwworich
        sei wit,
    muss die Kort ewwe den Mann in dei Hend
        gewwe.

The dialect has indeed become a plastic medium for the expression of ideas.

Edith Romig Fink also wrote skits, eight longer ones and four one-act plays, all in folk style, for performances in the Western Salisbury Church. Some of her plays were repeated as many as twenty times before enthusiastic audiences—folk drama of significance. Verona P. Laubach wrote prize-winning plays on common themes. John Y. Kohl wrote *'N Inside Chob* as well as radio skits and two other full-length plays. Thomas Brendle wrote dialect dramas, as did also Preston A. Barba. Because the dialect was chiefly spoken language it could be suited to dramatic presentation. However, few serious themes were taken up; most of the work was folksy and provincial.

While the Pennsylvania Dutch dialect drama was thus coming of age, other writers appeared who brought dialect literature to new levels of competence and self-consciousness. Lloyd Moll, whose works were first brought out in a newspaper column, was a physician turned poet and his novelette *Am Schwartze Baer* (At the Black Bear) is competently done. Ralph Funk began to rhyme in the 1920s and he lived to see his works published by the Pennsylvania German Folklore Society. Arthur D. Graeff called himself the poet of the Tulpehocken and many of his poems came out in his newspaper column, including songs to well-known tunes.

In 1938 the newly formed Pennsylvania German Folklore Society published a volume of dialect verse entitled *Gezwitscher* (*Twitterings*) by John Birmelin (1873–1950). Here Pennsylvania German literature reached the zenith of its achievement, expressing the full promise that Harbaugh had envisioned. This was followed in 1963 by *The Later Poems of John Birmelin*.

Unquestionably, John Birmelin was the most versatile poet to use the Pennsylvania Dutch dialect. Musician by profession, trained in metrics, taught to spell correctly (no mean feat!), and gifted with an astonishing vocabulary, Birmelin carried dialect verse, both here and in Germany, to levels hard to equal. He takes his place in the roster of poets who make claim to permanent fame. Humorous, nostalgic, romantic, satirical—these old-fashioned words apply to his work, marking him as a typical folk poet, set off from the main stream of dialect versifying by his competence and skill. His translations from Mother Goose, from Robert Louis Stevenson, and from Palatine dialect verse into the Pennsylvania patois lift him above the usual run of verse-smiths. It is in his three narrative ballads, "Regina Hartmann," "Der Laaf Kaaf" (The Walking Purchase), and "Celia von Bernville" that he achieves greatness. Here he takes folk stories and gives them exquisite expression. John Birmelin represents the late flowering of the Pennsylvania Dutch dialect, now soundly American, an ornament to the literature of his province. He was our best poet, writing,

> Mei Land, ich sing von dir,
> Siess iss die Freiheit mir,
>   Do will ich sei:
> So wie die alde Leit,
> So fiehl ich aa noch heit,
> Bin dir zu yedra Zeit,
>   Immer gedrei.
> (My Country 'Tis of Thee . . .)

9

Sauerkraut, Schnitz, and Shoofly Pies

The Pennsylvania Dutch are famous for food. However, they did not erect great bulwarks of foodstuffs from early days. Abundance was a later development. For the evidence suggests that from the time of the founding of the colony to the American Revolution—except for Protestant feast days of baptism, wedding, funeral—the Pennsylvania Dutch lived quite frugally. Traveller Cazenove said:

> they live on potatoes, buckwheat cakes, instead of bread. They deny themselves everything costly.

The rich cuisine with which they have been credited, if ever it did exist, was a later development.

There were excesses. The old pastors never did stop railing against too much feeding at baptisms, weddings, funerals. These special events were marked by a glut of food and drink; the visitors from afar had to be refreshed. Mittleberger, one-time organist at Trappe, gave this description of a funeral custom that now has gone astray:

> While the people were coming in, good cake cut into pieces is passed around on a large tin plate to those present, each person receives then, in a goblet, a hot West India rum punch into which lemon, sugar, and juniper berries are put, which gives it a delicious taste. After that sweet cider, heated, is passed.

These, though, were unusual events.

It is easy for us who are Pennsylvania Dutch to romanticize about Pennsylvania Dutch food. The famed fertility and abundance of our farms during the second half of the nineteenth century, the harvests that still are gathered help us recall with some degree of exaggeration the groaning tables of our youth whereby we remember the abundance at grandmother's. These were the feast days that stick in our minds; we tend to forget the simpler meals.

So, while it is true that Pennsylvania Dutch cuisine was different and even noteworthy, while the Dutch did make their land into a garden, when we read the early travelers who passed through here we understand that this affluence came after an earlier period of frugality. At the same time, our cooking was noticed by George Washington, who used Pennsylvania Dutch soldiers as messboys and who took Pennsylvania Dutch cooks back to Mount Vernon. Any honest historian must agree that our cuisine was a late development; still, while they did not use "bought" foods, the travelers agreed that they had enough to eat.

Dr. Johann Daniel Schoepff, who traveled formally through eastern America in 1783 but who had been here earlier with the Hessians, reported that gardening was in its infancy, perhaps even a neglected art. But his meaning becomes plain with his next remark, where he says that gardens were strictly utilitarian, with no effort to landscape. He wrote:

The wavy decorations were put on pie plates so that each family could identify its own pieces. Generally one or two dozen pieces were made with similar designs, all for one family.

agement. . . . Several of our vegetables first were introduced by the German troops—e.g., kohlrabi, broccoli, and the black raddish. But certain of our good fruits are lacking . . . such as plums, apricots, walnuts, good pears, the domestic chestnut, gooseberries, and others. . . . The American is satisfied with great yields of his cherry, apple, and peach trees.

Was Dr. Schoepff thinking of the so-called "English" walnut, and was he ignoring the local Pennsylvania chestnut?

He wrote that the Philadelphia market was held twice a week, Wednesdays and Saturdays, when all the bells of the city were rung to announce it.

Most of the vegetables and flowers of southern Europe have been introduced. Many of them do well and have even been improved, but others grow worse under careless man-

People from a distance, especially the Germans, come into Philadelphia in great covered wagons, loaded with all manner of provender, bringing with them rations for themselves and feed for their horses—for they sleep in their wagons. Besides, carts and horses bring in from all directions the rich surplus of the country. . . . Meats are supplied not only by the city butchers, but by the country people as well—for America is not yet cursed with exclusive guild rights. . . . The American on the whole, like the English, consumes more meat than vegetables and the market furnishes them the choicest store, cut very neatly. Besides the

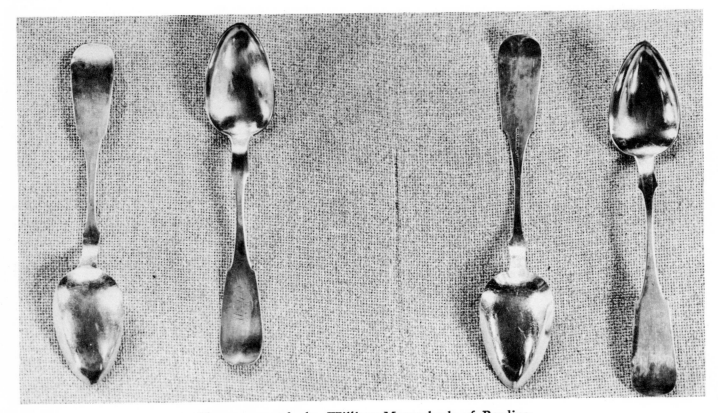

Teaspoons made by William Mannerbach of Reading.
Photograph courtesy the Berks County Historical Society

Outdoor bake oven at the Pennsylvania Farm Museum,
Landis Valley.

customary sorts of meat, Europeans find in season several
dishes new to them, such as raccoon, opossum, fish-otters,
bear-bacon, and bear's foot, etc., as well as many indigenous
birds and fishes. In products of the garden the market, although plentiful, is not of great variety, for divers of our
better European cabbages and other vegetables are lacking;
on the other hand all sorts of melons and many kinds of
pumpions [*sic*] are seen in great quantity, and fruits too.
(I, pp. 112–13)

Thus, even after the Revolutionary War there was no
want. He continued:

The inhabitants are not only well-clothed but well fed, and,
comparatively, better then their betters in Europe. . . .

Few families can be found who do not enjoy daily their
wheat bread, good meats, and fruits, cyder, beer, and rum.
Want oppresses but few. (I, p. 113)

During this earlier period, then, Pennsylvania was
mainly agricultural, exporting much wheat. In fact, its
chief exports were listed as follows: wheat, flour and biscuit, peas, beans, Indian corn, salted meats, bacons and
hams, dried and smoked game, salted and dried fish
(shad and herring), honey, and the like. If such foods
were being sent abroad, what was being retained? Still,
in view of the Dutch propensity to sell the better and eat

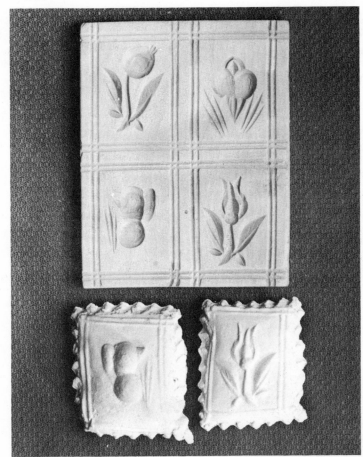

Springerle molds and cookies made therefrom. *Courtesy Mrs. Mary deTurk Hottenstein*

long winter ahead when there was no canning and no refrigeration? Root cellars were everywhere. Some vegetables were buried in the early fall.

Generally speaking, early Pennsylvania Dutch food may be classified by the way in which it was preserved. During the harvesting months the *Hausfrau* was busy preserving in one way or another the succession of crops coming from garden and field. Fowl was always plentiful; meats were somewhat of a problem, but dairy products were in constant supply.

At least four processes were used for preserving food during this earlier period: fermentation, drying, salting, and smoking. Perhaps a fifth should be mentioned: pickling. It was through these methods of preserving foods that the early character of the Pennsylvania Dutch cuisine arose.

Of course, fermentation was an ancient process, well

The traditional dove in a cookie cutter. *Courtesy Mrs. Mary deTurk Hottenstein*

the poorer themselves, we cannot conclude much about the quality of their table.

Oddities appeared, bred on the farms. Traveler Schoepff saw a cross between a cock and a duck, a perfect hen in the front, but in the rear it was formed like a duck. Its feet were half webbed, set far back on the body so that it waddled. This was a freak.

During these years drinks were noteworthy. There was large consumption of liquors. The people made good cheer with cider and with a drink made from the oil of cider—applejack—a "pretty strong drink." Nor was all the Indian corn fed to the hogs or shipped abroad. In 1810 York had 399 distilleries, almost one for every farm, and Lancaster County had 191. It was easier to turn corn into corn liquor than to transport it. In a prospering wheat economy, corn was not for human consumption as a grain.

Of course, the main problem of early food production remained preservation. How could foods be kept for the

Cookie cutters. *Courtesy Mrs. Mary deTurk Hottenstein*

known in Europe where grapes had been fermented and the forebears of the Pennsylvania Dutch were among the best vintners of Europe. As mentioned above, Pennsylvania insects made extensive cultivation of many kinds of grapes impossible.

The early Pennsylvania economy was wheat-dominated. To this must be added the inherited tradition of baking with yeast, making leavened baked goods. When we put these two together, it is inevitable that fermented doughs became the hallmark of Pennsylvania Dutch baking. Home-made yeast added to various kinds of flour —from summer wheat, winter wheat, rye, or buckwheat —was fermented first in the large dough-troughs of wood and then transferred to straw baskets. From these fermented materials came the many breads and "raised cakes" that are characteristic of our cooking.

Friday was of course baking day. So Thursday after-

Cupboards, cabbage-cutter, and other kitchen utensils. *Courtesy Mr. Wallace Wetzel*

Cabbage cutter, pie plates, kitchen tools. *Courtesy Mr. Wallace Wetzel*

noon large amounts of dough were mixed in wooden troughs and then set out in straw baskets to work. This was for breads and cakes. Left to rise overnight, as the yeasty doughs fermented, they were ready for baking Friday morning. A huge fire was started in the outdoor bake oven; its stones were thoroughly heated; then plates of leavened dough were put in and soon the aroma filled the yard—the breads and cakes were being baked!

However, flours were supplemented by other substances: mashed potatoes, oatmeal, eggs, bran, raisins, and so on. Biscuits of all sorts were made.

One kind of bread was unleavened: Dunkard communion bread served at the religious love-feasts. Here each square of bread was marked with five nail-prints symbolizing the five wounds of Our Lord. Moravian love-

mon cakes, and, of course, raised doughnuts, which must be distinguished from unraised crullers.

Doughnuts were for *Fassnacht* (Shrove Tuesday), one Catholic custom surviving in Protestant Pennsylvania. Doughs were set out in straw baskets on Monday for raising, traditionally cut into squares or rectangles, and then fried in deep fat instead of baked. They were served for breakfast with hot coffee on Shrove Tuesday. There is an approved method of serving *Fassnacht* doughnuts— split in half and generously spread with honey.

"Raised" cakes were also baked outdoors on Friday, while "fancy" cakes were done in the kitchen and were not raised. Layer and loaf cakes were made with baking sodas and powders, which were store-bought substances. But they were flavored with domestic substances—apple-butter, walnuts, hickory nuts, cider, spices, chocolate, and the like. They were served on occasion and for the "company" of Sunday afternoons. If the contrast between plain and fancy has any meaning, it suggests the difference between "raised" and "fancy" cakes.

Two characteristic bits of Dutch baking were not done with fermented doughs—the lowly pretzel and shoofly

Earthenware crocks like these were used for storing foods, including sauerkraut.

feasts used leavened breads served with coffee in the sanctuary.

"Raised" cakes became a Pennsylvania Dutch specialty. They were made for dunking and so were known as "coffee cakes." Here is where Pennsylvania Dutch baking excelled, for nowhere else was the baking of fermented doughs sweetened with sugar and with the imaginations of the bakers. These plain "raised" cakes must be distinguished from fancy loaf or layer cakes, the latter generally being made in kitchen ovens for "company." Usually the family table was adorned with one kind or another of the many "raised" or yeasted cakes and rolls: "Light cake," coffee wreath, funny cake, "Moravian cake," Moravian sugar cakes, crumb cakes, "Schwenkfelder cake," cinna-

Decorated sauerkraut crock from around the middle of the nineteenth century.

The restored kitchen in the Pennsylvania Farm Museum,
Landis Valley, and home-baked bread.

cakes or pies, the latter being one of our symbols for Pennsylvania Dutch culture. The pretzel is, of course, European, perhaps even Latin, in origin; at one time it was used as a gift, especially in the Mosel valley, which cuts through the European homeland of the Pennsylvania Dutch. There may be some question as to its early appearance here, for as a word it is dated as coming into use some time after the Civil War.

Shoofly Pies are different. These are soundly Pennsylvanian. And there are many ways of making them. Not really pies, they are a poor man's cake, made in the earlier days with sorghum, later with molasses, and with brown rather than granulated sugar. Because of their ubiquity I have used them as a symbol in the title of this book. Here is a tried recipe for shoofly from Lehigh County:

In kitchen fireplaces like this one in the Historical Society of Berks County the early Pennsylvania *Hausfrau* prepared her meals.

Mix crumbs made from one and a half cup of flour, one cup of brown sugar, one quarter cup of butter or lard. Then take one half cup of New Orleans molasses, one half cup of hot water, scalding one half-teaspoon of soda in molasses and water. Fill two pre-rolled pie crusts with the molasses mixture and put crumbs on top. Bake until firm.

Next to "raised cakes" and breads made with yeasted flours, the chief of fermented Pennsylvania foods was our national dish, sauerkraut, fermented shredded cabbage. Cabbages were easily grown and fermentation easy to encourage; indeed, sauerkraut is best when it is in that condition where nothing more can happen to it! It was fermented, as soon as cabbages matured, in large earthen-ware crocks. One put about three inches of shredded cabbage at the bottom of a crock, salting lightly. Next, the kraut was pounded with a stamping tool until all juices were squeezed out. Layer was added upon layer of kraut, then stamped until the salty juices rose. When the crock was full it was covered with a cloth, covered again in turn with a round board weighted down with rocks, then left to ferment in a warm place. In about a week a scum formed. The cloth was washed and the crock put in a cool place. In about two weeks the kraut was ready. Some experts used grape leaves instead of cloths to cover the kraut.

Another vegetable sometimes fermented like cabbage

was turnips. This was not so popular as the kraut.

Another method of preserving foods before the days of refrigeration and canning was by drying.

Dried corn was strictly Pennsylvanian, an example of the old custom of dehydrating vegetables and fruits. It is said that this came from the Indians, but this is not proven. All sorts of foods were dried: beans, peas, and fruits. This method was also well known in Germany —and who has not tasted dried string beans cooked with home-cured ham? A dish fit for kings!

Drying fruit has given us the most characteristic Pennsylvania Dutch dish, *Schnitz un Gnepp* (dried apple slices and dumplings), cooked with a generous slab of home-cured ham. If there is any dish that characterizes the traditional Pennsylvania Dutch cuisine it is this, which came to us from the old land and served well during the earlier period. As with most dried foods, there is a trick to cooking Schnitz, and that is to soak them overnight in water. Then in the morning one began to boil a chunk of ham (dinner was always at noon) for about two hours, and then dried apple slices were added to the brewing ham. Later some brown sugar was added. The dumplings were mixed from egg, butter, and flour into a moist, yet somewhat stiff, batter and then dropped into the baking-ham brew. Characteristically, during the earlier period dumplings were "raised," making them soft and airy. Some would soak the Schnitz in cider before cooking.

During the earlier period, meats coming from domestic animals were supplemented by wild game. There was much hunting. In fact, traveler Schoepff wrote,

There is no lack of . . . game; elks wander hither at times.

Trivets and other kitchen utensils. *Courtesy Mr. Wallace Wetzel*

The turkey-cock is seen more frequently here than near the coast. The passage-dove is found here in pairs. (I, p. 161)

Indeed, almost all wild game was used as food, even finding its way into the markets of the city.

Still, wild or domestic, meats had to be dressed, so butchering was a winter activity, a frequent one. Very early in the morning the assemblage would gather; great

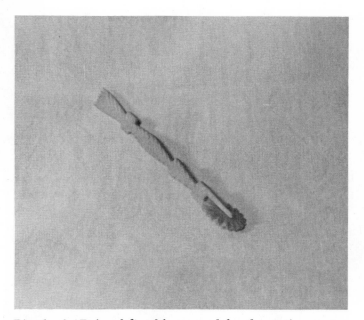

Piewheel (*Boiraedel*) of bone used for decorating pastry for pies.

tubs of water were steaming in the yard. Everybody had his job. The animal was neatly dispatched after having been maneuvered into proper position; generally he was axed to death. Blooded, de-bristled, and cleaned, the animal now was turned over to the women; the intestines were emptied and cleansed, and then made ready for sausages. The carcass was skillfully dissected; chops, steaks, and bacons were cut off; all scrapings were kept for future workings. The next day the various meat dishes were prepared: sausages of all kinds, tripe, and finally the famous but misnamed "Philadelphia scrapple" was prepared, so called because there is where it was sold.

Now scrapple was an ancient pork dish that was just as soundly Pennsylvania Dutch as haggis is Scotch. The latter consists of the head, liver, and lungs of a sheep mixed with oatmeal and other meats, baked, and served hot. Unfortunately, no Robert Burns has come in Pennsylvania to celebrate *Pannhaas,* which literally means

"pan rabbit" (which it is not). This corrupts the German *panharst,* which means pan or pot roast. As with the Scottish haggis, Pennsylvania *pannhaas* wastes nothing; all scraps are put into it, including the liquids left in the various kettles after boiling the meats. To these some "good" meats were often added, as well as some meal— buckwheat or cornmeal. This mixture was stirred as it was boiled to a heavy consistency, then was set out on bread pans to cool and harden. Fried scrapple was a frequent White House breakfast during the administration of Herbert Hoover, descendant of Andreas Huber who entered Pennsylvania in 1738.

Other early methods of preserving foods were used by the Pennsylvania Dutch but they were shared by other peoples and were not especially characteristic. Little salting of meats appeared, and because we were not seafaring folk, we did to ham what the Scotch did to herring.

Much dried fruit and vegetables were stored in wicker baskets for the long winters.

Things remained somewhat frugal during the earlier period, although even then characteristic dishes appeared. However, with the developing economy the Pennsylvania Dutch *Hausfrau,* like most women, experienced two great moments of liberation. The first had nothing to do with food; she was freed from long winter days in the *Spinnstube,* making textiles and clothes for her family. With the invention of the Jacquard loom and other devices, she was freed from her endless hours at the spinning wheel. It was at this time that she began to ornament her textiles.

Then, after the Civil War, the Dutch *Hausfrau* was also freed from endless hours in garden and kitchen. The coming of the glass jar and of the tin can, by which foods might be preserved, and the development of commercially produced foods, liberated her from the common cycle of putting up foods from spring to summer.

While the glass jar had appeared with Ezra Dagret in 1817, and while Isaac Winters had experimented with canning as early as 1837, it was not until after the Civil War that foods were preserved commercially. In 1872 Heinrich J. Heinz, a Pennsylvanian, began his commercial establishment for preserving foods, and in the same year Lutz and Scharmer, also Pennsylvanians, began similar industries. In fact, Pennsylvania Dutchmen took the lead in the commercial food-preserving industry.

The commercial preservation of foods changed the domestic life of all American housewives, including the

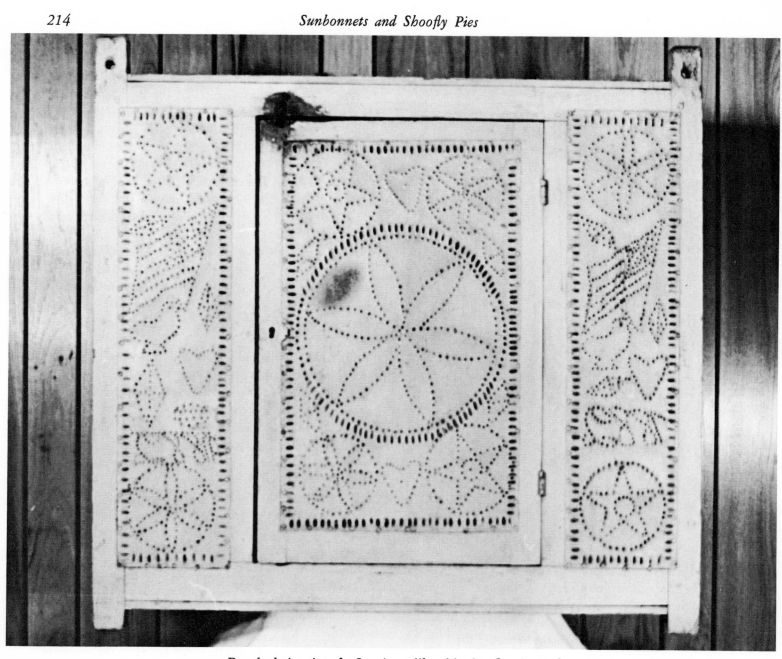

Punched tin pie safe. In pieces like this shoofly pies and
other baked goods were stored until eaten. *Courtesy Mr.
Walter C. Moser.*

Pennsylvania Dutch. It liberated them from the necessity
of stocking the larder against winter's needs. And the
social consequences of this change cannot be exaggerated.
It made the family garden almost obsolete. No longer
were wife and daughters busy from spring to fall. No
longer was their direct orientation and purpose toward
agricultural work. This one event changed an agriculturally oriented economy to a commercially oriented one,

doing away with root-cellars, bake ovens, and the like.
This great revolution in domestic life has been passed
over by the historians, but its consequences were enor-
mous. In Pennsylvania Dutch culture this aspect retains
its significance, because some religious groups still refuse
to use the products of technological food-preservation industries, regarding such procedures as unnecessary.

Now, it is my contention that in the period after this

great revolution we lost the main character of the Pennsylvania Dutch cuisine; I suggest that the character of our food arose from the way it was put up rather than from the way it was cooked. Most of our characteristic foods—sauerkraut, scrapple, schnitz, and "raised cakes" —come from special processes of preparation before cooking. The affluence and prosperity of the Pennsyl-

Springerle molds. *Courtesy Mrs. Mary deTurk Hottenstein*

vania rural scene came after 1865. Then the family-size farm of around one hundred acres came into its own. Here work was satisfying. Here expansion of activity developed, which carried food production beyond the more primitive levels of development that had prevailed during the earlier period.

Most dishes were still in German tradition, inherited from the Old World. Some, however, were new creations. Pies, for example, are a Pennsylvania institution. Almost unknown in Germany, being instead English in

origin, they were taken over by the Pennsylvania Dutch *Hausfrau* and imaginatively realized, typical products of the Americanization process, there being no native Pennsylvania Dutch word for these except the imitative *Boi.*

Pie baking became an art. The real artist in pastry does not measure; all is subtly mixed instinctively, rolled out and carefully kneaded in, and then decorated by brass or bone *Boiraedel* (pie wheels), crimped, curled, twisted, and sometimes even decorated with dough cutouts shaped like flowers and hearts.

And what endless variety of fillings, too! In early spring rhubarb with its tartness, then sorrel, strawberry, cherry —black, sour, white—and raspberry, blackberry, elderberry, apple, raisin, pumpkin, mince. There were of course seasonally fresh fruits, which moved from vine, garden, and orchard to table without much delay. However, to these fruit and berry pies were added the great dishes—oyster pies and corn pies, which were not desserts but main dishes, meals in themselves. The endless variety

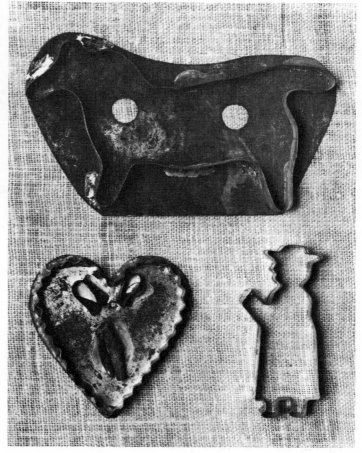

Cookie cutters. *Courtesy Mrs. Mary deTurk Hottenstein*

Springerle mold and cookie. *Courtesy Mrs. Mary deTurk Hottenstein*

of dessert pies, however, was augmented by custards baked in pastry, to which fruits were added with great imagination. Have you ever eaten raspberry custard? Aand what child who grew up in Pennsylvania Dutch country will ever forget what was done with the left-over pastry? The remaining dough was rolled out into pastry, fitted into pans, filled with a mixture of flour, sugar, milk, and butter, and then carefully baked. This creation bore a precise name: *fress es graad,* gulp it down right away, which is just what the children did.

Compared with the English, Pennsylvania Dutch cooks were poor pudding makers. Rather, they disguised fruit in many ways: dumplings were much favored, combining the German tradition of the dumpling with the Pennsylvania love of fruit. Apple dumplings covered with rich sweet cream are more than just an ordinary dessert.

Baking Christmas cookies was a Pennsylvania Dutch monopoly. During the weeks of early Advent all sorts of cookies were made, cut out in various shapes and figures, some of which bore small relationship to the Christmas tale: stars, sheep, shepherds, animals of all kinds, hearts, and flowers. Originally these figured cookies were set beneath the Christmas tree as a pastry ornament, a long-forgotten custom. Sometimes they were pressed out on wooden forms known as *springerles,* a hold-over of an old Catholic custom where such cameos in dough were given as sacrificial gifts in the churches. Sometimes an interesting figure thus impressed was of *der Ewige Jäger,* the rider on the horse.

The frugality of the Pennsylvania Dutch *Hausfrau* scorned "bought" cheeses. Why buy what one can make? She made do with home products and, by making frugality a virtue, created one of the classical Pennsylvania Dutch food combinations—*schmierkaess un lattwaerich,* cottage cheese and apple butter. Living on a family farm where dairy products were basic, she first skimmed her milk and made rich yellow butter which she sold at market, all properly marked by butter molds. What was she to do with what remained? There was no refrigeration, so she made a cheese from the skimmed milk, one of the cheeses that called for sour milk curds.

And cottage cheese was easily made. Thick sour milk was heated over a low fire until the curds and whey

Late designs in springerles, which border on the humorous. The chimney sweep is an interesting figure, prelude
to the coming of Father Christmas. *Courtesy Mrs. Mary
deTurk Hottenstein*

Cooking applebutter and preparing apples at the Pennsylvania Farm Museum, Landis Valley.

parted. Then the curds were bagged, hung up to dry, and when they were separated they were hung in the springhouse. When they were to be used, a cupful or so was taken, salted, and both sweet and sour cream were added, until the cheese had the consistency of saft paste.

Now came the second ingredient, *lattwaerrich,* apple butter. This also was soundly German, coming from the Palatinate, where it often was made of prunes, pears, and apples. This way fruits could be stored.

Making apple butter was a neighborhood social event, a festive occasion. All the neighbors were invited, especially the young people. Fair sweet apples were pared and *schnitzed,* cored. Two barrels of cider were set to boil. The apples were put into the boiling cider and stirred continuously. Then came the precious aroma. Put into crocks and set in the springhouse, there was enough of the dark brown butter to last all winter. And what child will ever forget swabbing out the huge cooling kettles with bare hand and licking the sweet leftovers?

Now for the stroke of genius. Take some freshly mixed cottage cheese and spread it on a thick slice of homemade bread. Top this with a layer of rich brown apple butter. Spread it so thick that it strikes the *owerden* (barn door roof) as it goes on! Here you have a classic, nourishing, and healthy *Schmierkaess un lattwaerrich,* the basis of many a lunch.

Pennsylvania Dutch soups were more than just appetizers; they were meals in themselves. Hearty and full-bodied, used for the main meal, and generously made from meats and vegetables, butter, milk, even sugar and eggs, they form some of the most characteristic of our foods. It was what was added to the basic stock that was important: *riwwele,* dumplings, potatoes. *Riwwele,* small dumplings, were more characteristic than noodles, and they were to the Pennsylvania Dutch what *Spätzle* were to the Swabians.

Chief among Pennsylvania Dutch soup dishes, and also made from many recipes in different forms, was *Grumbeere Supp* (potato soup). To the basic humble potato many things were added—onion, carrots, peas, asparagus, herbs. He who has not tasted a solid bowl of Dutch potato soup, well spiced, does not know what Pennsylvania Dutch women can do with humble ingredients.

Then there is pretzel soup, an unusual dish. Take pretzels, crush them, and add them to a boiling mixture of butter, flour, milk, and water, seasoned to taste. Hearty eating!

In a wheat-dominated economy it is understandable

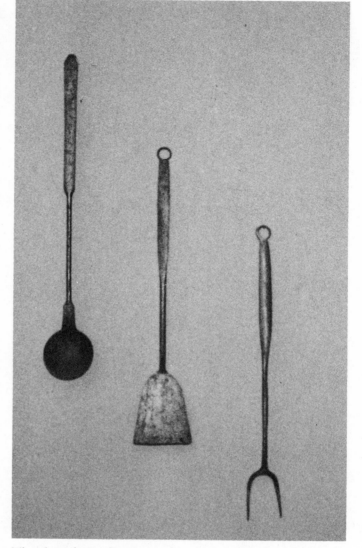

The three basic fireplace tools: ladle, spatula, fork. *Courtesy Mr. Wallace Wetzel*

that batter cakes of all sorts would become basic dietary items. During the older days one huge cake was made on a common griddle of varied kinds of flour, supplemented by flavoring of fruit, eggs, and the like. Fritters were made with raised doughs and here the Pennsylvania Dutch *Hausfrau* outdid herself. Have you ever eaten "grape leaf cakes"? Take some young tender grape leaves, wash and dry them, spread them with jam or fresh fruit, roll into a jelly roll, dip in batter, and then fry in deep fat until they are golden brown. Sugar them and serve hot. Almost any kind of fruit and preserve can be used for fritters; do not forget the classic corn fritters.

Coming from northern Europe, the Pennsylvania Dutch were not olive-oil conscious, so their salads and greens were not used as they were among the peoples of southern Europe. Rather, out of necessity, we created sour cream and hot bacon dressings. Some people are astonished to learn that crisp fresh lettuce is covered with a hot bacon dressing; but have you ever eaten fresh young dandelion greens, raw, covered with a hot dressing of fried bacon, egg, flour, sugar, salt, and cream soured slightly with vinegar? Here we come to the acme of salad-eating, hot dressings on salads where greens from the field were used: dandelion, called *Pissebett,* watercress, wild lettuce, and catchfly.

There is also a myth about seven sweets and seven sours—again an imaginative ascription of customs to the

Pottery batter pitcher for making waffle and pancake batter.

"Hooded" buttermolds including a small one for marking individual pats of butter.

Punched tin coffee pot, said to have been made by a man named Angstadt. *Courtesy Mrs. Walter C. Moser*

Pennsylvania Dutch. Of course, no feast in the Dutch country was complete without some sour things and some sweet things. There were many characteristic sours like chowchow, pickled beets, pickeled melon rinds, and so on. Also, there were sweets like applebutter, pearbutter, elderberry jelly (very hard to make jell). Still, there was no studied effort to produce a given number of sweets and sours.

Beverages provided escape for the culinary imagintion. Unfortunately the sour wines of Europe were not popular in colonial times; Anglo-Saxons preferred rum and tea. Cider and its derivatives became a substitute for wine, and the local apple crop replaced the grape as the

Pennsylvania butter molds in various designs. *Courtesy Mr. and Mrs. Tom Schmoyer*

basis of beverages. Nor were the Pennsylvania Germans tea drinkers; they preferred coffee, althtough the coffee tax of 1765 forced them to seek substitutes. Early newspapers printed recipes for making coffee substitutes like roasted rye meal, to which, when properly cooked, egg yokes were added. Pennsylvania Germans were skilled in making syrups that were concentrates for cooling summer drinks. Who has not enjoyed a good cool glass of raspberry drink made from homemade syrup? Or currant syrup, rhubarb syrup (nice and tart), and grape-juice concentrate!

Pennsylvania Dutch cooks, then, were both frugal and imaginative, creating from what their abundant farms produced a basic cuisine. However, we must not romanticize the Pennsylvania Dutch food, just enjoy it.

10

Healing Laughter

What people laugh at is an index of their spirit, of their cultural consciousness, because it shows what they cherish and what they scorn. Ever since philosopher Bergson wrote his book on laughter, we have come to understand that it tells much about the culture of a people. And one mark of Pennsylvania Dutch culture from the start, which has had quite a revival as the years have passed, is their capacity to laugh at themselves. Today the mark of being Pennsylvania Dutch is to belong to a *Grundsow* lodge or some other kind of assembly, where stories, some tall and some spiced by that special brand of Pennsylvania Dutch risqué humor, are told.

Pennsylvania Dutch people have laughed at themselves and have been laughed at. For they were known as "dumb Dutch," mainly because their language was mixed. Indeed, to be funny, the Pennsylvania Dutchman had merely to speak in dialect. Even the exquisite poetry of John Birmelin, rich in moods, is always not far from humorous and he had a hard time establishing the seriousness of his longer narrative works.

From the start the dialect was laughed at. The naturalist Dr. Johann David Schoepff, erstwhile Hessian officer, traveling through Pennsylvania, gives an illustration of the butchered language that was then used:

Ich hab' wollen mit meinem Nachbar tscheinen und ein Stück geklared Land purtschasen. Wir hätten, no doubt, ein guten Barghen gemacht, und hatten können gut darauf ausmachen. Ich war aber net capable, so'me Summe Gelt aufzumachen, und konnt nicht länger expecten. Das thät mein Nachbar net gleichen, und fieng an mich übel zu yuhsen, so dacht ich, 's ist besser du thust mit aus.

This bit was written by one who knew High German, and it translates:

I wanted to join my neighbor and purchase a piece of cleared land. We would, no doubt, have made a good bargain, and could have made out well. But I was not able to raise the sum of money, and I could not delay longer. This my neighbor did not like, and he began to use me badly, so I thought it would be better to do without.

Or the other classic that Dr. Schoepff cites:

Mein Stallion ist über die Fens getschumpt, und hat dem nachbar sein Whiet abscheulich gedämätscht.

Translation:

My stallion jumped over the fence and badly damaged my neighbor's wheat.

The first recorded humor of the Pennsylvania Dutch is found in the humorous inscriptions on pottery. Here are a few:

Wer etwas will verschweigen haben, He who wants something kept secret
Der darf es seiner Frau nicht sagen. Dare not tell his wife.

The fellow riding the billy goat says to the black man, "Fellow, do not cause my goat to shy or I'll knock your head in two." The German reads:

Kerl, mach mich mir meinen Bock nicht scheu
Sonst schlag ich dir den Kopt entzwey.

From a private collection

Ich fert die breid stross hin und her *Und doch wirt mir der beitel lehr.*	I rode the broad street far and wide And still my pocketbook grew empty.
Ich koch was ich kan *Est mein sau net so est mein mann.*	I cook what I can; If my sow does not eat, my husband will.
An diesem disch gefällt mich nicht, *Der Koch der wäscht die Finger nicht.*	This table does not please me; The cook does not wash his fingers.
Es ist mir bang *Mein wieschte dochter grigkt kein mann.*	I am afraid that my ugly daughter Will get no husband.

Wer des lieben ungesund, *So thätens Doctor meiden;* *Und wan den wibern weh thät,* *So thätens sie nicht leiden.*	If loving were unhealthy Doctors would forbid it; And if it harmed wives They would not permit it.

Here is a parody on the Lord's prayer:

Lieber Vater in Himmelreich *Was du mir gibst das ess ich gleich.*	Dear Father in heaven; What you give me I immediately eat.

Here are the translations of several inscriptions:

This dish is made of earth,
When it breaks the potter laughs.

Cartoon, late eighteenth century, that says: "He who has a nasty wife already has hell on earth."

Hot lang gelebt und viel gezankt;	She lived long and argued much;
Nau, geh do weck, mei liewe Leit,	Please go away, my good people,
Sunscht steht sie uff und zankt mit euch.	Else she will rise and argue with you.

It was known that some husbands were not only henpecked; some of them were stupid. Thus, when a Pennsylvania Dutch farmer was elected to the General Assembly of Pennsylvania when that body was meeting in the State House in Philadelphia, he, sensing his language difficulty, dutifully attended every session. One day the business was a debate about "moving the house." The new member was perplexed. He rose from his seat, walked outside and went around the building, looking carefully at its foundations. Returning to his seat he said to his neighbor, "If those fellows think that they are going to move this House they have another think coming."

In 1810 an unknown Pennsylvania publisher brought forth *Das Leben und der Thaten der berühmten Till Eulenspiegel,* which was printed for amusement of children. Till was indeed a legend brought over from the old country, but he had been a real person, Dietrich Eulenspiegel, who had lived in Brunswick during the fourteenth century, dying around 1350 in Möln. In 1483 a work dealing with his exploits had appeared and he became a popular figure in children's love. In 1515 an edition of tales about him came out in Strassbourg.

Till was the prototype of the clever rogue who always beats the devil at his own game. Till's exploits were celebrated as much in Pennsylvania as in Europe. Here are a few of them as recorded here:

Till and the devil agreed to farm for shares. The first year Till said that he would take for his share what grew under the ground, to which the devil agreed. So Till planted potatoes, beets, and radishes. Next year the devil insisted that he have what grew under the ground, so Till planted beans and cabbages. The third year the devil claimed as his due what grew both under and above the ground; so Till planted cucumbers, melons, and other creeping vines.

Next, Till and the devil bragged about their swimming. They agreed to settle matters by a swimming meet, to see who could swim the longest distance. Before they started Till said that he would have to eat a calf. "Why?" the devil asked. "I'm not going to swim for a week without any food in my stomach," Till replied.

Till and the devil bragged about their ability to withstand heat. To settle the argument they both entered

All maidens on earth
Gladly would become wives.

Happy is she who still is single,
Sorrowing she who is married.

I would rather stay single
Than give the pants to the wife.

A pipe of tobacco is as good for one
As a dollar spent on the girls.

I have ridden over hill and dale
And still have found no wife.

The henpecked husband is perennial and not especially Pennsylvania Dutch. Often he is butt of jokes, but this one got his revenge. The following tombstone inscription tells its own story:

Doh leit mei Fraa, Gott sei Dank,	Here lies my wife, may God be praised;

The gaudiest of all barns in Weisenberg Township, Lehigh County.

Sheriff H. Getwicks of York, with sidearms. *From a private collection*

Mr. and Mrs. Beard, of York. *From a private collection*

Nineteenth-century paintings

Peter Coffman: Pastel portrait of a young lady, 1833. *Courtesy Mrs. Walter C. Moser*

Two modern Pennsylvania revivalist painters

Primitive paintings by "Pennsylvania Hattie" Brunner.
Courtesy Mrs. Martha Silvernail

The egg tree was an old Pennsylvania Dutch custom.
Here David Ellinger captures the spirit in a water color.
Courtesy Mr. Ellinger

an oven over a roaring fire. The heat was so intense that Till began to edge toward the door. The devil, sensing victory, asked, "Where are you going?" Till replied, "To get more wood; I'm cold."

The Pennsylvania Dutch also laughed at the stupid Swabians, those inhabitants of the province southeastward from the Palatinate. As the English laugh at the dour Scots, so Palatine people laughed at Swabians.

One day seven Swabians decided to measure the depth of the well. Having neither tape nor rod, they racked their brains for a way to measure it. Finally they decided to make a human chain. One Swabian lay crosswise at the top of the well and the others hung on to him. They found this was hard work and the fellow at the top was perspiring freely. Finally, to get a better hold, he decided to spit on his hands. Then the whole caboodle fell into the well.

A group of Swabians had come to a gate in the wall of a large city with their wagon, on which they had, crosswise, a large beam. The beam was wider than the gate and they couldn't get it through. Thinking it over, they decided to knock down the walls on both sides and

The humor of the period of the Revolutionary War was grim and deadly, and it took public form. Here the traitor Benedict Arnold is castigated. *Courtesy the Historical Society of Pennsylvania*

Are these the stupid Swabians, American style? These carved nine pins, six only surviving, were done in Pennsylvania sometime during the late eighteenth century. They are carved in the shape of a boot, with individually conceived heads. *Courtesy the Shelborne Museum*

then take it in. When they were just about done a Palatinate farmer came along, turned the beam lengthwise, and they went in.

One Swabian wanted to make wagon tongues. He went into the forest and cut himself a piece of timber. When he came home he found that it was two feet too short. So he laid it aside and went into the woods to get another piece of timber. He brought it home. This was two feet two long. So he cut off two feet from the one and nailed it on to the other.

Two Swabians bought a wheelbarrow but did not know how to use it. They took it home with one of them

carrying it by the handles and the other by the wheel.

Swabians, they say, put hay on one shoulder and straw on the other so that when they march they can tell the hay foot from the straw foot.

When the British king employed Hessian mercenaries to fight his American battles, the Pennsylvania Dutch learned to ridicule the stupid Hessians. One night during the war a company of Hessians was being attacked by the Americans. They were alarmed. They advanced file on file, firing as they came. They found that they were attacking heaps of manure.

In 1829 George Wolfe of Northampton County was

running for the office of governor. He was in Harrisburg while his family was in Easton. Young Georgie, his youngest, was at the post-stage depot waiting for the news. It came. His father was the newly elected governor

To the memory of Johannes Spatz, husband of Magdala Spatz (sparrow). Perhaps the tombstone cutter thought that the family name was Daub (dove).

of Pennsylvania. He rushed home and into the kitchen, saying, "Mom, are we all governors now pop's elected?"

The reply is classic. "No! Just me and pop."

Preacher stories are legion.

The minister and elder John went to Synod, John for the first time. On the way home, as they drove in the buggy, they discussed what had taken place. The minister gathered from the tone of the elder's conversa-

tion that he had not been too impressed with the affair. So he asked, "John, didn't you like it?"

John's reply was honest. "No. I didn't! I'll tell you. Preachers are like manure. Spread out over the land they do a lot of good, but on a heap, they stink."

As an up-country parsonage was burning, the fire out of control, the elder, standing next to a dismayed minister, turned to console him. "Reverend, we'll build you a modern house, and furnish it well."

"I know," said the distraught cleric, "but there's a barrel of sermons in there."

There was a consistory meeting in the parsonage,

Says Lucifer, on meeting a newly arrived person in hell: "You do not seem to be afraid to come in!"

Newly arrived one: "No! It is a great satisfaction for me to know that I have come finally to the place to which so many people have recommended that I go."

which stood in need of repair. The issue was whether they would build a new parsonage or just repair the old one. It was hotly argued. The leading elder, also the leading contributor, was opposed to the new house. Just then a storm broke, and a piece of plaster was loosened, falling on the elder's head. The elder looked up and said, "Perhaps the parsonage does need some work."

The minister, sensing intervention from above, said in proper sanctimoniousness, "Good Lord! Hit him again! Hit him again!"

The Pennsylvania Dutch people had many preacher stories, but none were more widespread than those which dealt with Moses Dissinger. With William H. Stoy,

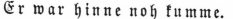

Der Paíre hot for en Trunk Waſſer gefrogt g'hatte, un ſagt, wie er getrunke hot—,,Ah=h=h! En kühler Trunk Waſſer duht 'me Mann awer gut an 'me heeße Dag !''
,,Ja'', ſagt die Frah, ,,ich bin juſcht ſorry, daß es Waſſer wennig trüb war — die Kinner ware juſcht im Brunne g'weſt for abkühle !''

The Pastor had asked for a drink of water, and when he had drunk—"A-h-h-h! A cool drink of water does a person good on a hot day!"
"Yes," said the woman, "I'm just sorry that the water was somewhat clouded—the children have just been in the spring to cool off."

Ja, grad ſo.

Der alt Mann—Was, hoſcht du ah ſchun des Sc g'lernt ?
Der klee Buh—Un du, hoſcht du es Schmoke no g'ſtoppt ?

After 1885 the Reading *Adler* almanac published cartoons. Here is one entitled "Yes, exactly so."
    The Old Man: "Have you learned to smoke already?"
    The Small Boy: "And you haven't given it up yet?"
Note that the caption in this cartoon is in dialect. Some are also in High German.

Moses Dissinger was the prototype of the fervent evangelical preacher.

Moses Dissinger had been born in Schaefferstown, where he spent a wild youth before he was converted. He became a moralistic evangelical preacher, sharp-tongued and quick in repartee. And the stories about him are classic, some entering print in the Almanac of the *Reading Adler*.

When a prayer-meeting dragged, Moses is reported to have said, "You hem and haw like a set of old mill wheels when there's not enough water to keep them running."

One time, holding a service, some rowdies created a disturbance. Moses paused to say, "Once upon a mountain the devils which had been driven out of men went into swine and the sea. Lo, for these many years now they were lost, but behold, they have been found! Back there they sit and the devil still is in them."

Sei Limit.

„Der Doktor hot g'jagt, daß ich müßt Milch trinke zwee Stund vor jedere Mahlzeit. Ich bin nau jchün dra' for fufzeh Minute, un ich will verdollt jei wann ich noch en Droppe meh jchlucke kann!"

The doctor said that I have to drink milk two hours before mealtime. I have been at it now for fifteen minutes and I'll be darned if I can swallow another drop.

Once a lady parishioner complained that her pastor never called on her. The open secret was that she kept a dirty house. Moses accepted an invitation to dinner. This is how he asked the blessing: "God bless this dirty woman. God bless this dirty food. And God bless poor Moses who has to eat it."

Once Moses went to a funeral where the services, based on a Scripture passage, were conducted by a cleryman from one of the more formal denominations. Moses was amazed. Next Sunday he preached on the same text in his church, with these introductory remarks: "Now I'm going to preach on the text which the priest out yonder chewed up so badly. God in heaven knows how much pity I have felt for this text. It has seemed to me just as if you had thrown a bagful of oats to a hog and left the bag tied. The old hog will sniff around it, smell that there is something there, but cannot get at it. Just so

this godless preacher went around this text, smelling that there is something there; he sniffs it over, chews it all up, and yet he fails to find the grain. But today justice shall be done to this text."

Moses fought a real devil. One day he was going down the street in Allentown. Some loafers asked him, "Well, Moses, how is the devil doing today?" Quick was Moses' reply: "Well boys, I'm glad that you are concerned about your father."

Moses also did battle with the fire-house gang. Once the firemen asked him to preach to them. Here is part of what Moses said: "My dear hearers! The Lord is ready to pardon, gracious and merciful, slow to anger, and of great kindness, but unless you fellows change the courses of your lives and reform you will get to a place where there is a fire that you will never be able to put out."

One Sunday morning Moses appeared in the pulpit

Wann der Klee des danne naus g'wißt het.

„Sag, Mäm!"
„Was?"
„Is jell net die Hoorberjcht, was ich mei Benze uf= g'jpart hab befor un hab jie dir kaaft for dein Geburts= dag?"

If the little fellow had known beforehand:
"Say, mom!"
"What?"
"Is that not the hairbrush for which I saved up my pennies and which I bought for you at your last birthday?"

with a black walnut in his hand. "Now," he said, "this nut represents the three churches." Then, taking off the husk, he said, "This is the Lutheran church. No good! We throw it away." He cracked the walnut. "This hard shell is the Methodist church. It's no good either. We throw it away too." Then he paused, and added. "This kernel is our church. It's wormy and rotten. So we have to throw this away too."

There is also the tale of Moses and the well-known thief. The thief was in church regularly. So one Sunday Moses came in with a rock and set it on the arm of the pulpit. Then he began. "There is a man in this congregation who stole a colt and if he doesn't confess and repent I'll throw this rock right at him." At this a woman turned to her man and said, "John, he means it."

Moses fought demon rum with eloquence. His sermon against drunkenness is classic. Here is a part of it. "Just look at those drunkards! These the devil has so mixed up that one might think that they could not be restored during their whole lifetime. Many of them not only have drunk away all human sense of honor so that they can do anything mean and dirty that the dirty devil in hell wants them to do, without feeling any shame; they also have guzzled away their whole understanding. . . . Now take a good look at their outward appearances. . . . They have noses like red peppers, ears like *Fastnacht* cakes, bellies like barrels, and they make faces like foxes eating wasps; but in spite of it all they go on drinking. They jump for the bottle like bullfrogs for red rags. . . ." Then, after saying how the Lord can make honorable men out of them, he concluded: "By the power of the Gospel the most wretched drunkard can be saved and gifted with the power so that he could swim in a stream of rum reaching to his mouth without any desire to drink it."

Many a joke has been passed about the Lutherans and Reformed, the two main Pennsylvania Dutch religious denominations, which often worshipped together in the same building on alternate Sundays. One common joke was that in saying the Lord's prayer the one said *Unser Vater* while the other said *Vater unser*. Also jokes about the stubborness of the parties were common.

Here is the classic story on this theme:

A Lutheran and a Reformed family were neighbors. The Lutheran family adopted an orphan girl to raise while the Reformed adopted an orphan boy. The children grew up together, played together, went to the same school and Sunday School, seeing each other frequently.

When time came for catechetical instruction one went Lutheran and one went Reformed, thus learning that there was a difference. And the ministers exploited any difference.

One day about a year or so after their confirmation they took a walk together. They went down through the meadow to a small creek. It was a hot summer's day. The boy said, "Do you want to go in swimming?"

The girl said, "Yes, but I didn't bring my suit."

The boy answered, "Never mind! You go behind the bushes there and undress. We'll go in nude."

When the girl came out from behind the bushes the boy whistled and said: "Say! I didn't know there was this big a difference between Lutherans and Reformed."

Professor Joseph Henry Dubbs had a favorite story about the Pennsylvania Dutch farmer who sent his son to Mercersburg to school. He was proud that his son was a student at so famous a place, and was especially proud that he was being taught the Latin language. When the son came home for a vacation the father asked him, "What is this Latin that you study?"

"It's a foreign language."

"What do you do with it? How do you study it?"

"We take Latin and put it into English."

"You show me, now."

The lad said, "Now take a Latin sentence like *puella est bona.*"

"What does *puella* mean?"

"It means 'girl.'"

"That's easy! The girl eats beans." (*est* means "eats," *bona* means "beans" in Pennsylvania Dutch.)

Another source of humor was the village half-wit. He was the butt of many jokes. This made him edgy. The local minister used to tease Bill Miller in a good-natured way, but Bill took it somewhat badly. One day Bill came down the street with a basket neatly covered with a red cloth. The minister greeted Bill, saying, "Good morning Bill, what's in the basket?"

"That's what I got it covered up for," was Bill's quick reply.

The older almanacs that were published by the Pennsylvania Dutch printers were full of jokes, and, after 1888, the Reading *Adler* almanac pioneered with cartoons that had captions in all three languages: High German, dialect, and English. Indeed, the humor came from all sources: High German stories were printed verbatim; stories in European dialects were also reprinted; but both High German and dialect anecdotes were printed that were clearly of American origin. This American literature has not yet been collected or studied.

Here is a story in High German from the *Adler* calendar for 1905, which I give in German and translation:

Der bekannte Hofrath Gebhardt in Berlin, der zwar einen guten Tisch führte, dessen Wein aber viel zu wünschen, übrig liessen, lud einen Freund zu sich zu Tische. Der Gast fand der Wein überaus sauer. Mehrenmals von der Hausfrau zum öftern Trrinken aufgefordert, sagte endlich der Gast: "Ich danke sehr; mir gehts wie den Engländer. Ess ich (essig), trunk' ich nett!"

Translation: The well known councillor Gebhardt in Berlin hardly kept a good table, and his wine left much to be desired. Once he invited a friend to dinner. The guest found the wine much too sour. Several times the wife offered him more to drink. Finally he said: "If I eat (*essig* means vinegar), I do not drink."

This typically European story contrasts with the soundly American one that follows, written in dialect:

"Auf wen wart'st du den, Schane?"
"Ich wart auf an' Herren mit an' grossen Schnurbart, der an cigaret raucht, I möcht gern an' Stummel hab'n"
"Warum muss's den Aner mit an grossen Schnurrbart sein, raucher sie besser Cigaren?"
"Ne, aber sie lassen's net so weit herunnerbrennen."

Still, this story sounds strange to ears that know the dialect only by hearing, for it is spelled for German readers. Its translation is as follows:

"On whom do you wait, Johnny?"
"I wait for a gentleman with a large beard who smokes cigarettes. I would gladly have a stump."
"Why must it be a gentleman with a large beard? Do they smoke better cigarettes?"
"No, but they do not let them burn so far down."

European humor sometimes retained its Old World moods, and there was a double cultural heritage present here. Thus this make-believe old bill from a bookseller:

"The Way to Heaven," repaired	80 cents
"Schiller," bound in calf's leather	1.10
"The Old and New World," mended	65 cents
"The German Empire," cut and pressed	1.10
"The fire-spewing mountain," with iron cover	2.25
Old and New Bible, bound together	80 cents.

Another joke possibly of European origin:

Judge: "And why do you go around the city streets at night?"

Accused: "I'm afraid to go home at night."
Judge: "Are you married?"
Accused: "Ach, Sir Judge, you are too!"

Another bit of European humor from the almanacs is the following:

First Traveler: "If you want to stay overnight in this inn you can make up your mind not to get any sleep; the drunken fellows make such a hellish noise that you will have to hear every sound."

Höflichkeits = Austausch.

Gefängniß=Warden (zum Sträfling bei dessen Entlassung)—Und nun hoffe ich, daß Sie ein anständiges Leben führen und ein nützliches Mitglied der Gesellschaft werden.
Entlassener Sträfling — Danke Ihnen; ich wünsche Ihnen das Gleiche!

Prison warden to a prisoner on his discharge: "And now I hope that you will lead an upright life and become a useful member of society."
Released prisoner: "Thank you, and I wish you the same."

Second Traveler: "Wait a minute—an idea has come to my head." (Very loudly to the innkeeper) "Mister innkeeper! Will you be so kind as to wake us early in the morning at daybreak? Coming here we lost a hundred-mark banknote outside in your courtyard, and we'll have to look for it right early in the morning."
Shortly thereupon noise in the bar subsided. The drinkers were all outside with lanterns looking for the banknote.

These obviously European stories are mixed in with

Die knißige Buwe.

Kleene Buwe — Gebt awer nau gut acht, Mister, daß Ihr net in sell Loch nunner fallt!

The kibitzing boys: "Now take care, mister, that you don't fall in that hole!"

anecdotes obviously written in America. Most of these American anecdotes were in dialect and were of local origin. Here is the story of the suspicious bottle, from the *Adler* Almanac for 1895:

A short time ago a farmer from the sticks came into the city on business. Before he went home he had to see someone up town, so he climbed up on a Penn Street electric car so that he could ride to the place more pleasantly and rest his weary legs. Across from him sat a woman, a dried-up, thin, pointed-nose woman, already quite old. She had a packet of printed temperance leaflets and other stuff in her hands, and she looked mighty pious and made a sour face.

From out of the old man's coat there peeped a bottle. He was almighty hot, so that he nearly burst. All at once he said, "It's surely hot in your city!" The people all looked at him but no one said a word. The old woman across said nothing either. Soon, though, she reached her arm across and handed him several of her tracts.

"Thanks," said the old farmer. "This is surely a funny calendar. Is it like those from the Eagle Press?"

"No!," the lady then said in English. "This is to save your soul. Touch not! Taste not! Handle not!—it says here." And then she pointed with her finger to the bottle, which showed out of the old farmer's pocket.

"Oh! Now I see," said the old man. "But that bottle is not for me."

"Woe unto him who gives his neighbor strong drink," the old woman said.

"No," said the old farmer, "it's not exactly my neighbor! The bottle is for our baby. I just married a pretty young

Die fünf Sinne.

Das Gesicht.   Der Geruch.

Der Geschmack.   Das Gehör.

Das Gefühl.

The five senses: Sight, smell, taste, hearing, feeling.

En Opinion vum Sunndags fische.

„Ich denk net daß es letz is for zu fische uff Sunndags, wann mer es religiously duht. Ich bet immer for en Beiß un sag Dank wann ich en Fisch krick.‟

One opinion about fishing on Sundays.
"I don't think that it's wrong to fish on Sundays if it is done religiously. I always pray for a bite and say thanks when I get a fish."

wife about a year ago and she says that she wants to raise the baby on the bottle—and where the dickens did I put the rest of the apparatus?" All the while he was looking around in his pockets and soon he found a long rubber hose with a nipple at the end, and he put it before the nose of the old woman, with the words, "Have you ever in your life seen such a thing?"

She was as frightened as if a rattlesnake had bitten her. She said nothing more to the farmer and left the car like a bolt of lightning as soon as she had a chance. And the whole car of people laughed and rejoiced over the farmer and his lovely young wife and baby at home.

Another example of dialect anecdotes from almanacs is entitled: Joe does not Believe in *Hexe*:

Mister Printer! One day as I was mowing oats a man

called me over to the street and asked me whether this was *Hexestädtel* (a witch village). This so angered me that I said to him, "Nothing doing with *Hexestädtel!* There is no such place. This place is called *Heckerstädtel* (Bush village). We are not so stupid, nor so superstitious, nor so far behind the times as to believe such foolishness!"

Der Busch Cousin — Well wie gleichschts dann do im Busch?

Der klee Schtadt Buh—Well, wann's juscht meh Häuser und Polismänner und Schtriet-Cars un "Bleib vum Gras" Seins un so Dings het, deht ich's forschtreet gleiche!

The country cousin: "Well, how do you like it in the country?"

The small city boy: "Well, if there were more houses, and policemen, and streetcars, and 'keep off the grass' signs, I'd like it first rate."

Then the man asked me what we did believe in and I told him: "We believe in a person minding his own business, that all persons should work hard, go to church regularly, do all good to their neighbors, and that all people should do unto others as they want them to do unto them."

The man then said, "Are there no *Hexe* in your neighborhood?"

"No, there are none," I said to him, and then I asked him who it was that could or would bewitch people, what a witch looked like, and how they got around.

The old man then said, "Generally they are old hypocritical women and old widows. Sometimes old men pursue this business."

I called mom and told her what the man had said about widows, and mom began to throw stones at him and called him a thickhead, dolt, fool, and everything else that she knew. She further told him that if he came along this way again and were to stop by she would scald him with boiling water. "Aren't you ashamed of such stupid talk? Don't you know about Christianity? Ey, our pigs and Holstein cows are not as stupid. Our cats and dogs do not believe in such things and know better than you!"

I tell you, printer, that that fellow took off and looked like a whipped dog who has a pig's ear pinned to his tail. I'll bet you that he'll not soon come to *Heckerstädtel* to look for *Hexe*. If anyone ever calls my mother a *hex* I'll punch him black and blue, and green and yellow, and red and brown, and I'll break a couple of his ribs, break his head so some of the stupidity can leak out.

So those people who still believe that there are such things as *Hexe,* and that people can bewitch others are retarded in wisdom and deep in stupidity. We should stick such people in the corn husker and then press them like cider and so squeeze all the foolishness out of them.

So far the account in the almanac. Why did the editor think he needed to write against witchcraft? Were there still those around who believed in it?

The campaign against the "dumb Dutch" took many forms. There is also a classic tale about the yokel who tells his friends back home about his trip to the big city. Sometimes the city is Philadelphia, sometimes Reading. The almanacs have both. Here is Jim Schappel of Hamburg telling about his trip to Reading:

"We went to Readin' last month, but just fer shopping and not fer doctoring or the like. I walked up and down the Penn street all day. I sure was tired. We came to the depot to get the train for Hamburg. It was so full of people that there was no place to sit. Mom found one place, and finally I saw such a high chair that was empty. I was hardly seated when such a black fellow came and began to rub at my shoes. He rubbed and rubbed. He put the blacking on them and then made them shine. They shined like his head. Then he rubbed them with brushes and with a rag until I could see my face in them. I thought fer such work I should give him something, so I reached in my pocket and gave him a dime. Then the train came and we climbed aboard. At the Hamburg station my boy met me with the buggy and we rode home. I went upstairs right away and took them shoes off and put them in the closet. Now, I had them fer Communion and fer Homecoming at the church. And if it doesn't rain they'll keep until the next time when I get to Readin'. Then I'll sit in the high chair again."

Der poleit Porter.

Die Frah am Depot: — Kann ich die do Train nach Reading nemme?

,,Well, die Engine nemmt sie for common, awer ich denk net daß ebber objecte deht wann du's emol browire wid.''

The polite porter.
Lady at the depot: "Can I take this train to Reading?"
"Well, the engine generally takes it, but I don't think anyone will object if you give it a try."

One of the classic tales about the Dutch is probably a true story, and it is about an Allentown brewer who was famous for his temper. He would become very angry and then cool down, becoming penitent again. When the telephones first came out he got one for the office in the brewery. But, knowing his weakness, he was afraid to use it, for he felt that he might hurt someone. One day, however, alone in the office, he just had to make a call. He placed it and got the wrong number. That was too much. He told the operator off.

That evening when he got home his neighbor, the president of the local phone company came over and said to him that he had heard that he was angry over the phone and had insulted one of the operators. The brewer was contrite. He said that next day he would surely apologize.

Getting to the office early he put in a call, asking for the operator. "Hello! Are you the operator that I told to go to hell yesterday?"

"Yes, I am, sir."

"Well, I'll tell you. You don't have to go."

Another classic is also a true story. A young man went to college in Lancaster. He was made steward of the old Franklin club, an eating club for students. In this capacity he went to the Lancaster market regularly.

One day he came up to an older Amish lady. "How much are eggs today?" he asked.

She told him her price.

Schlimme Geschichte.

„Ei! Ei! Un dort is ah noch der Bauer wo g'ſ
daß er deht mich ſchieße, wann er mich widder u
Aeppelbaum antreffe deht!"ſ

"And over there too is that farmer who said that he
would shoot me if he ever caught me in his apple tree
again!"

"How many eggs do you have?" he asked.

"Fourteen dozen," was the reply.

"I'll take them," the young man said. As they were
putting the eggs in his basket the old woman asked,
"How many people sit down at your table?"

"Forty," was the reply.

The old woman shook her head "And such a young
man, yet, too," she said.

These then are samples of what the Pennsylvania
Dutch laughed at, an index of their culture.

11

The Good Old Days

The high point of the influence of Pennsylvania Dutch Culture on American life came between the years 1820 and 1840, when an unbroken chain of Dutchmen, descendants of Colonial immigrants, sat in the governor's chair: Joseph Hiester, 1820–23; John Andrew Schultz, 1823–29; George Wolfe 1829–35; and Joseph Ritner, 1835–39. These men expressed in their political opinions the values inherent in older Pennsylvania cultural moods: under Wolfe's administration came free public education; Ritner's views on holding slaves were praised by Quaker poets. Liberal and forward looking, these men were followed, although indirectly, by Francis Shunk, 1845–48, and William Bigler, 1852–55.

With the end of the Civil War a new mood was apparent. Nostalgia for the past arose. Now a hybrid culture was impossible. The union had been saved. Regionalism was dead, north as well as south, and new democratization was on the way. Newer immigrants were arriving, fresh from lands that were "foreign" in moods and ways, and older Pennsylvania Dutch people discovered that they now were old Americans with distrust for the ways of the Old World.

Decline of the German-language culture set in. School had to be conducted in English. After 1837 no one dared speak German in school at all. So when boys and girls studied in English, the end of Germanic culture was sure. And longing for the old German-language school, which Henry Harbaugh has immortalized in his poem about the old schoolhouse at the Creek, grew stronger as these good old values were being overwhelmed by newer ones in the common American culture. As a consequence, old Germanic ways came to be more and more isolated from American life, and the dialect, last vestigial remnant, became a symbol of all that was good in the older ways.

This nostalgia varied from group to group. Some churches soon went over to English worship. The Old Order Mennonites still use German, or a kind of German, today. Some have come to terms with the technological society; others drive horses and ride buggies. And for some people the measure of Pennsylvania Dutch culture is the degree of resistance to mass technological society that is apparent.

So if it be true that Roman Catholicism reflects feudal values, and that Calvinism reflects mercantilism, then I should suggest that an anti-feudal and anti-bourgeois value scheme is implied in the plain sects. Were they not the forerunners in the peasants' revolt of the sixteenth century? They oppose the stratification of professional life; they have no paid clergy; they do not strive for worldly success; they do not go to war; they are reluctant to make use of technology. These are in truth negative values, and we can say that they are cultural primitivists.

Yet such rebellion against middle-class values, which was so violently opposed by Martin Luther, lingers on among the plain Pennsylvania Dutch. The opposition of Amishmen to technology is never quite total. They

The Americanization process is fully developed on this
Lehigh County barn.

use their neighbors' telephones and pay for them. Old
Order Mennonites, also buggy people, ride in automobiles
—other people's. And they repair power mowers for
others. Some Pennsylvania Dutch retain loyalty to these
older values while others willingly and eagerly come to
terms with the newer ways. Whatever may be said about
longing for the "good old days," for ways of living not
overshadowed by technology, must be qualified by the
knowledge that many answers can be given to this
question.

About 1870, then, just as the Civil War was over,
Pennsylvania Dutch culture became reflective and self-
conscious, looking backward to battles lost and won. So
our culture became a historical phenomenon, a matter
for study, and most of its materials were in the German

language. No amount of argument can refute the fact
that the Pennsylvania Dutch culture was related to the
High German language.

This period in our history has been covered in a competent history which, in spite of some one-sidedness, man-
ages to present a good picture of the time: Homer Rosen-
berger's *The Pennsylvania Germans, 1891–1965.*

The use of High German was slow to die out. In 1880
there were still eighty-seven periodicals appearing in the
Pennsylvania heartland in that language. By 1900 only
fifty were left. In 1909 no German journal survived in
Lebanon county. By 1913 the Reading *Adler,* bastion
of the German press in Pennsylvania, folded.

During the same period Pennsylvania Dutchmen
shared the public life of the Commonwealth. They con-

tinued to sit in the governor's chair: John J. Hartranft (1873–1879); John A. Beaver (1887–1891); and Samuel W. Pennypacker (1903–1906).

As the use of German began to wane, as German-language schools passed away, the dialect became culturally vocal. Perhaps the earliest scholarly attention given to the dialect was a brief essay on Harbaugh's *Harfe* by S. S. Haldeman, professor of comparative philology at the University of Pennsylvania, which appeared in the *Transactions of the American Philosophical Society, 1869–1870*. This was followed two years later by a sixty-nine page book, *Pennsylvania Dutch—A Dialect of South*

Germany with an Infusion of English (Philadelphia and London). In these works dialectal self-consciousness was emerging, at just the same time that culturally self-conscious literature was appearing.

One of the early independent giants in Pennsylvania Dutch studies was Professor Oswald Seidensticker (1826–1894), who taught German literature at the University of Pennsylvania. His *Bilder aus der Deutsch-pennsylvanisch Geschichte* (New York, 1885) was pioneering and in many ways is still unsurpassed, especially in its insight into the Colonial period. His *The First Century of German Printing in America, 1728–1830* (Philadelphia,

A covered bridge near the Trexler Game Preserve in Lehigh County. *Photograph courtesy Mr. Edward W. Schlechter*

Looking south from the covered bridge at Welker Dam,
Lehigh County, over the late autumn Pennsylvania Dutch
countryside. *Courtesy Mr. Edward W. Schlechter*

1893), while superseded and supplemented, remains the
one basic book for serious students of Pennsylvania Dutch
culture. This work shows the depth, nature, scope, and
spread of High German literature in America. More than
any other scholar, Oswald Seidensticker awakened the historical consciousness of the Pennsylvania Dutch; he also
took part in the anniversary celebrations of the Crefeld
migration to Germantown in 1883. His book on the
German Press in America now needs to be supplemented
with a list of the works written in Pensylvania and published abroad.

In 1891 a call went forth for the founding of a Pennsylvania German Society. This has become the oldest
organization of the Pennsylvania Dutch. Its avowed purpose was to change the image of the Pennsylvania Dutch.
Marked by filio-pietism from the start, the organization
voted to restrict its membership to "descendants of early
German and Swiss settlers in Pennsylvania." This excluded Dr. Seidensticker, the finest scholar in the area.
Thirty persons signed a "call," and the organization was
formed with George F. Baer, president of the Reading
Railroad, as chairman. The issue of heritage as a require-

Old Order Mennonite Meeting House in Berks County.

ment for membership was hotly debated, and there was fear that the society would become peppered with German nationalism.

The earliest publications of the new society were boastful in an almost offensive tone. In 1895, however, probably as the result of Seidensticker's work, H. M. M. Richards proposed that a research program be developed, and soon the society began to publish its "Narrative and Critical History," which was to consist of about twenty-five fine historical volumes, the heart of the society's early work. These volumes were dominated by two themes: religious groupings and the migration. Under the vision of Frank Reid Dieffenderfer, Julius F. Sachse, and Richards, these earlier volumes went a long way toward ful-

filling the promise of this society. It was in truth remarkable that untrained scholars could develop such a skilled program.

It is difficult to estimate how many Pennsylvania

What well-dressed Pennsylvania Dutch girls wore around 1880. Mollie and Lizzie deLong were thus photographed by Charles A. Saylor in Reading.

One-room Amish schoolhouse in Lancaster County.

Dutch there were at the beginning of the twentieth century. Dr. A. B. Faust counted 18.4 million Germans in all of America, but this is somewhat of a romantic estimate. Beidelman in 1898 said that there were about one

In his pottery works in Doylestown, Henry Chapman Mercer used Pensylvania designs. Here he used Johann Valentin Haidt's portrait of Anna Mack as the basis for a tile.

and a half million in Pennsylvania, while Oscar Kuhns estimated that there were two million. The difficulty is compounded when we see that the 1900 Census gave 643,754 Germans in a total population of 6,310,115. Were these only German born?

The decision of the Pennsylvania German Society to limit its membership to descendants of early German and Swiss settlers kept the society from becoming a tool of German nationalist interests. It also separated Colonial Germans and their descendants from newer arrivals. In 1901 the German-American Historical Society was formed by those who had been excluded from the Pennsylvania German Society. This new organization became a brash expression of German imperial ambitions. Its literary organ was *The American German Review,* which was edited by Marion Dexter Learned, able scholar at the University of Pennsylvania, who gave energy and drive to the study of cultural relationships between Germany and the United States. This journal appeared between 1903 and 1918. Learned's biography of Francis Daniel Pastorius remains standard. By turning away from modern Germany, the Pennsylvania German Society proclaimed its American heritage.

During these early years of self-consciousness, Pennsylvania Dutch was being discovered in depth. In 1891, as I have noted, Edwin Atlee Barber discovered old pottery. In 1896 J. H. Sieling reported on the work of "Baron" Stiegel. In 1897 Henry Chapman Mercer wrote on the medieval art of *Fraktur* in the *Proceedings* of the American Philosophical Society. Also, at the same time, Dr. Mercer was reviving the older ceramics at his Doylestown pottery, using old designs from stove plates. He

Henry Chapman Mercer here used designs from Pennsylvania stove plates on his tiles. This was some of the earliest revival of Pennsylvania folk art.

even reproduced Moravian paintings by Valentin Haidt on his tiles.

Generally speaking, during this period American historians continued to ignore the field of Pennsylvania German studies, thus forcing students to overstress their subject. Even under the guidance of John W. Jordan, a Moravian, the Historical Society of Pennsylvania kept its focus of interest on Philadelphia and its history.

vania Dutch, wherein she ridiculed the sectarian scheme of values. The continuing opposition of the Pennsylvania Department of Public Instruction, even under the leadership of Nathan C. Schaeffer, added to the disparaging of the sectarian view. In 1877 the Schwenkfelders had forsaken their opposition to infant baptism; in 1891 they had accepted formal communion; and by 1901 they were paying their clergy. Indeed, opposition to public service

The Governor and his protégé. Samuel W. Pennypacker and friend at a conference on Pennsylvania Dutch affairs. From an old photograph.

At this time also, a notable decline in sectarian consciousness began to take place, notably among the Schwenkfelders. While Julius Sachse was publishing his work on the sects, while James I. Good, Henry Eyster Jacobs, and others were promoting denominational causes, the burgeoning culture of the world began to make inroads on sectarian attitudes. Old-fashioned values were being scorned. In 1904 Helen R. Martin published *Tillie The Mennonite Maid—A Story of the Pennsyl-*

has so weakened that now a descendent of the Schwenkfelders sits on the armed services committee of the United States Senate.

Around the turn of the twentieth century a new magazine began to appear, called *The Pennsylvania German,* ably edited by P. C. Croll, Lebanon historian. Later the editorial work was taken over by Howard W. Kriebel of East Greenville. Pressured by strident German imperialists to advocate German nationalist ideals, the jour-

At the Pennsylvania Farm Museum, Landis Valley.

The Schwenkfelder Library, Pennsburg, depository of much that is precious in Pennsylvania Dutch history.

The late sculptor William Swallow and his prize-winning ceramic piece, The Amish Boys. He was the most success-ful of the revivalists who used Pennsylvania Dutch themes in their work. *Photo by Edgar T. Clewell*

nal managed to keep its independence and published good fresh material. In 1914 it collapsed "for lack of capital." While it lasted it kept alive deep interest in Pennsylvania Dutch affairs.

Meanwhile, broad new horizons were opening up. Attics and closets were being ransacked and magnificent archival collections were taking shape. The most energetic of the early collectors was Samuel W. Pennypacker, one of the founders of the Pennsylvania German Society and former governor of the Commonwealth. Descendant of an early Germantown paper maker, he gained reputation as judge, historian, and vigorous administrator of state affairs. His literary and scholarly work was founded on his own broad collections; much of the pottery now has found its way into the major museums and his assembling of Schwenkfelder books and manuscripts now forms a goodly part of the collection at Pennsburg. He was an excellent linguist, knowing German, Latin, and Dutch, and he was also a trained lawyer who wore his learning lightly. It is to be regretted that the Commonwealth of Pennsylvania did not see fit to take up its option on his collection when it was offered for sale in 1919.

With the passing of the first generation of leaders in the Pennsylvania German Society, and with completion of the plan for a "Narrative and Critical History," interest sagged. Also, the establishment of new archival centers and the opening of great collections were giving broader scope than the original purposes of the Society envisaged. During the period of American participation in the First World War, the Society did not meet. Publication stagnated. One historian confesses that "no significant, widely circulated book or article" appeared in 1919. Annual meetings were halted, resumed only in 1920.

By 1926, however, newer aspects of Pennsylvania Dutch studies began to appear, hesitant at first, but growing with the years. When the Pennsylvania German Society met in the Pennsylvania Building at the Sesquicentennial in Philadelphia, they were treated to the first exhibition of Pennsylvania Dutch folk art. Even then that showing was subordinated to the "liberty bells" of eastern Pennsylvania. However, there were several celebrated pieces that have now found their way into museums, loaned by established antique dealers like A. H. Rice of Bethlehem, Beulah Jacobs of Allentown, and Hattie Brunner of Reinholds. Several pieces now famous were on exhibition: the Daniel Oyster Lafayette Clock, the Jacob Mäser desk, and Hausmann coverlets. More im-

portantly, this exhibition served to stimulate many new collectors.

In 1926 Elmer Schultz Johnson became president of the Pennsylvania German Society. He had returned from a long stay in Germany to create the magnificent Schwenkfelder Library. At the same time, under the leadership of Bishop Taylor Hamilton and others, the fine Moravian Archives in Bethlehem were taking shape. Cornelius Weygand, University of Pennsylvania profes-

The late Dr. Preston A. Barba, whose column *'S Pennsylvanisch Deitsch Eck* ran for thirty-four years in the *Allentown Call,* the finest of the historical columns devoted to the literature, lore, and history of the Pennsylvania Germans. Barba encouraged writers in the dialect, especially John Birmelin and Lloyd Moll. He circulated their work to more than a hundred thousand persons through the *Call,* as well as through the "book paper" edition to libraries and archives. *Courtesy the* Call-Chronicle Newspapers

sor, wrote *The Red Hills,* wherein he expressed a mood of romantic pride in the beautiful Pennsylvania countryside. In this same year, 1929, the Pennsylvania Museum of Art published a small work on its exhibition of Pennsylvania Dutch folk art, and Esther Stevens Frazer was helping Mrs. Robert W. deForrest of New York assemble her things now in the American wing of the Metropolitan Museum of Art. Henry Francis duPont was an avid and eclectic collector, making his fine museum of American interior decoration, including the Kerschner parlor and the Hottenstein drawing room from Pennsylvania Dutch homes. Also, Esther Stevens Frazer discovered the Jones-

looking toward the establishment of a foundation for work in the field of Pennsylvania history.

In 1935 the Pennsylvania German Folklore Society came into being, publishing its first slim volume the next year. Its officers were mostly men trained in the professions—professors, clergymen, and scholars, but the many members were mostly interested laymen. It was not a "learned society" and it made no genealogical requirements for membership. The Society had a somewhat

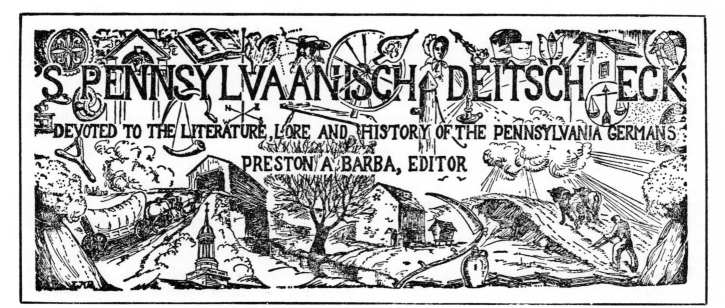

Masthead of the column edited by Dr. Preston A. Barba
in the *Allentown Call-Chronicle*.

town school of chest painters. Others were avidly collecting manuscripts and books.

The time was ripe for an expansion of horizons. Not only were new archives and collections being made, but vast new collections were coming into the public domain and we were learning that Pennsylvania Dutch history was more than sectarian and religious, dealing with artifact as well.

During these later years of the 1920s, the Pennsylvania German Society had subsidized headquarters in Norristown and in two years it caught up with its arrearage in publication. The future seemed bright again.

In 1931 the Pennsylvania German Society was reorganized. Some loyal workers were excluded. This led to a collapse of delicate negotiations, then in process,

broader view of Pennsylvania Dutch "folklore" than the older organization, and it planned to publish the newer dialect writers then appearing, John Birmelin, Clarence Iobst, and Lloyd Moll, as well as works on various aspects of folk art. Most volumes were edited by Preston A. Barba, who brought in his scientific scheme for spelling dialect. Growing rapidly, the Folklore Society soon impressed the public with the quality of its work. Its volumes came with some regularity and were attractively printed.

About the same time that the Pennsylvania German Folklore Society was starting up, a second important instrument was established, a vehicle for much that was solid and substantial, *'S Pennsylvaanisch Deitsch Eck* in the Allentown *Morning Call*. This column began March

23, 1935, and it continued for more than thirty years, far and away the finest achievement in the field. Its editor was, again, Preston A. Barba, who produced an eclectic column that interested laymen as well as scholars. Broad in scope, rich in its use of sources, and fearless enough to print High German and dialect materials, this was far more than one man's musings. Dr. Barba let the facts speak out. He was also fortunate in having a stable of dialect writers who were producing fine materials: John Birmelin, Lloyd Moll, Ralph Funk, Clarence Iobst, and many others. Probably his most important contribution was the system of spelling he worked out with the help of Professor Buffington; here for the first time the dialect could be read by readers of High German and English with equal comprehension.

Although the house seemed to be divided, competition led to mature work. In 1937, working under a generous foundation grant, Dr. Emil Meynen produced the magnificent *Bibliography of German Settlements in North America* (Leipzig). This gathered up every work in the field to that date, exclusive of the imprints, and it was a noteworthy contribution. It included materials dealing with Hessian mercenaries, an area not generally classed with the Pennsylvania Dutch. In 1942 a *Bulletin* of the New York Public Library brought out "Pennsylvania Dutch Folk Art and Architecture." This selected bibliography showed the new impact that the arts and crafts were making.

Although Thomas J. Wertenbaker, a Virginia Dutchman, gave adequate attention to the Pennsylvania Dutch theme in his *The Founding of American Civilization— the Middle Colonies* (New York, 1938), most other American historians continued to underplay the theme. Thus when the *Harvard Guide to American History* appeared, there was precious little attention to this area.

Meanwhile the great archival collections were growing. Mr. Charles W. Unger of Pottsville had been an avid collector of books and manuscripts relating to the Pennsylvania Dutch. In 1945 he sold his collection to Mr. Harvey Bassler of Myerstown, a total of forty-five tons of materials. This collection was offered to the Pennsylvania German Society and was put in the Fackenthal Library at Franklin and Marshall College, Lancaster. In 1955 an agreement was made by which the college generously accepted the collection and integrated it into its holdings, making these materials available for scholars. Over thirty thousand items have been noted.

By now the dual thrust of Pennsylvania Dutch affairs was becoming evident. During this period self-conscious-ness emerged. Tension between scholarly and popularizing aspects appeared. This suggests that there are two spheres of activity. The first is the attempt to tell the truth about the Pennsylvania Dutch, to go beyond popular stereotypes and misconceptions. For there still is much that is untrue in the popular view of the Pennsylvania Dutch.

Popularization took many forms—novels, plays, folk festivals, newspaper columns, fairs, *Grundsow* lodges, *Fersommlinge,* and so on. These were efforts to keep alive popular awareness of Pennsylvania Dutch culture, based upon the old idea that by birth a Pennsylvania Dutchman has a heritage and tradition that set him apart from others.

Popular novels were many: Katherine E. Blake, *Heart's Haven,* 1905; Katherine Loose (George Shock), *House of Yost* and *Hearts Contending,* 1910; Elsie Singmaster, *The Long Journey,* a novel dealing with the migration, and *The Magic Mirror,* 1934; Mildred Jordan, *One Red Rose Forever,* a fictionalized life of "Baron" Stiegel; Conrad Richter, *The Free Man;* Adelaide H. Wonsettler, *Liberty for Johnny.* Perhaps the high point of Pennsylvania Dutch self-consciousness was the appearance of Joseph W. Yoder's *Rosanna of the Amish,* a work privately printed by the author.

Children's literature was not neglected. Marguerite de Angeli wrote her lovely *Henner's Lydia,* also illustrated by her drawings, one of the more successful children's books. Katherine Millhouse also did children's works.

The Pennsylvania Dutch became self-conscious, meeting in numerous *Grundsow* lodges and *Fersommlinge,* where they heard stories told by tellers of spry and racy tales. Buttressed by heaping dishes of sauerkraut and *speck,* most of these assemblies took place around February second.

Folk festivals proliferated. The Folk Festival at Kutztown has drawn persons numbering in the six figures; it has overcome an earlier propensity for the bizarre and grown more authentic in its exhibits. Other "Dutch Days" have kept the spirit alive, and amusement parks have also celebrated these people.

Museums and Historical Societies have stressed Dutch artifacts. The American Museum in Britain in Bath, England, is proud to exhibit its two fine rooms of Dutch Stuff as well as to show many fine quilts and coverlets. The Pennsylvania Trail of History, managed by the Pennsylvania Historical and Museum Commission, includes Ephrata and the Pennsylvania Farm Museum at Landis Valley.

Cooking apple-butter at Dorney Park, Allentown, a revival. *Photograph courtesy Mr. Edward W. Schlechter*

Many individual artists have used Pennsylvania Dutch themes in their work. Henry Chapman Mercer started by utilizing stove-plate designs on his tiles. William Swallow used Amish boys for his prize-winning sculpture and he created an imaginative piece by putting barn signs on a milk-cow. David Ellinger has revived the techniques and moods of old folk art and our "Pennsylvania Hattie" Brunner of Reinholds has been doing primitives in traditional style for many years.

All this popularizing has gone a long way toward changing the image of the Pennsylvania Dutch. It still rests on the mystique of heritage, on the view that was expressed in the requirement for membership in the old Pennsylvania German Society limiting membership to descendants of German and Swiss immigrants. This may have been necessary because American historians were continuing to ignore the cultural contributions of the Colonial Germans. This unfortunate stress on heritage excluded some able scholars in the field, men like William J. Hinke and, as mentioned above, Dr. Seidensticker. It was perhaps unavoidable because of the neglect of this field by scholars.

Mr. Paul Wieand's Folklore Group spinning the plate
in a game at Crackersport, Pennsylvania.

Mr. Paul Wieand's Folklore Group reviving the old-time
folk dances.

Mr. Paul Wieand's Folklore Group reviving the old dance
called the "candle dance." The one who holds the key
when the candle drops wins a prize. The key was passed
from hand to hand. This is an ancient German dance.
Photograph courtesy Mr. Paul Wieand

So the work of many individuals, societies, groups, and
assemblies, popularizing as well as scholarly, has changed
the image of the Pennsylvania Dutch. Now Professor
Robert Spiller can say in his *Literary History of the
United States* (III, p. 286) that the most fully explored
"foreign" culture is the Pennsylvania Dutch. May I object to the word "foreign," quotes and all? Men with such
"foreign" names as Muhlenberg, Pershing, Eisenhower,
Spatz, Eichelberger, and Devers do not have to apologize
for a hyphenated Americanism! The old difficulty that
has faced the Pennsylvania German Society from its start
continues.

Unfortunately, this prejudice against "foreign" influences has kept Pennsylvania German studies, and the
basic research implied, in the hands of Germanists. Our
societies were manned by professors of German; American historians showed little interest and did not share the
work. Is it because they would not or could not read
the sources?

May I suggest that Pennsylvania Dutch culture now
is less a living reality and more a subject for scholarly
work? If when the Pennsylvania German Folklore Society was being founded in 1935 it could be said that
there was enough work for twenty-five scholars for

Pieces of pottery made by Mrs. Naaman Kaiser, one of
the chief makers of revival pottery.

twenty-five years, now there must be an even more ex-
pansive prophecy. The achievements of both the Pennsylvania German Society and the Pennsylvania German
Folklore Society, adequate as they are, have only scratched
the surface. It can now be said that there remains enough
work for a hundred scholars for a hundred years if the
assembled materials are to be soundly worked. For one
thing, great new archival collections have been made, or
have come into the public domain, and these need exploi-
tation, for now we can tell the full story of these "foreign"
people in eastern Pennsylvania. Not only will new regional consciousness come forth, but also a new understanding of American history itself.

The first basic task that faces us, then, is archival house-
keeping. Now that these fine collections have been
gathered, both in Pennsylvania and in Europe, oppor-

tunity exists for a first-class bibliographical work. Professor Seidensticker's *The First Century of German Printing in America*—still indispensable for those who would
learn to know the scope of our thought-world—needs
fundamental revision. It should be carried down to the
end of the nineteenth century. Moreover, it needs to be
supplemented with lists of books, sold by booksellers,
that were imported from Europe, as well as with those
works written in Pennsylvania and published in Europe.
In this latter category five hundred works come to mind.

We are in desperate need of a manuscript survey that
will tell us what is in the Schwenkfelder Library, the
Moravian Archives, the Bassler-Unger collection, and the
Rare Book Room of the Philadelphia Free Library, as
well as a detailed listing of what the Library of Congress
has of reproductions from various German archives. The

newly acquired German archival holdings need study; what is the use of doing a biography of Conrad Beissel of Ephrata without knowing of his correspondence with Count Zinzendorf? Most German collections are now in the public domain, but some remain in private hands.

Such a manuscript survey should stimulate work in these sources, if only piecemeal, and so deepen our understanding of American history. My purpose is not to boast about what the Pennsylvania Dutch have achieved but to get our sources used for an integrated study of American civilization.

There are many areas of neglect.

We know little about nineteenth-century newspapers. Few complete files survive. Their feature articles show that here is a great deal of fresh material that needs integration into historical studies. Both dialect and High German poetry needs to be studied more thoroughly. Anecdotal and narrative prose from newspaper and almanac needs work.

Books, newspapers, almanacs, manuscripts—all need to be surveyed; such bibliographical work may stimulate further research.

The second great opportunity that faces scholars in the field of Pennsylvania Dutch studies deals with demographic questions, with the people themselves. It is well known that the Palatinate was decimated during the Thirty Years War, being filled up again after 1648 with settlers who came from Alsace and Switzerland. We therefore need surveys of this migration into the Palatinate. Then, starting from the year 1683, migration to

Lester Breininger revives the old art of pottery, capturing the spirit of older pieces in museums and private collections with boldness and creativity. *Courtesy Mr. Breininger*

Going to church, 1971.

Going home from church, 1971.

Waiting for their parents to come out of an Old Order Mennonite Meeting.

Pennsylvania took place. We know the names of about forty thousand persons, telling us when they arrived in the port of Philadelphia. The rest is confusion. One European scholar has found the places of origin for ninety-five percent of these "pioneers." His work needs augmentation. Can we not find out where these people put down, when they were naturalized, and when their sons and daughters went west? Can we not put this information on punched cards and then play with them, finding out patterns of the migration—why, for example, people from the Frankenthal-Lambsheim region went to Oley to settle, why those from the Kusel region went to Bern Township, Berks county? Such knowledge would be fruitful not only for historians but also for family historians.

Linguistic studies also languish. Although dialect dictionaries proliferate, we still do not know the range where dialect was spoken. We have not even charted the extent of the use of High German before 1830. We know almost nothing about our High German literature, in spite of several anthologies, which only scratch the surface. Ephrata poetry remains a mystery, Moravian poetry a huge enigma. We cannot even approach the Moravian custom of extemporizing verse in worship services because we know so little about it. Nor have we studied the mass of High German verse in nineteenth-century newspapers, separating verse originating from European sources from that which was written here. We know nothing about the influence of German poets on Pennsylvania verse, although nineteenth-century newspapers reprinted much German verse. Also, in spite of several anthologies, no comprehensive index of dialect poetry has yet appeared. There is enough work in the area of dialect and High German poetry to keep more than two dozen scholars busy for ten years. Conrad Beissel was not only the greatest poet writing in a "foreign" language in the Colonies; he was the most prolific colonial poet, bar none. Yet his name does not appear in American literary histories.

The folklorists, each in his own way, have presented their special points of view with less objectivity than might be wished for. No good study of medicine has been made by a scholar trained in the history of medicine. George deBenneville's *Materia Medica* gathers dust in a Philadelphia library while his chemical and medical manuscripts in the Schwenkfelder Library are not being looked at. No one is informed about the history of homeopathic medicine in Pennsylvania, especially about the relationship of Hahnemann and pietism to this area.

Nor do we know anything about Paracelsian chemistry in Pennsylvania; Abraham Wagner, Schwenkfelder physician, was the grandson of a notable Silesian chemist.

Pennsylvania pietism still awaits its historian. Julius Sachse's works were not adequate to the theme and much new material has been discovered and published. The mass of manuscripts now in the public domain in Herrnhut and also in the A. H. Francke papers, available in reproduction from the Library of Congress, makes new approaches mandatory.

Hundreds of personal diaries and collections of letters cry out for translation, asking for integration into the American historical scene. These documents will illuminate, not just the field of Pennsylvania Dutch studies,

Restoration of the Strassburg Railroad in Lancaster County.

but the whole of American history. Pastor Helfferich's *Lebensbild,* for example, so illuminates the nineteenth-century scene that it should be made available to those who do not read German. And at last, the Bethlehem Diary, the single most important source for Colonial history in Pennsylvania, is coming out in English.

The subject of the Pennsylvania Dutch and the American Indians has not been fully covered. While vast sums of money are spent for archaeological research, the mass of historical documents in the Moravian Archives dealing with this theme is ignored. Nor is there even a bibliography of works translated from German into the Indian dialects, and we know very little about the Indian language school at Bethlehem.

There are cookbooks galore treating of the Pennsylvania Dutch cuisine, but we do not have a major study of Pennsylvania Dutch agriculture. Indeed, the entire economic field of study, including the crafts, is sadly neglected. The best book on pottery, still reprinted, was done in 1903. There are no modern monographs on pewter, painted and punched tin, or iron (wrought). There are societies that concentrate on tools, but we still have little that is authentic on the nature of Pennsylvania Dutch tools; Dr. Mercer made his great museum in Doylestown in vain. The Kentucky rifle has been much studied, but its predecessor, which was used so effectively in the Revolution, has not yet been identified.

So it goes. Great areas of basic research remain. Our scholarly tasks only increase as new materials are found and new insights provided. The fault is in the scholarly imagination, not in the paucity of material.

However, several theoretical reorientations have to be made if we are to gain full vision. First, we must understand that, linguistically speaking, Pennsylvania Dutch studies embrace far more material in High German than in dialect. For two centuries our literature was in High German and dialect was afterthought. The present emphasis on dialect is a distortion. We must keep the proper place of formal German literature in our studies.

Second, we have to face the fact that we are confronted with two jobs: research and popularization. Pennsylvania Dutch culture is both a subject for study and an inheritance. We also must grasp the relationship between these two, namely, that proper appreciation rests on correct scholarship and honest research.

Third, serious efforts must be made to integrate the Pennsylvania Dutch story into histories of American civilization. Here we ask not for exaggeration of our place in American life, just honest appraisal of our role.

Finally, then, we may come to measure the future by the past. Then we may say that, as the false image of the Pennsylvania Dutch has largely been changed through the hard work of many minds, so, too, new appreciation of the scope of our influence on American life and thought may yet come.

For this many of us wish with full hearts.

Epilogue

So, it's sunbonnets and shoofly pies! By these terms I have intended to symbolize Pennsylvania Dutch culture. However, as we come to the close of this cultural history, I must confess that both items are ambiguous, inadequate symbols to carry this meaning.

Sunbonnets were worn in summer only. Winter headgear for women was different. Some sects replaced the sunbonnet with a prayer cap indoors. Also, shoofly pies were a late arrival in the culinary art, coming when molasses and brown sugar came. However inadequate, though, these things do symbolize the culture of the Pennsylvania Dutch.

Ambiguous as these symbols are, they cannot be compared with the ambiguity of the basic phrase in the subtitle—*Pennsylvania Dutch.* Who are these people? *Pennsylvania Dutch* has several meanings.

First, there is the demographic sense, by which we mean the 237,775 persons of Germanic background who were counted in the 1790 Census, and their descendants, wherever they may be. Projecting this figure, we get about twenty million modern Americans who may be classed as Pennsylvania Dutch.

Next, there is the geographical sense. Here we mean those who live in eastern Pennsylvania, where Germanic peoples dominate.

Third, there is the linguistic sense. Here we mean those who speak a non-English language, the Pennsylvania Dutch dialect. These people go to *Grundsow* lodges and are regaled with tall stories about our people.

A fourth meaning is possible—the buggy Dutch, the plain people who oppose modern technology.

Many questions still come forward. None of these definitions sums it up. Can we ascribe a terminal date, say 1830, after which an immigrant was not among the Dutch? What do we do with later political refugees, the 48ers, who settled down in eastern Pennsylvania and melted into the older population? Where do we put the Harmony Society, which put down in western Pennsylvania but was pietist in spirit and mood? Where do we put the Hessians, with their massive materials? Dr. Meynen in his bibliography classifies them as Pennsylvania Dutch. What do we do about the Canadian settlements, those pacifists who followed the trail of the black walnut northward, buttressed as they were by newer immigrations? How do we treat the migration of Pennsylvania Dutch into the burgeoning west, for if four million Pennsylvania Dutch lived in this province then at least fifteen million are part of modern America.

The problems are many indeed, and they go far beyond the stale old argument over *Pennsylvania German* or *Pennsylvania Dutch.*

Now I shall propose yet another problem, which can only add to the difficulty. I conceive of *Pennsylvania Dutch* as a historically dynamic, developing essence, which moved from primitive settlements to more established modes, from grubbing in the soil in Rockland Township, Berks County, to living at 1600 Pennsylvania Avenue, Washington. Not every Pennsylvania Dutchman made sgraffitto pottery, did *Fraktur,* lived in Pennsylvania, or goes to a *Grundsow* lodge! I shall have to suggest that the conception *Pennsylvania Dutch* embraces the element of time, changing with the centuries. It seems to have meant one thing for Pastorius, another for Benjamin Franklin, another for Henry Harbaugh, and still another for Dwight Eisenhower. That is why I have tried to make this book a history, seeking to express the temporal dynamic that I believe resides in *Pennsylvania Dutch.*

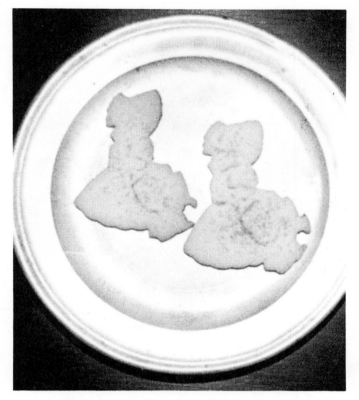

Christmas cookies in sunbonnet mood.

was popular—suggested that culture is the best that has been said about life. As I see it, culture is the spirit of a people expressed in form, artifact, and illuminating events. Culture projects the human spirit.

History is more than ambiguous; it is mysterious. It is both *res gestae* and *historia rerum gestarum*—events and their interpretations. History is more than the past; it is the meaningful past.

In the final analysis, I suggest that Pennsylvania Dutch cultural history, which I have subsumed under the title *Sunbonnets and Shoofly Pies,* is meaningful not only

Shoofly pie ready for dunking, with deep saucer and cup on cup plate. In older days dunking was in saucer, not cup.

Still, if the term *Pennsylvania Dutch* is ambiguous, what about *culture?* Here I mean more than refinement of mind, manners, and intellect. Matthew Arnold, in *Culture and Anarchy*—written before modern sociology

for those who have Pennsylvania Dutch heritage, but also for those Americans who are interested in the variegated past of this nation.

Index

Christianbrunn, 100
Christiansen, Hans Christoph, 100
Christman, Oliver Lewis, 11
Chronicon Ephratense, 51, 99
Church Record, 1787, 107
Church, Friedens, Wernersville, 79
Church, Northampton County, 78
Church, Western Salisbury, 79
Church, Zions, Allentown, 79
Cist, Carl, 120
City Cousin cartoon, 234
Civil War, 155
Claudius, Matthias, 194
Claus, Jacob, 149
Clewell, Edgar T., 245
Clewell, Edward, 201
Clockcase, folk designs on, 136
Codorus, 37
Comets, meaning of, 180
Continental Congress, 34
Cornwall Furnace, 140
Coffeepot, punched tin, 220
Coffee tax, 221
Coffman, Peter: pastel by, Color Plate XV
Colinson, Peter, 85
Colonial Craftsman, The, 103
Commissarissen voor het fonds van buittenlandsche Noeden, 34
Complete German Grammar in Two Parts, A, 120
"Concord," The, 26
"Conestoga": word described, 23, 34, 52, 103, 111
Conewago, 27, 103
Conflict between "the city" and the hinterland, 120
Cookie cutters, 207
Cooper, James Fenimore, 68
"Coots Town," 39, 107, 111
Coots, G., 107
Corn crib, 103
Corn, dried, 212
Counting-out rhymes, 167ff.
Cowan, Philip F., 11, 173
Crefeld, 21, 26, 240
Crisp, Stephan, 20
Crocks for storage, 209
Crop rotation, 103, 110
Crown Point, 87
Culture, Pennsylvania Dutch: changing character of, 74; becomes reflective, 238; dual thrust of, 251
"Cures," 175, 178
Curieuse Nachricht, 22
Custards, 216
Customs, New Year, 180

Dagret, Ezra, 213
Daimler, Gottfried, 137, 138
Darmstadt, 37
Datestones, German inscription on, 189
Daub, Professor Carl, 129
Daub, William A., 11, 32, 70, 227
Davenant, Ambassador, 21
Days of the week, counting the, 170
DeBenneville, family, 39; George, 69, 70
De Campaign Briefe fun Pit Schweffelbrenner, 192
Décime ecclésiastique, 19
DeForrest, Mrs. Robert W., 172, 247
Declaration of Independence, 87
DeHaas family, 39
DeHaas, General Philip, 90
Dell, William, 72
DeLong, Lizzie, 241
DeLong, Mollie, 241

DeLong, Peter, 81
Dencke, Jeremiah, 68
Deshler, Colonel David, 2
Deshler, Fort, 141
Deshler, Susanna, 2
DeTurk, Abraham, 39
DeTurk, Isaac, 34
DeTurk family, 42
Deutscher Kinder Englischer und Deutscher ABC Buchstabier-Lese und Sprechbüchlein, Der, 122
Deutscher Algegenwärtiger Sprachlehrer, Der, 122
Dewees, name, 25
DeWitt, Dr. Christopher, 50
Dialect: Pennsylvania Dutch. *See* Pennsylvania Dutch
Dictionary, Muhlenberg and Schiffer, 122
Dieffenderfer, Frank Reid, 241
Dietrich, W. W., 29, 42, 102, 199
Dillbeck, Isaac, 26
Dissinger, Moses, 228ff.
Distilleries, 206
Draus und Daheem, Gedichte in Pennsylvanisch Deitsch, 194, 196
Dried foods, 212
Drinks, strong, 206
Drugs, 180
Dock, Christopher, 80, 147
Donner, W., poem by, 189
Dorney Park, 249
Dower Chest, 148, 149
Doylestown, 127
Doylestown Morgenstern, 190
Durham Furnace, 140
DuPont, Henry Francis, 247
DuPont, Henry Francis Winterthur Museum, 11, 165
Dunkard, 56, 91
DuSimitiere family, 39

Eagle, Reading. *See Adler*
Ealer's Tavern, 105
Earltown, 34
Easton, Charity School at, 85, 104; *Unpartheyische Easton Bothe,* 119, 122, 127
Eberbach, 56
Ebner, Allentown printer, 122
Eckerlin, Gabriel, 59, 99
Eckerlin, Israel, 65; "Scriptures of the Zionitic Order," 65, 99, 100
Eckerlin, Michael, 35; widow of, 51; four sons of, 51, 99
Eckstein, Elizabeth, 63
Economic patterns, conflict of, 94
Economy, Old, 121
Edlemann, Daniel, 130
"Egler's," Allentown tavern, 105
Eichelberger, Georg, 90
Eichelberger, name, 251
Eichendorf, 194
Eichholtz, Jacob: painted tin ascribed to, Color Plate XIII
Eisenbrown, P. T., 196
Eisenhower, Dwight, 259
Eisenhower, name, 251
Elias with fiery wagon, 171
Elemente der deutschen Sprache, Der, 122
Ellinger, David, 11; Color Plate XVI, 249
Elisabeth furnace, 140
Elisabeth, wife of Friedrich V, 17
Elwetritsch, hunting the, 171
Emerson, Ralph Waldo, 196
En Quart Millich un en Halb Beint Rahm, 201
En Trämp Story, 200
Ephrata, 34, 39; restored buildings at, 52, 54, 56; "Roses of Sharon," 56; Householders, 56, 61; Press, 64, 65; as hospital, 91, 99; economies at, 99ff., 100; center of printing, 119